RECLAIMING ASSIA WEVILL

JULIE GOODSPEED-CHADWICK

RECLAIMING ASSIA WEVILL

SYLVIA PLATH, TED HUGHES, AND THE LITERARY IMAGINATION

LOUISIANA STATE UNIVERSITY PRESS
BATON ROUGE

Published by Louisiana State University Press

Manufactured in the United States of America
First printing

DESIGNER: Mandy McDonald Scallan
TYPEFACE: Whitman
PRINTER AND BINDER: Sheridan Books, Inc.

Cataloging-in-Publications Data are available from the Library of Congress.
ISBN 978-0-8071-7056-4 (cloth: alk. paper) — ISBN 978-0-8071-7227-8 (pdf) — ISBN 978-0-8071-7228-5 (epub)

The paper in this book meets the guidelines for permanence and durability of the Committee on Production Guidelines for Book Longevity of the Council on Library Resources.♾

For Keith Chadwick,

Josephine Barbara Jean Chadwick,

and Jude Valentine Chadwick

CONTENTS

ACKNOWLEDGMENTS

My profound gratitude lies with my prepublication readers. I am grateful to James W. Long and others, including the specialist outside reader who expertly straddles Plath studies and Hughes studies, making any perceived divide nonexistent. You made this book the best it could be. Also of especial note are Marcia Eppich-Harris, Jay R. Howard, Nicholas Lawrence, and Peter K. Steinberg, among other first readers of this book. Your generosity and liveliness of mind and spirit ensured that this work was conducted in the most advantageous of circumstances. You are my readers, colleagues, and friends; while I am thankful for your collegiality, I am thankful for your friendship most of all. I am grateful to Eilat Negev and Yehuda Koren for reviewing the manuscript but also for their collegiality, congeniality, generosity, and expertise.

My admiration and thanks belong to Louisiana State University Press and the stellar people associated with it. You produce and champion beautiful and important books at a time when scholarly publishing needs support. It is an honor to be one of your authors. James W. Long deserves to be acknowledged twice: he is superlative. Thank you to the brilliant freelance editor Elizabeth Gratch for lending her expertise to this book. Thank you to Lee C. Sioles for her unparalleled work and artistry with production. Special thanks to Catherine L. Kadair for her superb work.

Thank you to the Estate of Assia Wevill for its support in the way of approval and permissions to work with and feature materials authored by Assia. It is a privilege to have your support.

I thank David Wevill for our correspondence and for permission to work with photographs he took of Assia.

I wish to thank the outstanding Courtney Chartier, Kathleen Shoemaker, and the staff of the Stuart A. Rose Manuscript, Archives, and Rare Book Library at Emory University. You are magnificent, and your graciousness is remarkable. I am grateful for access to the treasures housed in the Ted Hughes archive and for the help provided by the terrific staff of the Rose Library during my extended visits in 2016 and 2018.

Thank you to the Lilly Library at Indiana University for accommodating my requests to read materials and view artifacts in the Sylvia Plath archive in 2016 and 2018. Thank you, too, for accommodating my students' visit; the Plath archival materials are riches indeed.

The University Library of Columbus earns my deep appreciation. Every item I needed could be secured, including rare books and materials. Thank you also for your outstanding work with interlibrary loan, especially concerning unusual requests, and for your support of research in the humanities. The University Library of Columbus is a truly impressive resource.

Thanks also to the Indianapolis–Marion County Public Library, which is a community good that deserves accolades. Every book I requested for this project was secured, and the library goes to great lengths to cultivate an impressive collection of books for its readers.

This project was funded by a 2015–16 New Frontiers Exploratory Travel Fellowship from Indiana University Bloomington (IU) and by faculty development funds from Indiana University–Purdue University Columbus (IUPUC). Thanks are due George Towers, who supported my sabbatical, and this work specifically, including providing support for a travel fellowship, overseas conference travel, and faculty development funds. I am indebted to him. Vicki Kruse aided the research of this book in purchasing materials for it and in providing other necessary support, and I am grateful for her help, skill, and talents. Thanks, too, to my IUPUC colleagues-turned-friends at large for collegiality and friendship. Also, I thank Feminism Club at IUPUC and its community partners; they continually remind me of the importance of work, such as this study, in the world outside of academic scholarship.

I must respectfully thank several others: my aforementioned Division Head George Towers; Reinhold Hill, Vice Chancellor and Dean of Indiana University–Purdue University Columbus; Kathy Johnson,

Executive Vice Chancellor and Chief Academic Officer at Indiana University–Purdue University Indianapolis (IUPUI); and Nasser Paydar, Chancellor of Indiana University–Purdue University Indianapolis and Executive Vice President of Indiana University, all of whom are advocates for faculty rights and supporters of high-quality faculty work in all areas, including humanities scholarship. These people make IUPUC-IUPUI a great place to be.

Special acknowledgment and thanks go to the IUPUI Office of the Vice Chancellor for Research for its strong support of this research. Special thanks are due Steven B. Chin, who lent his expertise and brilliance to this project; I thank him for his efforts in working with me to identify and apply for funding in connection with this project.

Thank you to the IU Office of the Vice President for International Affairs for funds that allowed me to travel overseas to present work and learn from others in connection with the material of this book.

Also, my students at Indiana University–Purdue University Columbus deserve recognition: over the years, I have learned from them, and as a result, I am a better teacher and scholar as time progresses. The students who took Sylvia Plath Studies during the fall 2016 semester shared my enthusiasm for Plath studies, and they cocreated the spaces in our service learning course within which we could engage in the study of texts, people, and concepts that showcase the real-world importance of literature. Thank you, Amanda Ballard, Bailey Burnett, Emily Pedigo, Alicca Rice, Melissa Sinclair, and Courtney Watkins. Thank you, too, to Brandi Rund, Clayton Ham, Seth Kerr, and the other students from the Introduction to Poetry course in spring 2017 for discussions that demonstrate how Plath's poetry resonates with twenty-first-century readers.

For professional community and its rewards, I am grateful to Kathleen Connors for codirecting the Sylvia Plath Symposium at Indiana University in 2012 and to Maeve O'Brien for her leadership in organizing the Sylvia Plath: Letters, Words and Fragments Conference at Ulster University in Belfast, Northern Ireland, in 2017. To Plath scholars and biographers around the world, you make Plath studies important, exciting, and rewarding, and I am proud to be counted as one of you. In this vein, I am inspired by the exemplary scholarship, efforts, and friendship of many Plath scholars. Among others, thank you to Janet Badia, Heather Clark, Gail Crowther, Amanda Golden, Karen V. Kukil, Carl Rollyson, Peter K. Steinberg, David Trinidad, and Emily Van Duyne for creating new vistas for vibrant research and for your conversations about Plath and her circle with me (and my students). For his discerning work on Assia, I am indebted to Jonathan Bate; thank you, too, to Hughes scholars who produce impressive work and who exhibit generosity in their interactions with other scholars. As for primary work, I remain impressed by the power, resonance, and significance of Frieda Hughes's poetry and paintings. Regarding work on Assia, I am in awe of the biography produced by Yehuda Koren and Eilat Negev. In similar fashion, I wish to acknowledge Kristie F. Fleckenstein, Sr. Stella Gampfer, Deborah M. Mix, Rai Peterson, and Diane Prenatt—thank you for the example you set for me.

On a personal note, I am grateful to Laura Combs, Marcia Eppich-Harris, and Mary Kennedy, the women who became the sisters I always wanted, for our friendships and for all the times we have had over the past twenty years, from college to grad school to today, and for all the times we will continue to have together. Those, in total, are what motivate me to return to hard work, again and again. Thank you to my brother, Terry Goodspeed, for being part of my family. Family and friends who are the equivalent of family are the biggest blessings of all.

My heartfelt gratitude for everything belongs to my husband, Keith; my daughter, Josephine; and my son, Jude: you are the brightest stars in my sky. And so this book is for you.

RECLAIMING ASSIA WEVILL

CHAPTER 1

RECOVERING ASSIA WEVILL

An Introduction

> . . . But the man laughed—
> The song was worth it.
> The woman felt cheated.
> —from "Two Eskimo Songs," by Ted Hughes

This book began when it became clear to me that scholarly interest in Assia Wevill's role as actor and muse in the biographies and poetry of Sylvia Plath (1932–63) and Ted Hughes (1930–98) would never wane. From the outset, Assia Esther Gutmann Steele Lipsey Wevill (1927–69) was positioned as an integral part of the Plath-Hughes myth, a myth that prevented her from receiving acknowledgment of her own victimhood and recognition for her own artistic contributions.[1] Ironically, the Plath-Hughes myth, perhaps the most sensational biographical and literary interpersonal and family drama in twentieth-century poetry, could not survive if Assia were not a major player in it. Fortunately, Assia's life story has been recovered, retooled, reconstructed, and related beautifully by Yehuda Koren and Eilat Negev in their book *Lover of Unreason: Assia Wevill, Sylvia Plath's Rival and Ted Hughes's Doomed Love* (2006) and in their newspaper articles in *The Guardian*. What remains to be examined is the substance and significance of Assia's life and contributions to poetry and art, particularly in American and British literature. Of equal importance but in a different vein is the need for a feminist recuperation of her reputation, artistic work, and influence. What we have done to Assia in scholarship, research agendas, and teaching—our literary imagination, in short—is a disservice to our field. As teachers and scholars, we have perpetuated victim blaming and have scapegoated Assia in sexist fashion, and we have either eclipsed or minimized her importance in literary studies, women's studies, and work on Plath and Hughes.

My aim is to offer new scholarship on the writer and artist Assia Wevill in order to establish her significance in letters and to accord her a more proper place than femme fatale or scapegoat for marital discord and suicides. The arc of this enterprise is indebted to feminist recovery work as well as to scholarship in trauma studies. Additionally, this study sheds light on Assia's and Hughes's relationship with each other and with Plath. Because Plath as well as Hughes occupy privileged places in the American and British literary imaginations, research about Assia, an important figure in Plath's and Hughes's work and lives, has far-reaching implications for literary and biographical insights and scholarship on two famous poets: the Pulitzer Prize–winning Plath and the British poet laureate Hughes have always been of interest to scholars and teachers, and so they, unlike Assia, are well established in the literary canon and acknowledged as important figures. Assia puts them into relief; that is her current role to play.

If we adhere to the tenets of feminism and current trends in trauma studies, we need to reconsider and/or reclaim Assia (her life and work): she was a woman who was artistic and talentedly so, and her life serves as a panorama of gendered politics from which we can learn. While she created, designed, wrote, and translated visual art, advertisements, and poetry, her roles as muse and collaborator with Hughes—and Plath—eclipse her contributions and her own status as an important literary and historical woman. Her life, contributions, and legacy have been demonized and victimized, much as she was a victim in her actual life too. I address the following complex question as I work through and untangle the Assia Wevill–Ted Hughes–Sylvia Plath triangle: How might Assia's life and work shed meaning on our own times concerning gender roles and power in heterosexual relationships; femininity and its challenges, dangers, and pleasures; and our knowledge about and understanding of trauma and its manifestations and representations in life and art?

A bit of context: I come to this project as a feminist scholar working on Plath, which, from my point of view, is quite a startling revelation with respect to the focus of this book. One is not supposed to take up Assia and recuperate her in positive terms if one is dedicated to fleshing out Plath's victimization and traumatic responses, as I have done in the past.[2] But when one spends time in the archives at Indiana University or Emory University, it becomes increasingly apparent how Assia has been elided from the professional and public record in many ways. Her own voice has been silenced: in life, in the archive, and in the public domain.[3] Texts authored by her, specifically her journals and letters, remain unpublished and are difficult to access. Others speak for her and about her, most notably Hughes and Plath, and they tax Assia with their own grievances. Part of what I hope to accomplish with this study is the acknowledgment that what we have done to Assia in professional scholarship, in texts that circulate on the internet, and in our classrooms is antifeminist and a profound and unkind injury to another woman who deserves better than what she encountered in her life—and we deserve better than what we encounter in ours.

What I endeavor to do here is to rethink Assia from a feminist, literary studies perspective and bring that to bear on important texts so that a dialogue about gender, women's bodies, identity, and power in interpersonal relationships and their subsequent representation in literature emerges. This is a book about identity politics and women, primarily: women as subjects and victims many times over. Concerning recovery work, I have attempted to show how Plath wrote about Assia in her poetry and to what extent Assia proves to be a critical influence on Hughes and his work. Moreover, analyses of artifacts that contain Assia's personal stamp or that are authored by her are highlighted in chapter 4 and are incorporated into this study whenever possible. These avenues forge new pathways into research on Assia as well as bolster existing work and indicate new directions in Plath studies and Hughes studies.

What follows is a mapping of how Assia has mattered and how she might be reapproached. For instance, in chapter 2, I focus on Assia's place in Plath's *The Collected Poems* (1981) and showcase how Assia emerges as the embodiment of Plath's desires, fears, and trauma; in this case, Assia is Plath's Other Woman, an adulteress and a fantasy upon which Plath projected what she wanted, hated, and could not make sense of within a gendered world. The third chapter treats Assia's signature role in Hughes's impressive oeuvre, namely *Capriccio* (1990), *Birthday Letters* (1998), and his highly regarded collected letters. Chapter 4 gives us Assia in her own voice, in textual materials created by her, and in self-styled images of her and her daughter with Hughes, Alexandra "Shura" Tatiana Elise Wevill (1965–69). In other words, we will view Assia as an author and as a subject. Specifically, we will encounter her as she chose to represent herself in her letters; in artifacts produced by her or directly related to her in the archive; in her translation of Yehuda Amichai's poetry (1968, 1969); in her artistic products (i.e., visual art); and in her unpublished journal entries. The last chapter assesses Assia's legacy in the twenty-first century, presenting materials and developments that draw attention to her. Examples include the distribution of the big-production film *Sylvia* (2003); the publication of *Lover of Unreason* (2006); the publication and staging of the drama *Doonreagan* (2013); the airing of the BBC documentary *Ted Hughes: Stronger than Death* (2015); and the appearance of what I will call fanfiction dedicated to Assia.

HOW ASSIA HAS BEEN STAGED: A REVIEW OF THE LITERATURE

The first public address, in English, to Assia after her death occurred in the poem "The Death of A.G." (titled "The Death of Assia G." in Hebrew) in Amichai's *Songs of Jerusalem and Myself* (1973). Koren and Negev reference this poem as the work that ignited their investigation and study of Assia: her name and details about her were purposely obscured.[4] As they point out, Amichai's friendship with Hughes would have led to such discretion, and twenty years would pass before her full name would appear in the title of the poem

(Koren and Negev 224). Fortunately, Assia is now readily identifiable, which fulfills a rhetorical function of the poem: the speaker of the poem wants others to know someone important died, and he invites us to share in his grief over the loss and to puzzle over the incomprehensibility of her suicide. As a poetic lament on the occasion of Assia's death by someone who knew her, the poem opens with the speaker explaining that he has just left off crying, and the silence is strange to him. He declares, "I want to make propaganda / for your death" (5–6). The desire for her to be remembered—to not be eradicated from the world of poetry (she was, after all, the English translator of his poems and his friend)—resonates. The poem commemorates Assia's life in a sense: hers was a life worth remembering and mourning; she is worthy of this poetic tribute. All traces of her, then, are not erased: the speaker in the poem will not let her go without protesting her death and the impact it has on him because she was important to him. In lamenting her loss, Amichai mixes his warm regard for Assia with this public, poetic eulogy. He treasures her letters, he suggests, distinguishing them from others. Those letters from others are "set apart for life"—for the living, for the duration of his life, perhaps—but he qualifies life without Assia as "not so long, / and maybe not better" (9–10). The last stanza closes with the speaker's stark bewilderment: he cannot fathom what she has done or why she has done it.

With respect to what has proven instrumental in solidifying Assia's position as the villain in the Ted Hughes–Sylvia Plath drama, we will turn to a brief survey of early work that set the stage for Assia's critical victimization. Factors that enable what I call the traditional approach to Assia include her elision as a significant biographical subject; the eclipse of her personhood; and the disregard or lack or acknowledgment for her own artistry and/or her significance as muse to Plath and Hughes.

Letters Home, edited by Plath's mother, Aurelia Plath, appeared in 1975, and it was pruned: intensely and scrupulously edited, few mentions of Assia appear in print. An exception appears in the 7 November 1962 letter. At its close, Plath writes to her mother: "Living apart from Ted is wonderful—I am no longer in his shadow, and it is heaven to be liked for myself alone, knowing what I want. I may even borrow a table for my flat from Ted's girl—I could be gracious to her now and kindly. She has only her high-paid ad agency job, her vanity . . . and everybody wants to be a writer . . . I may be poor in bank funds, but I am so much richer in every other way, I envy them nothing. My babies and my writing are my life and let them have affairs and parties, poof!" (479). In this excerpt we see what we might not expect: that, at this particular moment, Plath professes to pity Assia and to look down upon her.[5] Plath refrains from categorizing Assia as a talented writer, despite the fact that Assia held a high-powered copywriting job. Plath apparently recognized Assia's desire to be known by her pen ("and everybody wants to be a writer") and prevents giving her that identity, thereby becoming the first on record to diminish her professional achievements. Insisting that she is "richer" in every way except money, Plath declares that she envies Assia and Hughes nothing at all because, she implies, they may have ephemeral "affairs and parties," but she has her children and her writing to provide meaning and depth to her life. From Plath's poems and from memoirs and recollections of friends and associates, we know that Plath struggled to conquer her demons and that she was not always "gracious" and "kindly" to either Assia or Hughes, as Assia attested in her journal (Koren and Negev 117). Plath's take in the letter to her mother contributes three aspects to the Assia story, as told by Plath and Hughes: first, Assia is superficial and vain (perhaps part of her femme fatale image); second, Assia was never a true writer, so she could only envy the talented Plath and Hughes their writing abilities; and third, Assia's relationship with Hughes was not a partnership but, instead, that which Assia abhorred: a "slinky affair" (Assia qtd. in Koren and Negev 101). Assia wanted to marry Hughes more than anything else in her life and served him, for roughly the same number of years as Plath did, as a partner and the mother of his children. Although Hughes unkindly dubs her "this Lilith of abortions" in "Dreamers" (*Collected Poems,* line 27), Assia assumed caretaking duties for Frieda and Nicholas, Hughes's children with Plath, addressing them lovingly in her will ("Will of Assia Estre [*sic*] Wevill"), and bore Hughes a daughter, whom Assia cherished.

Edward Butscher produced two books that included Assia early on in Plath studies; his books formed part of the first fleet to center on Plath. In his first, *Sylvia Plath: Method and Madness* (1976, revised and reprinted 2003), he changed Assia's name to Olga, in an attempt, as stated in the 2003 editor's note, to protect "people from legal repercussions" (x). However, Assia continues to be identified as Olga in the same prefatory note. Despite its blatant unkindness to Assia—one description dismisses her fabled body as "dumpy" and another dismisses her attraction to Hughes as transference (because Assia "had always wanted to be a 'real' writer" [315])—what sets this book apart is its reliance on contents from a letter about Assia by Edward Lucie-Smith, one of her colleagues. Lucie-Smith provides biographical details and emphasizes her beauty and her perfectionism: "In terms of personality, he recalls her as a perfectionist about everything, from her immediate surroundings to her relationships with others, which made her somewhat self-conscious about her minor physical defects" (315). While Butscher places blame squarely on Assia for destroying Plath (i.e., destroying her "last illusions" about marriage and her husband [313]), this book offers other details and ways to think about Assia, although Butscher refrains from endorsing an alternative view—or a fair one. For instance, he asserts: "[Assia] is a rather tragic figure, one who can no longer testify in her own behalf, having also committed suicide [. . . .] Still, it is difficult not to be slightly prejudiced against her in view of the disastrous effect she had on Sylvia's life" (314). In his second book, a collection of essays, *Sylvia Plath: The Woman and the Work* (1977), Assia is infrequently mentioned. The only sustained account of her comes from Elizabeth Compton Sigmund, who identifies her as a seductive "villainess from beginning to end" (24).

Bitter Fame (1989) by Anne Stevenson offered a markedly different picture of Assia; the book as a whole sympathized with Hughes more than Plath. Sanctioned by the Plath estate—which was managed by the Hughes family, with Olwyn Hughes, Ted Hughes's sister, as literary executor—this biography was almost cowritten: Stevenson insisted that the book was a work of dual authorship between Olwyn Hughes and her in the author's note. Brief, sympathetic accounts are related by people who knew Assia best, including her last husband, David Wevill: he describes her as "brave, resourceful, warm, with many shadows" (243). We are told, too, that "Assia's quality meant that [for Plath] this 'rival' was more likely than other, imagined rivals to turn into a real one" (244). In no other early account that historically grounds the Plath-Hughes marriage mythos is Assia presented in a positive or sympathetic light. Instead, she is repeatedly dismissed as crude by David and Elizabeth Compton, who admittedly did not know Assia very well or spend prolonged time with her. In *Method and Madness*, the couple finds that Assia was "a very high powered presence in any room, quite unbearably another Sylvia, in a much nastier way, much cruder in dominance" (David Compton qtd. in Butscher 314). Assia's beauty changes into crudity in contrast to Plath's refinement. Countering the negative portrayals of Assia that put Plath in a much better light due to their contrast (though they appear more similar than one might expect), Stevenson informs us of what Suzette Macedo, a friend to both Plath and Assia, told her: "[Plath] scorned Ted for having left the perfection of what they shared for 'a whiff of Chanel.' Suzette was surprised, for she remembered Sylvia's exclaiming enthusiastically about Assia the previous year, 'An amazing woman—she has her passport on her face.' Suzette was quite aware that David and Assia Wevill were both in a terrible state about the affair. Suzette tried to tell Sylvia that things were not as black and white as she imagined, but Sylvia would not listen" (273). The recollection here dates back to October 1962; Plath was living alone at Devon with her children at the time and would not have been inclined then to consider her husband's mistress an "amazing woman." Indeed, Jillian Becker remembers that Plath refrained from using Assia's name in talking about her ("Sylvia would never speak Assia's name"), further rendering her a muted presence but a powerful one, nonetheless. All the same, Assia "was hateful" in Plath's eyes (Stevenson 293). In a somewhat similar vein, Richard Murphy records in his brief memoir, which Stevenson appended to her biography, that Hughes also refrained from mentioning Assia's name in discussing the breakup of his marriage to Murphy, "but [Assia's] role was implied" (Stevenson 350; Murphy 225). In his full-length memoir, Murphy remembers that the "Babylonian beauty of Assia's raven hair, dark eyes and voluptuous bosom astounded me" (229). In his memoir, also part of the appendices to Stevenson's book, Lucas Myers, who sidesteps naming Assia, writes: "Sylvia's rival has been misrepresented. She was a touch too elegant for her own well-being, fundamentally very vulnerable, needed a lot of affection, and could remember SS boots outside the railway carriage compartment as her family, half Jewish, approached the Swiss border" (319–20). This assessment captures a version of Assia that emerges when one seeks out Assia's own voice and imprint in various media or in the archive.

Ronald Hayman's *The Death and Life of Sylvia Plath* (1991, new edition published in 2003) harbors gems of information pertaining to Assia in the way of interviews, especially with Fay Weldon. Hayman sketches a valuable overview of Hughes's poetry collection about Assia, *Capriccio,* too. These aspects differentiate this biography from the others about Plath that include Assia. Historically, Plath biographers were the first to break the ground in introducing Assia to Plath-Hughes scholarship: Hughes biographers followed suit and extended the examinations of Assia at a later date. Similar to the traditional accounts of Assia in Plath biographies, Hayman delivers the narrative of Assia as an exceptionally beautiful but difficult woman—one who is, by turns, mischievous, unconventional, untamed, flamboyant, confident, talented, lively, amusing, egotistic, impulsive, unscrupulous, and ladylike, whenever the notion struck her to be so. Assia's reputation as a homewrecker is also furthered in this narrative: Hayman relates that three of Assia's friends, Suzette Macedo, Julia Matcham, and Angela Landels, told him that Assia announced her intention of seducing Hughes to them in May 1962, in anticipation of the storied weekend in Devon (169, 241). What makes this assertion interesting is that Hayman follows it with the statement that, to people who knew her, Assia "didn't give the impression of being promiscuous" (169). This observation counters the one provided by Al Alvarez, who maintains that Assia threw herself at every man she encountered (240). Alvarez's point has been disputed by Koren and Negev, who cite Nathaniel Tarn, a close friend in whom Assia confided and who documented their conversations in his journal. Tarn maintains that Alvarez was spurned by Assia, who rejected his marriage proposal on 27 July 1962 (Nathaniel Tarn Papers).

Regardless of what actually happened, traditional accounts, such as this one, of Assia in the aftermath of Plath's suicide popularize the idea that Assia "was trying in several ways to take Sylvia's place." Among the examples given are Assia's attempts to befriend Plath's friends; become a patient of Plath's physician, Dr. John Horder; live in Plath's homes; and rely on "things Sylvia had used, including a hand-painted pot on the bedside table" (Hayman 199). The insinuations are that Assia was jealous of and obsessed with Plath, so much so that she wanted to copy her deceased rival.[6] However, these precise conjectures seem to be overblown in Assia's day-to-day life and, indeed, when true, caused her much distress. In fact, Hughes, in stipulating the conditions he saw as necessary to promote a harmonious household, dictated that Assia refrain from battling over changing the furnishings of a home she would share with Hughes ("Draft Constitution"). Jonathan Bate, Hughes's biographer, interprets this stipulation as "don't remove every last trace of Sylvia's taste" (266). In other words, Assia could not completely redecorate Hughes's domicile, should she move in with him. Unfortunately for Assia, two of the homes she established with Hughes in London and Devon were residences where Plath had also lived. While Assia preferred not to live at the Fitzroy Road "ghost house," as she called it,[7] or at Court Green in Devon, she had to make do with what was there if she wanted to live with Hughes.

As one can see, when Assia appeared at all historically, it was in the form of biographies about Plath. Paul Alexander's *Rough Magic: A Biography of Sylvia Plath* presents Assia, in her very first appearance in the book, in a misogynistic, body shaming way: "[David Wevill's] wife, Assia Gutmann, was a woman whose beautiful elegant face more than compensated for what one [unidentified] friend remembers as 'hips like the rear end of a 158 bus'" (265). And again, we find three chapters later: "Assia—[was] a beautiful if thick-waisted woman who disguised her figure by wearing long, flowing coats" (276). There cannot be a need for us to dwell on Assia's putative large hips except to find fault with her and detract from the almost universal admiration of her beauty; this move can only be designed to make us think less of her, especially if beauty is (supposedly) the only attribute worth admiring that she possesses. We take away the message that we *should* think less of her as a woman, and the various authors who have documented her impact on Plath's and Hughes's lives and texts have given us the means to do so. To add fuel to the fire, Alexander offers the anecdote that Assia "strait-jacketed" Hughes in her nightgown—approaching him while he was alone on the morning of the Wevills' fateful weekend visit to him and Plath in Devon—pulling up her nightgown and letting it fall over him, "trapping him inside the nightgown with her" (277). Despite these damaging visual images—and incorrect, it seems, according to what Assia told her friends and what Hughes himself recorded of that weekend in "Dreamers"—Assia is given this sentence, arguably to her credit: "Because of her background in the arts, Assia had assumed more than a passing interest in Hughes's career" (345). My book will explore Assia's role as muse to Plath and Hughes, in addition to considering her own contributions, in later chapters. As for Assia's contributions, Alexander dismisses them in his book, with the understanding that Assia was inferior to Plath (and haunted by her).

In many ways and by different strategies, Hughes scrubbed Assia from his and Plath's official record. Anne Stevenson reported in an interview with Janet Malcolm in the early 1990s that there was a concerted effort to spare Hughes the pain that mention of Assia would bring: "I'd known about Assia's suicide for years. All the poets knew about it—but out of pity for Ted no one ever spoke of it. Ted didn't demand that people be silent, but he asked me to keep what I said about Assia [in *Bitter Fame*] to a minimum, and I obeyed [. . . .] Ted had ten years of absolute hell after Sylvia died" (qtd. in Malcolm 103).

What Stevenson discloses is of interest to us: in effect, the memory of Assia and her contributions were being circumscribed after she died because of the perceived effect she would have on Hughes, personally and professionally, real and imagined. Treated differently in life and death in virtually every way than Plath, Assia's importance has been eroded: she simply does not exist in public documents or in the public sphere as she might. Although Stevenson suggests that Hughes refrained from issuing an edict that prevented people from talking about Assia, he all but prevented such talk. Even during her lifetime, he asked Assia to burn his personal letters to her; the thought of Assia saving his letters (and keeping a journal) "oppresses me," Hughes wrote to her (*Letters* 236).[8] He also requested that she not speak about him or their relationship to anyone else ("Draft Constitution"). Seemingly, in an attempt to avoid having his love letters traced to him, Hughes's letters to Assia are typically unsigned. The consequence of destroying the letters, should Assia have complied with the request, would ensure that no trace of their correspondence existed, thereby erasing their relationship and its dynamics from any record. Assia's biographers document to what extent Hughes obliterated Assia from the record of his life, despite her prominent role in it: he did not properly acknowledge Assia as his partner, the woman who lived with him for years. Indeed, Assia's seven-year relationship with Hughes was as long in duration as Plath's was with him, and Assia cared for him and his children in England and Ireland following Plath's death. The care Hughes took in shaping his life story, leaving Assia out of it, became apparent in his carefully cultivated Emory archive: the letters from him to Assia were purchased years later and added to the archive after his death. Regardless of Hughes's efforts to prevent Assia from being part of a record, people knew about Assia, and information slowly leaked out about her, as it did in the libel suit Hughes faced in connection with the film adaptation of Plath's *The Bell Jar* in the United States (Koren and Negev vi, 225). The present study aims to offer a scholarly avenue into Assia's significance and relevance and to restore her as an important figure in her own right in literary studies and women's studies.

What I wanted to do here is set out the historical and traditional ways in which Assia has been portrayed and interpreted in the twentieth century (and, in chapter 5, the twenty-first century)—when she has been depicted at all—because these formed the monolithic model or mold of how we think about and approach Assia and the gendered implications of her situation. These early books developed the foundation from which later conversations, authors, teachers, and readers took their cue. In retrospect, what we find is that Assia has been used to serve many purposes: to prove Plath's goodness in contrast with her own purported badness; and to assume the function of a scapegoat in a messy marital-literary situation that not only informed some of the best and most famous American and British poems of the twentieth century but also became the fodder for important (and riveting) biographies of important lives.[9] The historical ways that Assia as a person and literary figure has been approached are limiting and reductive for scholars, students, and general readers because they present, broadly, one story line, which allows one pathway into investigations into material texts and actual lives. More egregiously, demonizing Assia upholds, vindicates, and ultimately sanctions the practice of scapegoating women who do not fit a mold we like, who do not act or look the way we think they should, or who become the vehicle or embodiment of all the things we despise (whether or not they do embody such values). If we are willing to act this way in our scholarship and endorse this type of viewpoint and story in our teaching, we must ask how this misogyny has poisoned new generations of readers, scholars, men, and women who live and act in a world that already does not respect its women and girls the way it should.

THEORETICAL CONSIDERATIONS AND THEORETICAL FRAMING

Perhaps this project is indebted, in part, to the trajectory of expansion in new modernist studies because its author is a modernist by training. The agenda of new modernist studies includes expanding the authors studied and considered as modernist; expanding the definitions and geographies of modernism; and expanding the time frame of modernism as an active movement. The desire for expansion may be the extent of influence of new modernist studies on this study, however, because a far greater indebtedness belongs to feminist literary studies. What we have now, approximately a half-century after Assia's and Plath's deaths, are the critical concepts and theoretical frameworks that provide us with a means of reexamining, reconfiguring, and recuperating a woman's life through textual representations in many forms: poems, letters, and journal entries, in addition to photographs and other texts. Fay Weldon, a friend of Assia, observes in an interview with Elaine Feinstein in 1999 that feminism could have bolstered Assia's and Plath's resilience. She believes they "would have been less likely to kill themselves if the feminist movement had been strong in those years, since feminism would have helped them to realize that they could cope on their own and there would have been a network of support to question whether any man was worth such a sacrifice" (Feinstein 165). Feminist support in its many forms—institutional and structural, cultural and social—could have dramatically altered the course of many women's lives, including Assia's. As it was, the effects of second-wave feminism had yet to manifest, and Assia struggled with her mental health during low points in her life. Like Plath, Assia had a history of past suicide attempts and died by suicide,[10] but Assia also committed filicide by taking her daughter with her, an act that echoes what is depicted in Plath's poem "Edge" (composed 5 February 1963). To Assia, the prospect of leaving Shura behind in an inhospitable world was unfathomable. Writing to her sister on 11 March 1967, Assia expresses her love for Shura: "She is all I have. I adore her, as I only adored [my mother])." To her father, in January 1969, Assia writes, "I've often thought of this [. . .] the criminality perpetrated on my little Shuri—these thoughts often stopped me." But she concludes her suicide and filicide note: "I couldn't leave little Shura by herself" (qtd. in Koren and Negev 164 and 205). From here, I will highlight the feminist thinking that most directly informs this study of Assia and representations of her in the literary sphere.

A concept embedded in women's studies can aid us in rethinking

Assia and her signification: "positionality" is that condition "in which people are defined not in terms of fixed identities, but by their location within shifting networks of relationships," and these "can be analyzed and changed" (Maher and Tetreault 164). If we present Assia to our students in the classroom or to each other in scholarship as a figure we should identify and somehow know in the poetry of Plath and Hughes, then we need to be cognizant of how we are positioning her. Positionality reminds us that it is impossible to fix Assia's identity to a static subject position or to a flat character type: she was someone or something dynamic and different to Plath, Hughes, friends, and acquaintances as well as to her daughter and to herself. What I hope to offer in this book is a sense of Assia as a complex woman who deserves to be located within a shifting network of relationships, texts, and artifacts that require us to revisit her, thereby analyzing and changing her position within the traditional script delivered in American and British letters.

The ways that Assia has been represented in scholarship by critics and in poems by Plath and Hughes illustrate how injurious language can be. In *Excitable Speech*, Judith Butler elucidates how injurious speech and address function, including language that "depends on the use of names, calling another a name[;] other forms seem to rely on descriptions or even silences" (28). We should consider, she suggests, which words and representations wound and offend, and so we should turn to concrete utterances and, as Butler does, interrogate them. She points out that the "mode of address" directed to a given person fixes that person via interpellation and subject constitution. Victims of injurious speech experience being "derogated and demeaned," and this scenario is one in which we find Assia. Yet the possibility for a reversal, a liberation, emerges: "If to be addressed is to be interpellated, then the offensive call runs the risk of inaugurating a subject in speech who comes to use language to counter the offensive call" (2). I engage in the spirit of this type of revisionist or recovery project with this book, but Assia herself embarked in writing to reflect her own subject position and, at times, to reconstitute herself in her diary entries and letter writing. But because we have a relatively small number of letters and journal entries penned by Assia available in archives, I will use other artifacts associated with her to make the case that a literary and feminist study of Assia counters the sexist turn that diminishes her as a woman who is worthy of respect or dignity; that prevents her from assuming her position as an influential woman in literature and culture; and that discredits her own contributions as an artist and writer who merits recovery. Moreover, we continue to blame the victim when we fault Assia for the tragedies of her life, an act we can address and redress as we learn more about our own contemporary expectations for women and femininity in our study of Assia (and Plath and Hughes).

Butler provides important definitions for this type of recovery project in *Gender Trouble*. Concerning *gender*, one becomes a woman; one is formed as such. "Gender," explains Butler, "is the repeated stylization of the body, a set of repeated acts within a highly rigid regulatory frame that congeal over time to produce the appearance of substance, of a natural sort of being" (45). She encourages us to consider deconstructing such natural-seeming constructions of gender, which we will do with respect to Assia because her own authored texts and products speak to gender and its representations, as do the representations of her body and life. *Representation* is also a critical term for the purposes of this study, being that it is the only way to access gender. According to Butler, "*representation* serves as the operative term within a political process that seeks to extend visibility and legitimacy to women as political subjects; on the other hand, representation is the normative function of a language which is said either to reveal or to distort what is assumed to be true about the category of women" (2). Representations of Assia in famous poems that appear to reveal and distort her femininity in the attack on her womanhood or personhood will be treated, with the goals being to identify and deconstruct the ideologies and messages embedded therein. As a result, we can cultivate new lines of thinking and engage in (re) positioning women for the benefit of the women and men we write for and about and teach. Assia's own self-reflexive texts, the images of her captured in art and photography, as well as the art and literature she produced complement the more canonical representations of her by Plath and Hughes.

A text that has proven formative in how I conceptualize the approaches to Assia presented here is Butler's *Precarious Life*, a sensitively written book in which Butler discusses post-9/11 American politics and ideologies. While her focus is quite remote from mine, its theoretical framing makes it an important critical companion to this study. Specifically, Butler claims that lives are "maintained and supported differently," and while some lives will be highly protected, others "will not even qualify as 'grievable'" (32). Coming from my past work in trauma studies, I was struck by the fact that Assia's life is not typically viewed as "grievable," which is disturbing when it appears that she was a victim too.[11] Butler theorizes that we exact violence on those "who are unreal" because "those lives are already negated" (33); in other words, those lives do not matter, and we can do what we want to them. However, in maintaining this powerful position of perpetrator, we continue to negate those lives again and again, and I believe this is what we are doing to Assia in biographies, in scholarship, and in our teaching of Plath's and Hughes's poetry—and in our neglect of Assia's accomplishments and contributions. We do not have to condone all choices she made; we can value Assia for various reasons. As Butler argues, "We do not need to ground ourselves in a single model of communication, a single model of reason, a single notion of the subject before we are able to act" (48). While I hope feminist recovery efforts pertaining to Assia continue to gain momentum (I will examine Assia's legacy and such efforts in chapter 5), I will read her through various feminist and poststructuralist lenses, grounded in embodiment theory, in chapters 2, 3, and 4, so that she may be reread and reinterpreted.

Additionally, Butler's ideas about loss and vulnerability are important here. I will quote her in full because this assertion is one that underwrites Assia's self-presentation in her letters and journal entries, which will be examined in chapter 4: "Each of us is constituted politically in part by virtue of the social vulnerability of our bodies—as a site of desire and physical vulnerability, as a site of publicity at once assertive and exposed. Loss and vulnerability seem to follow from our being socially constituted bodies, attached to others, at risk of losing those attachments, exposed to others, at risk of violence by virtue of that exposure" (20). In her archived letters and journal entries, Assia repeatedly acknowledges attachment to Hughes and her romantic dependence on him, to such an extent that her sense of self, as a woman and mother, are linked to him—socially (e.g., her lifestyle as a single mother who desired to marry Hughes and set up a home with him), personally (e.g., as the father of her child), romantically (e.g., as a partner and lover), and professionally (e.g., concerning literary projects for her and for him). To Assia, Hughes was the key to her and their daughter's happiness and security, and that belief was likely indebted to cultural beliefs about what makes for a successful woman's life. But there were also structural barriers that Assia encountered as a single mother and working professional in 1960s London that further destroyed her. We are constituted politically in terms of our sex, sexual orientation, socioeconomic class, and nationality, and so examining the "social vulnerability of our bodies," as Butler terms it, will expose the dangers and disadvantages, as well as the pleasures and advantages, of our situations. Assia and Hughes experienced incredible losses from their respective perspectives, as their writing evidences, and Assia's losses proved too much for her, as we will see in chapters 3 and 4. Butler's treatment of mourning will help us in approaching, in chapter 3, Hughes's representations of limited (i.e., restricted) mourning for Assia and Shura in his poems and letters. These are not the only ways in which to approach Assia (and Hughes), but I do think that they will provide startling new means of viewing her, which may incite and beget additional approaches other than the traditional ones. As for Assia, she desired the good life: financial stability, emotional support, respectability, and love. When these aspirations eluded her, she deemed them losses too great to overcome.

Assia's body and embodiment will be analyzed throughout this study, due to the impact her body has had on the literary imagination. Informing the theoretical undercurrents of these discussions of embodiment and subjectivity are many theorists, but the most important to this book are Iris Marion Young, Luce Irigaray, Rose Weitz, and Julia Kristeva. Young fleshes out how we might think about gendered bodies in *On Female Body Experience*. She argues that "deep social divisions of masculine and feminine gendered dispositions and experience, which have implications for the psychic lives of men and women" exist (Young 14). More concretely, I want to focus on her insistence that the "lived body is a unified idea of a physical body acting and experiencing in a specific sociocultural context; it is body-in-situation" (16). An approach to the "body-in-situation," or "lived body," pivots on material bodies and their subjectivity, while acknowledging, as Young does, that gender is separate from sex. She proceeds to argue that a sex-gender binary falls short of what we need it to do in feminist theory and women's studies, and she advocates, instead, for the concept of the "body-in-situation," the "lived body," because it attributes importance to how a person is formed and conditioned socioculturally while being clear that the person herself often cannot choose the conditions for behavior or dictate the expectations of others (18). Ultimately, Young argues that we need to consider social structures (or the lack thereof, I would add) in tandem with the lived body. According to Young, "Social structures position individuals in relations of labor and production, power and subordination, desire and sexuality, prestige and status" (20.) She continues, "The way a person is positioned in structures is as much a function of how other people treat him or her within various institutional settings as of the attitude a person takes to himself or herself" (21). What we see when we examine Assia's life and work and how that view has been disseminated in scholarship is that Assia both worked within and against social structures, including her positions within poetry circles, marriages, extramarital relations, and a domestic partnership—and the social structures involving her identities as a single, working mother; an advertising professional; a femme fatale; and a victim of her circumstances. In fact, Young believes these types of structures so determine our lives that she defines *gender* as "a particular form of social positioning of lived bodies in relation to one another within historically and socially specific institutions and processes that have material effects" (22). In the following chapters, we will approach Assia as a gendered subject who did not survive the world she found herself in but who acted, for much of her life, in ways that seemingly indicated she was thriving in a gendered world.

Similar to Young, Luce Irigaray maintains that a woman's "identity," her femininity, is "imposed on her according to models that remain foreign to her." She addresses a situation in which Assia became entangled while serving as muse to Plath and Hughes (I will delve into this scenario later on). Irigaray observes that women's "social inferiority" is reinforced by the fact that women are appropriated by "masculine" systems of representation. Women themselves can sometimes work within these masculine systems of representation, Irigaray explains, but to their own detriment (85). Assia, as the femme fatale, played to and was played by conceptions of femininity, which Irigaray defines as "a role, an image, a value, imposed upon women by male systems of representation" (84). This is the crux of the problem: Assia (or a woman somewhat like her) could never emerge in our literature, scholarship, or classroom discussions as anything other than unimportant at best and despicable at worst until we problematize her representations and legacy in the twentieth- and twenty-first centuries and understand what is at stake in such representations.

Underscoring what has already been discussed, Rose Weitz reminds us that women's bodies have always mattered throughout history: unlike men, women have had to grapple with the close association of their bodies to the conditions of their lives. Weitz concludes her survey of a Western history of women's bodies with the reminder that we need to examine the embodied experiences of women and consider how those experiences are socially constructed before "we can fully understand women's lives, women's position in society, and the possibilities for resistance against that position" (11). Historically, societies have dismissed women's bodies and their capabilities, physically and mentally, as inferior compared to those of men and have positioned men to be the purported owners of women's bodies. "Finally," Weitz argues, "societies have assumed that women's bodies inherently turn them into sexual seductresses who threaten men's bodies and souls" (3). With this history and its influence, it is little wonder we have demonized and scapegoated Assia so easily and successfully.

We have succeeded, with the help of Plath, Hughes, and traditional biographies about Plath, in abjecting Assia. As Julia Kristeva succinctly declares in *Powers of Horror,* "The abject has only one quality of the object—that of being opposed to *I*" (1). To identify with Assia, to feel sympathy for her, or to accord her a different place (or a repositioned or repurposed space) in the literary landscape would mean a demolition of what we have built her up to be: all that which we are not, that Plath is not, that Hughes is not. That which is abject is that which "disturbs identity, system, order. What does not respect borders, positions, rules" (Kristeva 4). While I will allude to the fact that Assia was a product of her time (especially in recognition of her belief that her life was a failure for having not secured Hughes in marriage), she also disturbed identities (i.e., Plath's, Hughes's, her own, and readers who never knew her) and did not adhere to geographical borders, gendered positions, or relationship rules in many instances. We will see that, in Plath's and Hughes's poetry about her, Assia fit the definition of the "abject" as defined by Kristeva: "Abjection [. . .] is immoral, sinister, scheming, and shady: a terror that dissembles, a hatred that smiles, a passion that uses the body for barter instead of inflaming it, a debtor who sells you up, a friend who stabs you" (4). Rita Felski refers to a "literature of shock" (110), a literature that evokes reactions to "what is startling, painful, even horrifying" (105), in *Uses of Literature.* Many of Plath's and Hughes's poems would fit within the category of "literature of shock," especially those poems involving or addressing Assia. Felski explores the affective responses of such literature on readers and points to several ways in which readers may respond. One response is to be left "floundering and speechless," unable to come to terms with what we perceive to be the ends of such literature: it disquiets us and becomes truly disquieting when we cannot discern how it might "further social progress." But there are other effects and affective responses such literature can have. According to Felski, the literature of shock can "blur the distinction between self and other" and "unravel the certainty of one's convictions rather than sustaining them" (110). Perhaps this book will show how the literature of shock invites us to blur, unravel, and dismantle self and other and the certainty of our convictions about Assia within two famous poets' bodies of work. As for furthering social progress along feminist lines, I hope that each chapter contributes to the feminist aim of recovering Assia, offering useful examples, analyses, and discussions while suggesting reasons we should be invested in this agenda.

Why Assia now? Interest in Assia will always exist because of her association with Plath and Hughes, and in this regard, materials are increasingly available as time progresses. For example, Hughes's poem "Last Letter," which surfaced in 2010, clarifies Assia's position within the Plath-Hughes drama: although, conventionally, Assia is held at least partially responsible for being the woman who killed Plath, it turns out that Hughes spent Plath's last weekend with another girlfriend, Susan Alliston, and Alliston recalled Plath phoning Hughes, very upset. Because the call from Plath was disturbing and because Hughes and Alliston did not want to receive a surprise visit from Plath, they left the flat and hid out in another, preventing Plath from making a last call or visit to her estranged husband before she took her life (Bate 210–11). Hughes was not, in fact, spending his time in the company of Assia when Plath died, but it makes little difference in how Assia is perceived post-2010. In the meantime, with respect to the recent outpouring of texts that treat Assia, we see that her life and legacy continue to stir interest. The fifth chapter of this book will trace Assia's representations in the twenty-first century.

Assia's life, work, and influence are relevant because her story teaches us about our expectations for women then and now. As Marianne Hirsch states, "Aesthetic encounters [. . .] elicit a sense of vulnerability [associated with "its own risk, that of ignoring differences in power and privilege" (338)] that can move us toward an ethics and a politics of open-endedness and mobility, attuning us to the needs of the present, to the potentialities for change, and to the future"

(334). Specifically, we are faced with determining which women we like and which we do not in socially determined ways, and we encounter the strategies by which value(s) is construed in gendered artistic performances. Assia's story achieves poignancy, as I read it, because a more developed treatment of her rewrites the trope of the villainous and/or seductive mistress and the beautiful but destructive woman. Instead of serving this reductive stereotype or archetype, we serve better justice to Assia and other women when we realize that Assia was a victim in her life, too, and what we have done, ultimately, is blame the victim for her traumatic outcome and ending. Victim blaming remains a particularly gendered problem in that it manifests itself most obviously in cases and situations involving violence against or toward women. By perpetuating a "blame the victim" scenario with respect to Assia, we are modeling a sexist, misogynistic, and injurious ideology that finds its outlet in the world outside of the book in courtrooms, police reports, and the public sphere of approval, leaving victims without support. We teach our students to blame the victim when we blame or demonize Assia: in this regard, we exact incalculable damage to ourselves, our colleagues, and our students. In order to move past this undesirable situation, Hirsch suggests that by engaging with literature that asks us to be vulnerable, to reimagine reality, we assume the power to envision different possibilities "that would lead to alternative futures" and "alternative pasts as well" (337). Joan Retallack posits the following call to arms for feminist literary scholars in *The Poethical Wager:* "Proposal for a healthy politics of identity: to demand the right to work on one's subject position rather than to live out its destiny" (116). Perhaps changing, complicating, and adding to the conversation about Assia Wevill, as well as to those about Plath and Hughes, follows this call to arms that might benefit literary studies at the macrocosmic level and our students and ourselves at the microcosmic level.

I will close this section by referencing the beginning, as seems appropriate to me when considering the repetitive nature of trauma (and trauma is a subtext of the work and lives of Assia, Plath, and Hughes). The epigraph to this chapter is taken from three lines of

Hughes's poem "Fleeing from Eternity." It is contained in the box of archived materials at Emory dedicated to Hughes and his relationship with Assia, and this poem was later published in *Crow* (1970), which was dedicated to the memory of Assia and Shura. After sifting through boxes of materials, including unpublished correspondence—most of it written by Hughes to Assia, not the other way around, with the end result being that her voice is silenced in what was once a dialogue of letters—I find that Hughes (a masterful poet, indeed) got it right in the three lines I have excerpted. Assia's life has been the song that other poets sing (e.g., Hughes, Plath, Amichai, and Murphy), and those songs have proven to be successful, or "worth it." In the published version of "Fleeing from Eternity"—titled "Two Eskimo Songs," of which "Fleeing from Eternity" is the first part—the narrator tells us, in symbolic terms, about a nameless woman.

> Then, lying among the bones on the cemetery earth,
> He saw a woman singing out of her belly.
>
> He gave her eyes and a mouth, in exchange for the song.
> She wept blood, and she cried pain. (Hughes, *Collected Poems*, lines 21–24)

The context of this poem requires us to consider the connections to Assia; the draft of it is in the archived box of materials about her and belongs in a poetry collection dedicated to her. In her death, Assia fascinates; she has an afterlife, in fact, in the literary imagination. To me, the "woman singing out of her belly" suggests the birth of Shura: there is a birth and a product that emerges, much as there is for the singing poet who will produce a song about a woman such as Assia. In his published poetic representations of Assia, Hughes "gave her eyes and a mouth" figuratively, thereby giving her, in exchange, poetic immortality in a poem, or "song." Truly, Assia's pain and suffering ("She wept blood") appear to resonate on the level of trauma, as I will address later. The first section of "Two Eskimo Songs" closes, as it does in manuscript form, with these lines:

> The pain and the blood were life. But the man laughed—
> The song was worth it.
> The woman felt cheated. (25–27)

The songs—poems by Plath and Hughes especially—show to what extent Assia became inscribed and scapegoated in the poets' work to fulfill their needs. In his 1996 interview with Negev, a highly unusual interview in that Hughes broke his silence about Assia, Hughes acknowledged that Assia was a literary subject for him but that he may not have done her or himself justice somehow: "Hughes confirmed that he also wrote many poems about Assia but said he was not sure that he 'wrote the ones [he] should have written'" (226–27).[12] None of his published poems involving Assia allows her the dignity to emerge as a fully rounded character or complex woman. With the exception of Koren and Negev's book, no outlet, other than this project, considers Assia in a sustained way. This book is the first to approach Assia as an important figure in literary studies from a feminist perspective and to recover her as an artist in her own right. No woman should laugh at how Assia has been cheated in poetry and in the literary imagination then or now.[13]

CHAPTER 2

SYLVIA PLATH'S REPRESENTATIONS OF ASSIA WEVILL

Perfection is terrible, it cannot have children.
—from "The Munich Mannequins," by Sylvia Plath

Of all the chapters of this book, this one is the most difficult to write because it examines Sylvia Plath's representations of Assia Wevill in her late poetry, and what we will find is that Plath, as both a feminist icon and a product of her time, both explores and trades upon what it means to be valued and devalued as a woman in discursive formations, specifically poetry. In Plath's poems about Assia, the speaker frequently activates binary oppositions, resulting in the speaker upholding conventional femininity and rejecting that which might oppose it.[1] And yet Plath resisted bifurcating herself in traditional ways: instead of choosing a family over a career, or vice versa, she chose both. While she was composing the poems primarily about Assia, however, Plath was smarting from the betrayal of her husband and friend and the breakup of her home. Therefore, it is not surprising that Plath would resort to animating gendered scripts in parceling out value in ways that malign Assia: perceiving herself as the injured party, Plath would want others to sympathize with her, not with the other people whom she held responsible for the injuries and damages. The poems "Words heard, by accident, over the phone" (dated 20 July 1962), "Burning the Letters" (dated 13 August 1962), "The Fearful" (dated 16 November 1962), "Childless Woman" (dated 1 December 1962), and "The Munich Mannequins" (dated 28 January 1963) were written after Plath intercepted the call from Assia to Ted

Hughes that heralded the affair. These poems are important in that they allow us a platform upon which to continue the examination of how gender is conveyed in the work of one of the most important poets in American literature and in twentieth-century world literature. Additionally, for the purposes of this book, the poems about Assia provide us the opportunity to investigate and interrogate how she is portrayed or gestured to in Plath's body of work. With Plath's evergreen popularity among academics and a general audience, the representations of Assia in Plath's Pulitzer Prize–winning *Collected Poems* are consumed far more often than dry academic treatises on gender identity or identity politics.

For her part, Assia felt she resided in Plath's and Hughes's shadows and saw herself as inferior to them (Koren and Negev 126). In her journal, she writes, "I'm immersed now in the Hughes's monumentality, hers and his. The weak mistress, forever, in the burning shadows of their mysterious seven years" (qtd. in Koren and Negev 122). It did not help matters that Assia was impressed and captivated by Plath's late poetry, particularly her *Ariel* poems, and that she understood herself to be a catalyst for it. As Assia's biographers recount, Assia "was mesmerized by Plath's *Ariel* poems and, though they vilified and attacked her and Hughes, she admitted that they were 'most incredible.' She flattered herself that she was the tragic muse. Opening a maroon-backed ledger, she read Plath's last journal, ending three days before the suicide. . . . She was shocked by the extent of Sylvia's hostility and hatred toward her" (Koren and Negev 116–17). Assia comes across as naive here, and her reaction to Plath's last journal indicates that she did not fathom to what degree Plath was affected by potentially traumatic events. About Plath and Hughes's relationship prior to the affair, Plath's friend Elizabeth Compton Sigmund remarks, "Their life was something so rare and different from anything I had come across before, and I knew that Sylvia depended on it so profoundly that it was impossible to imagine her life without it" (Sigmund and Crowther 20). In contrast to this account are comments about Plath and Hughes's relationship by Plath's mother, recorded on the *Letters Home* manuscript, which is housed in the Plath archive at the Lilly Library, Indiana University. After Plath discovered Hughes's attraction to Assia, Aurelia Plath writes that the problems in Plath and Hughes's marriage were nothing new; the problems had been triggered (the inference is that they had reemerged) by a series of recent incidents. Aurelia Plath reasons that Plath and Hughes needed to work through their problems, and the implication is that they needed to work them out together, as the problems are identified as theirs (Plath, "*Letters Home*—Part Seven"). From her perspective as her daughter's confidante, Aurelia Plath discerned a pattern of problems in the Plath-Hughes marriage, of which Assia was the latest manifestation. With these stories in mind, we now can position Plath's poems about Assia in a biographical context. As Stephen Enniss remarks, "[Hughes's] affair with Assia Wevill in the summer of 1962 had struck a deep blow to their marriage, yet it also unleashed some of Plath's most forceful and moving poems" (ix). We will examine some of these poems later in this chapter. What follows is an overview of the feminist theoretical framework; consideration of the contexts within which Plath was writing and we are reading; and a presentation of feminist interpretations and explications of what I refer to as Plath's Assia poems.

FEMINIST THEORETICAL FRAMEWORK, CONTEXT, AND DISCUSSION OF PLATH AND FEMINISM

Adrienne Rich argues that we need to revisit old texts and intentionally study them in other lights. Explains Rich, "Re-vision—the act of looking back, of seeing with fresh eyes, of entering an old text from a new critical direction—is for women more than a chapter in cultural history: it is an act of survival." According to Rich: "Until we can understand the assumptions in which we are drenched we cannot know ourselves. And this desire to self-knowledge, for women, is more than a search for identity: it is part of our refusal of the self-destructiveness of male-dominated society." Literature is a "clue to how we live, how we have been living, how we have been led to imagine ourselves, how our language has trapped as well as liberated us" (Rich 167). Rich is correct when she states that victimization, as it is experienced by women, is real, and the sources of it can be traced to our environment, society, language, and structures of our thoughts (176). As for Plath, Rich classes Plath's poetry as that which exhibits "man's power—to dominate, tyrannize, choose, or reject the woman" (168).

And it was a man's world in which Plath (and Assia) lived.[2] Following World War II, traditional gendered patterns of behavior and work were expected in concert with traditional family structures (Eekelaar 111). In fact, throughout the 1960s in Great Britain, approximately 40 percent of women participated in the paid labor force, whereas men's participation was 75–85 percent (Sorrentino 25). Heather Clark refers to the "tyranny of gender" as an obstacle for Plath to overcome; she notes that Adlai Stevenson exhorted Plath's graduating class at Smith College to become wives and mothers (33 n. 46). In short, Plath "was not expected to pursue her own career; subordination was the only option available to her if she wished to marry, which she did," concludes Clark (33). Thus, Plath's determination and success in carving out and maintaining a career while married and, later, caring for children is quite remarkable and very much a feminist achievement in that Plath chose her path(s) and worked toward self-actualization and empowerment. While Al Alvarez collapses Plath's "identity as a poet" with her "vindicat[ion] as a woman" after the birth of her children (*Savage God* 23), making the conflicting cultural identities appear seamlessly integrated, for Plath herself the mother-poet dichotomy, as entrenched as it was in the United States and England in the 1950s and 1960s, proved to be difficult to reconcile with her actual life.[3]

Trevor Thomas's memoir of Plath sets the sociohistorical and cultural stage for us. He remembers that Hughes accompanied Plath in meeting leasing agents when she was hunting for a flat for the children and herself. As a result, Hughes receives Thomas's praise in supporting his estranged wife because Thomas admits that any landlord "would be unlikely to let to a woman living alone with two children" (2), indicating the cultural climate and gendered structural obstacles

Plath was up against in London in the early 1960s. In this example, it is possible to see how important being partnered by a man could be. As Plath's neighbor, Thomas observed these types of instances, but he apparently also served as an occasional sounding board to Plath and so was privy to her feelings about Assia and Hughes. After Thomas invited Plath into his home (the flat downstairs from hers), Plath confessed her troubles to him. In conversing with Thomas about Assia and Hughes, Plath became "fiercely angry with an intensity that was quite alarming as she punched clenched fists up and down. 'It's that awful woman's fault. She stole him. We were so happy and she stole him away from me. . . . We were so happy, so happy. Oh, if only . . . if only she had never come.' And again she raged angrily about the other woman without ever naming her.[4] She raged about him, too, but in an ambivalent blend of blame, jealousy and wanting him back" (12). We can see how Plath's attitude toward Assia would shape the poems Plath wrote about her. But what we should take into account is Thomas's assessment of Plath and her love life: "For someone who in her High School and College days had a compulsion to come out tops with almost a complete run of straight A's, it must have deeply wounded her ego to be beaten in love . . . and by another woman" (13). From Thomas's perspective, women compete against other women in a homosocial triangle to win the man as a prize—love is their sport—but it is more than a vanity competition if we admit that Thomas's memoir, flawed though it may be, indicates systematic structural obstacles to security and personhood for women in his snapshots of daily life for Plath. Women simply are not positioned and socialized to have the same opportunities and advantages as the men in their lives do. For example, Thomas claims that Plath "needed a man about the house to render instant first aid" (9). Whether or not this is accurate, we see the type of gendered responses Plath would have picked up on from her neighbor and sometimes confidant. I suspect that it is this cultural environment and its dynamics that infect the Assia poems.

As Luce Irigaray reminds us, femininity consists of models (or scripts) that are imposed on women.[5] Because women do not enjoy as much privilege as men do culturally, socially, politically, or historically, they are appropriated by masculine systems of representation. Irigaray expounds on this concept: masculine or patriarchal systems of representation harm women, even if women attempt to work within the systems, or what I think of as codes (85). As a femme fatale, Assia is already coded or signifies in such a manner that she can never enjoy true power or privilege. By co-opting masculine representations of women in her Assia poems, Plath, though a feminist icon in her other work, shows that masculinist values and messages are absorbed by us all.[6] What Plath assimilates into her Assia poems are the very signs and values that subtract worth from Assia and women like her and that reaffirm and reinforce conventional, or traditional, femininity. Irigaray argues that for a woman to be valued in a male-dominated "exchange market," or "market of sexual exchange"—wherein women strive to be found desirable and chosen as romantic partners to men—they need to maintain their femininity. In sum, Irigaray declares, with respect to such a marketplace, "the value of a woman would accrue to her from her maternal role, and, in addition, from her 'femininity'" (84). The speakers in Plath's Assia poems laud the maternal role, and the poems consider the world as a sexual exchange market whereby femininity, good and bad, is shown to be the prevailing currency.

Plath's Assia poems are particularly intriguing in their strategies for deploying two versions of femininity, and they are dichotomous: one type of femininity is represented as desirable, and the other is represented as that which is undesirable. One is held up by the speakers in the poems as valuable and worth emulating, and the other type is shown to be despicable, destructive, and outside the boundaries of good taste. Irigaray surmises that women, treated as products to be consumed by men, have perhaps never been constituted as "subjects." From this perspective, women's "sexualized bodies underwrite the organization and the reproduction of the social order" (Irigaray 84), and so it would be expected that women writers might trade upon representations of femininity and sexualized bodies to marshal opinion or underscore a point or message, knowing, perhaps intuitively, that those representations will signify in specific ways. Consequently, regardless of how desirable or undesirable a female muse to a writer of either sex may be, she will almost always be at a disadvantage if she is marked as a feminine subject. Irigaray maintains the position that women are alienated from themselves and each other when they utilize masculine systems of representation, of which femininity and its depictions are a part: "Women's social inferiority is reinforced and complicated by the fact that woman does not have access to language, except through recourse to 'masculine' systems of representation which disappropriate her from her relation to herself and to other women. The 'feminine' is never to be identified except by and for the masculine" (85). In other words, Assia, as either a historical figure or an archetype, would not have been likely to be liberated in either Plath's or Hughes's poems in her role as feminine muse, even if the tragedies and the ensuing trauma had never occurred. When we read and study Plath's Assia poems, we should be cognizant of how femininity is represented and challenge ourselves to consider both the values saturating the depictions and the messages embedded therein, as we interpret them from our own subject positions. Ultimately, we will find that conventional femininity is championed in Plath's Assia poems, specifically values pertaining to domesticity and maternity.[7] In contrast, the speakers in the Assia poems depreciate the value and worth of the type of conventional but undesirable femininity associated with Assia.

Our goal, then, as Judith Butler phrases it, is to engage in "a critique of the categories of identity" (*Gender Trouble* 7), specifically gender within the scope of the present book. According to Butler, "Gender is the repeated stylization of the body, a set of repeated acts within a highly rigid regulatory frame that congeal over time to produce the appearance of substance, of a natural sort of being" (45). The representations of gendered and stylized bodies and identities in Plath's Assia poems deserve our attention because of their potential to reify traditional and polarizing views of femininity, making two versions of a conventional feminine script of gender seem natural and true. Through explicating the Assia poems, we come to understand the constructed core of gender, especially when we are aware of the biographical elements at play and at stake in the characterizations of Assia and the speakers in the Assia poems. We also will understand how representing gendered bodies and identities is a value-laden enterprise, intentionally or unintentionally designed for various effects. In the case of the Assia poems, one effect culminates in (re)producing Assia as a quintessential example of dangerous, bad, and undesirable femininity.

Erica Wagner comments, in her reading of Hughes's poem "Dreamers," that Assia, Plath, and Hughes "are now part of an irresistible myth" as Hughes himself saw it (230), and it is for this very reason that we should study the components of the myth with a feminist lens in order to discern what the myth teaches us—and can teach us—about cultural ideologies, especially those pertaining to gender and identity. We can complicate gendered performances and identities by revisiting representations of them and critically engaging them. For Plath, gendered performances and identity are, indeed, complicated: Plath was both attracted to and repelled by Assia. In October 1962, Plath tells her friend Helder Macedo, "I have conjured up Assia," in response to Macedo's account of a novel in which the characters "conjure up an alluring woman between them" (Stevenson 273). According to Anne Stevenson, Plath conceived of Assia as "her opposite—the Other" (273), but both the Plath figure and the Assia figure in the Assia poems attend to a gendered script and maintain their roles. This account and scenario remind us that all gender is a fraught construction and nothing more than a malleable script: it is a script that can allure and repel, by turns, and our reactions to any gendered iteration exposes more about us and our culture as an interpreter situated in discourse than it does the actual gendered entity being interpreted. Hughes acknowledged as much in his 13 July 1966, letter to Aurelia Plath: "With a story like Sylvia's, everyone treats it as a mysterious dream—a sort of free space for them to air their own nightmares & self-suspicions" (*Letters* 260). And what we have done to Assia in Plath studies is to transform her into the abject. "The abject," states Julia Kristeva, "has only one quality of the object—that of being opposed to *I*" (1). For Plath, Assia is the epitome of the abject if abjection is that which is "immoral, sinister, scheming, and shady: a terror that dissembles, a hatred that smiles, a passion that uses the body for barter instead of inflaming it, a debtor who sells you up, a friend who stabs you," as Kristeva phrases it (4). In my interpretations of the Assia poems, Plath molds speakers who are proxies or mouthpieces for herself, with the exception of the speaker in "Childless Woman," and so these are the very poems that we should re-vision, as Rich asks us to do, because Plath makes the personal political in her poetry. Interrogating and problematizing the female identities and their configurations in the Assia poems allow us to get at the heart of identity politics and how they manifest in Plath's work.

Kwame Anthony Appiah provides an overview of identification that resonates with what may be happening in the Assia poems. According to Appiah, "identification" is the process "through which individuals shape their projects—including their plans for their own lives and their conceptions of the good life—by reference to available labels, available identities" (66). It is important to people, Appiah affirms, "that they can tell a story of their lives that meshes with larger narratives" because identification factors into how people shape and evaluate their lives, to determine whether they have succeeded or failed (68, 69). Plath's Assia poems are a battleground for the processes of identification as well as the shaping and evaluating of identities, as we will see in the analyses and discussions of the Assia poems later in this chapter.

Plath's and Assia's stories are mired in gendered subjectivity. As Iris Marion Young defines it, *subjectivity* encompasses "who one is as an agent, the attributes and capacities one has for experience, the relations with others that contribute to one's sense of self." Gender is a general category, but subjectivity is particularized (Young 19). For instance, both Plath and Assia are women-identified women whose lives and work can be opened up by examinations of gendered subjectivity. In Plath's case, her Assia poems prompt us to reflect on gendered subjectivity for women—namely, identity issues tied to the female body: maternity and reproductive rights. For Plath's speakers in the Assia poems, motherhood is associated with empowerment, and "childlessness," including "barrenness" and choosing not to have children—whether by abstinence, birth control, or abortion—is relegated to the disempowered side of the binary opposition in the dichotomous, gendered world of the Assia poems. Of course, these treatments of female bodies deserve feminist analysis and critique.[8] What we see in Plath's representations of bodies like hers and bodies like Assia's is an outgrowth of what Young understands as women who experience their subjectivity differently. Young clarifies that "the group called 'women' is the product of a loose configuration of different structural factors" (21). Because subjectivity manifests differently depending on structural factors, such as family or marital status, socioeconomic status, nationality, and race, even women who adhere to gendered expectations can experience the world very differently, as we see both in the biographical lives of Plath and Assia and, more to the point of this chapter, the gendered subjectivities laid bare in the Assia poems.

Rita Felski's concept of a "literature of shock" aids us in our thinking about Plath's shocking poetry, with its "personal is political" pyrotechnics and unabashedly no-holds-barred treatment. In the next chapter we will see that Hughes's poetry is far more violent and gruesome—and overtly shocking—than Plath's, and his poetry fits neatly with what Felski has in mind regarding the literature of shock. But Plath's Assia poems are shocking: they refrain from redeeming or empowering all women, forwarding a feminist theme, or delivering a social justice narrative that illuminates or critiques realities. What we receive from the Assia poems are messages that disparage women, specifically that propagate the archetype of the beautiful but destructive woman; pit women against women in a manner that thwarts sisterhood and breeds competition in ways that support a patriarchal system; locate worth and value solely in traditional feminine domestic roles; and uphold the reproductive, maternal body as the ideal. It is shocking to find these aspects in the Assia poems because we hold up Plath as a feminist icon. Felski comments, "The literature of shock becomes truly disquieting not when it is shown to further social progress, but when it utterly fails to do so, when it slips through our frameworks of legitimation and resists our most heartfelt values" (110). The Assia poems may not be what we expect from Plath; we expect the feminist critiques embedded in the shocking "Daddy" and "Lady Lazarus." It is our responsibility, then, to generate the feminist critiques in our teaching and scholarship so that we might have productive conversations about how and why women are represented in the ways that they are—and what those representations mean.[9] Because Plath's oeuvre, especially her poetry, remains unflaggingly influential, we should attend to Felski's observation that literature "can bring home, with exceptional vividness and graphic power, psychic dramas of torment and self-loathing, destructiveness and disgust. . . . Rather than serving up the suffering at a distance, they allow us to witness it close up" (114). Indeed, the Assia poems are texts that display "psychic dramas of torment" as well as "destructiveness and disgust," and they allow us "to witness it close up." When we consider the real-life circumstances that inspired the Assia poems, we can honor Plath's anger by recognizing our unease with it as a cultural feature of Western societies, which are uncomfortable with women's anger and typically find it unreasonable for women to express it. Perhaps part of what situates Plath as a feminist icon is her refusal to censor herself or to tone down her anger over perceived injustice. A privilege of working with the Assia poems is that they allow us to take stock of our own ideologies, biases, and values. In them, too, we can ascertain biographical references that remind us that literature teaches us about the "real world," and in the real world, there is no such thing as a perfect feminist. The Assia poems are expert in their execution, and their intelligent design testifies, in part, to the power that gendered archetypes and conventional narratives about gender wield.

A sticking point for some feminists may be Plath's portrayals of a "childless woman" as less than (<) in value when compared to reproductive women.[10] What Judith Butler calls "feminism's claim to reproductive freedom" is not a small matter; indeed, Butler argues that "bodily integrity" and "self-determination" are constituent of political mobilization efforts for equality for all people (*Precarious*

Life 25). This is not an attempt to exonerate Plath from her depiction of Assia in the Assia poems, but we would do well to keep in mind the biographical context of the poems: Plath felt betrayed by Hughes and Assia, and she knew how to marshal gender discourses in her poems to affect the characterizations therein because she had already been formed by those very discourses. As Butler explains, "If we are formed in language, then that formative power precedes and conditions any decision we might make about it, insulting us from the start, as it were, by its prior power" (*Excitable Speech* 2). In other words, Plath is both formed by and trapped by the very discourses that she invokes, and the brilliance and genius of her (other) poetry broadly is that she is able to imagine and envision feminist alternatives through technically powerful and aesthetically beautiful texts. Perhaps the closest we can get to claiming the Assia poems as feminist is in their articulation of female voices and their premise that (some) women's lives do matter.

Is Plath a feminist? My own response is yes, which is likely the response of most feminist scholars who work on Plath. After more than a decade of teaching and writing about Plath and women's studies, my reductive definition of feminism umbrellas three overarching concerns: (1) equality (striving for it, maintaining it, celebrating it, etc.); (2) empowerment and advocacy for women and other underrepresented or underserved people; and (3) analysis of power, especially as it pertains to gender, which is often accompanied by a disruption of power structures or the staging of an intervention in them. Much of Plath's writing falls neatly into one or more of these feminist agenda items. The Assia poems are notable in that they do not neatly align with a feminist project broadly construed, other than they give voices to female speakers. Due to the contentious nature of the word *feminist*, it is understandable that people who knew Plath, who study Plath, and who value her and her work would occupy different perspectives on Plath as a feminist.

In a 2017 interview, Frieda Hughes adamantly states that her mother "wasn't a feminist"; after the publication of *Ariel*, young women, moved by that poetry collection, "could make her into anything they wanted" (qtd. in Jones).[11] Frieda Hughes refrains from delving into why she does not consider her mother to be a feminist, but there are passages in Plath's published work that suggest that Plath's views are complicated and do not lend themselves to distillation easily. On 19 February 1956, for example, Plath records in her personal writing: "I fight all women for my men. My men. I am a woman, and there is no loyalty, even between mother and daughter. Both fight for the father, for the son, for the bed of mind and body" (*Unabridged Journals* 199). Jillian Becker, a friend of Plath and a memoirist who details Plath's weekend stay with her and her family during the last days of Plath's life, refutes, like Frieda Hughes does, the notion that Plath was a feminist: "If feminists can savor an irony, here is one for them. . . . Had anyone prophesied [the ushering in of a "gynocratic age"] and told [Plath] that she would be one of its icons, I think she'd have been surprised and possibly annoyed." Becker adds, "Perhaps the myth of Sylvia Plath the Feminist will fade away as intellectual fashions change" (72). Plath herself sometimes articulates positions that may not sit right with feminists, lending support to Frieda Hughes's and Becker's contentions. In a late December 1962 letter to Helga and Daniel Huws, Plath writes about Assia and Hughes: "The woman he is with is on her third husband & has had so many abortions she can't have children. She is part of this set of barren women . . . that I am glad to get rid of. I guess I am just not like that" (*Letters of Sylvia Plath*, vol. 2, 945). Notwithstanding Plath's varied stances on identity politics and women's bodies, her work as a whole bolsters feminist inquiry and frequently forwards feminist visions in art and scholarship. As a result, Plath's status as a feminist is not likely to be stripped away. As Rose Weitz comments, "Despite the differences among feminists in ideology and tactics, all share the goal of challenging accepted ideas about women's bodies and social position" (9). Much of Plath's late poetry participates in just this kind of feminist project. Her Assia poems are the exceptions.

Plath's Assia poems have yet to receive the attention that many of the *Ariel* poems receive, maybe in part because only "The Munich Mannequins" was included in *Ariel*.[12] Taken together, the Assia poems present a sustained treatment of gender identity and associated themes, and the poems share interrelated features that link them to each other, as the examination and analyses here will illustrate. The poems also ask us to consider the circumscription of gender, as what we will see are images and representations that will feel very familiar and "natural" to us. Moreover, these poems encourage us to think about how femininity is depicted and to what ends we can (re)imagine feminist futures, especially as we work toward recovering scapegoated women or female victims from the confines of literary and cultural studies discourses and scholarship. Indeed, Elaine Feinstein observes, "Hughes had been afraid of the effects that publication of Sylvia's last poems would have on his children and on his own reputation, but the first to suffer from Sylvia's fame was Assia" (165).

"WORDS HEARD, BY ACCIDENT, OVER THE PHONE"

The accounts of Plath answering Assia's telephone call to Hughes revolve around a particular retelling.[13] Returning home by car from a shopping expedition in Exeter with her mother, Aurelia Plath, on 9 July 1962, Plath states that that she has it all. "I have everything in life I've ever wanted: a wonderful husband, two adorable children, a lovely home, and my writing," relates Plath (qtd. by Aurelia Plath in *Letters Home* 458). The beginning of the tragedy of Plath's—and by extension, Assia's—life begins when Plath answers the ringing telephone. Five years after Plath's death, Ted Hughes remarked to his friend Richard Murphy that "Assia had once rung [Plath] up, and this was why [Plath] had uprooted the telephone wires from Court Green" (Murphy 266). It was an event that Hughes never forgot. What happened that day has been immortalized in Plath's poetry: the caller asks for Hughes, and as Diane Middlebrook has it, "Plath silently passed him the phone: she had recognized the voice of a woman pretending to be a man, and knew who it was. When he ended the call, she ripped the wires out of the wall and fled upstairs" (174). In an alternative version, Plath "realised from the embarrassed moment of silence at the other end that the call was not meant for her. Accounts vary as to whether it was Assia putting on a deep voice or a male friend phoning on her behalf. Either way, it was clear that she and Ted were in, or at least on the brink of, a relationship. After the call, Sylvia ripped the telephone cord out of its socket and there was an explosive row" (Bate 188). According to Carl Rollyson, "Assia later told [Olwyn Hughes] that she had asked a man to call Court Green on her behalf" (293). Plath herself confides in a letter to Ruth Tiffany Barnhouse Beuscher, her therapist, on the same day she wrote "Words heard, by accident, over the phone":

> I picked up the phone & a nasty man's voice asked if Ted could take a call from London. Ted always wants me to find out who it is, so I asked, & the man said he was sorry, the person didn't want to say. I felt thick with my own dumbness & called Ted. It was a woman, saying "Can I see you?" He said she didn't say her name & he had no idea who it was. I was pretty sure who it was. A girl who works in an ad agency in London, very sophisticated, and who, with her second poet-husband, took over the lease on our London flat. We'd had them down for a weekend, and I'd walked in on them (Ted & she) Tête-a-tête in the kitchen & Ted had shot me a look of pure hate. She smiled & stared at me curiously the rest of the weekend.

In returning to the subject of the call in her letter to Beuscher, Plath states that the caller was "seemingly almost speechless when she got me" (*Letters of Sylvia Plath*, vol. 2, 791). She continues, "I have discontinued the phone, for I can't stand waiting, every minute, to hear that girl breathing at the end of it, my voice at her fingertips, my life & happiness on her plate" (792). The day after the telephone call from Assia, Frieda Hughes informed her grandmother that her mother and father were crying in the back garden, and Hughes packed a bag to catch a train to London on 10 July (Middlebrook 174, 176).

"Words heard, by accident, over the phone" creates an atmosphere that is permeated by filth, contamination, and degradation, as sustained by the imagery of the poem. A slow realization dawns on the speaker: the words uttered over the phone can never be taken back or erased; they are here to stay. The speaker indicates that the impact of the words spoken to her is great, so great, it seems, that this moment is one the speaker knows will "percolate in my heart" (13), that she takes it to heart, figuratively speaking. The poem refrains from giving specific details as to what the literal words are; rather, it concentrates on imagery and poetic sound devices to effect the scene of the call and the emotions the speaker is processing in the aftermath of it. The poem is not euphonic—a fitting poetic decision—though it teases us that it had the potential to be so, as we see in the occasional rhyme ("digestibles" [4] / "syllables" [5]) or internal assonance and melodic line ("It is he who has achieved these syllables" [5]). The subject matter of the poem does not lend itself to beauty and sensual pleasure, and so euphony is staved off.

The first line ("O mud, mud, how fluid!") sets the poem in motion, and the internal alliteration emphasizes that the dirtiness of what we will learn are the caller's words, words that "are plopping like mud" onto "the phone table" (7, 8). Biographical details are present, but they only serve to remind us that the event captured in the poem was momentous in the lives of Plath, Hughes, and Assia: the poem is based upon the actual event described earlier in this section. The speaker identifies "foreign"-born Assia in the second line and the apparent hesitation the Assia figure has in finding words (and the voice, too, perhaps) to address to the speaker of the poem: "Thick as foreign coffee, with a sluggy pulse. / Speak, speak! Who is it?" (2–3). The speaker realizes who the caller is by the end of the first stanza and declares, "It is he who has achieved these syllables," or words. The speaker assigns a male pronoun to the person who has brought about or initiated the words spoken, and the pronoun can refer biographically and contextually to Hughes as the purported instigator of the affair with Assia. (He does, after all, speak to her on the phone during this very call after Plath passes the phone to him, and after a fight with Plath about his motivations, he proceeds to meet Assia in London.) The pronoun also suggests the male voice Assia supposedly tried to appropriate. It is important to note that the poem turns on a man: "Is he here?" the speaker (or the caller) wonders (10). The stanza ends here, and the white space following the question becomes a pregnant silence, likely mirroring the speaker's shock and dismay. "Now the room is ahiss," the speaker tells us, resuming her role as a narrator in the following stanza (11). *Ahiss* may be a slight allusion to Assia's name (to people who know the backstory of the poem), and it also suggests onomatopoeia in the hissing of a snake, linking Assia with a sinister or evil biblical snake who will betray the speaker and play a role in the devastating consequences that ensue. The Hughes figure in the poem may be implicated in the poem as a perpetrator, but the Assia figure shoulders far more blame as a perpetrator in two or three allusions (lines 2, possibly 5, and 11), when compared to the possible allusion to a man in line 5 only. The dramatic arc of the poem, then, is a story about two women vying for one man, leaving the speaker in the unenviable position of victim in relation to the perpetrator(s) of the poem.

The themes of defilement and victimization—that someone from outside can forever change the domestic space of another to the detriment of that person, sullying a home and violating the speaker, in an instant—are conveyed by two poetic devices: caesuras and imagery. The caesuras evoke the bewilderment and impending horror of the speaker as she processes the situation, trying to make sense of both the words and their import. Each stanza contains a heavy marking of caesuras (e.g., "What are these words, these words?" [6]). Likewise, each stanza in the short three-stanza poem conveys images related to or signifying mud (stanzas 1 and 2) and excrement (stanzas 1 and 3). The home itself is referenced overtly in imagery in stanzas 2 and 3 for the purpose of locating the unfolding drama. The transformative nature of the call is found in the last stanza, where the speaker casts the image of the telephone as an instrument with tentacles that leaves spawn behind. These words, or "spawn" (13), penetrate the speaker's heart, and here we have an image of the outside forcing itself in, an appropriate image of trauma that figures a symbolic rape in the poem, replete with the speaker's protest of the act in the last line ("You are too big! They must take you back!" [15]).[14]

"BURNING THE LETTERS"

After learning about Hughes's interest in Assia, Plath exacted revenge. When she returned home from dropping Hughes off to catch a London train following Assia's fateful telephone call, Plath built a bonfire, fed by Hughes's papers that she took from his study. Among these papers were envelopes addressed to Hughes in Assia's handwriting; the contents of the envelopes were missing (*Letters of Sylvia Plath*, vol. 2, 791). She also burned her present for him, a novel-in-progress, *Falcon Yard*, which recounted their happy early days together. Aurelia Plath watched the destruction of the papers with dismay. According to Middlebrook, "Another source, who got the story from Plath herself, adds that along with the papers she took, Plath had scraped from Hughes's desk a scum of skin flakes, nail pairings, and fallen hair, which she cast onto the bonfire while intoning magic spells; and that one paper fluttered into the air and fell to the ground, singed but readable, displaying the name of her rival, 'Assia.'" (173, 175). Leaving Frieda with her grandmother, Plath arrived at the home of her friend Elizabeth Compton Sigmund, who recalls, Plath "told me that Ted was in love with another woman, that she knew Assia and was terrified of her. She wept and wept and held onto my hands, saying, 'Help me'" (qtd. in Middlebrook 176). The Plath figure in "Burning the Letters," the poem about this scenario, takes action, but burning said letters is an act of revenge that is completed out of a desire to destroy the "hate" (12), or hateful content the letters contain, from the speaker's point of view, in order to establish "a good place now" in the room where they were found (22). In "Burning the Letters," we know that the speaker has felt victimized, gullible, and disillusioned, by turns: she has been "strung just under the surface" like a "Dumb fish" (23, 24), while "Riding my Arctic / Between this wish and that wish" (28). Clearly, the speaker did not get what she wished for and has been mightily disillusioned, leaving her angry, hurt, and determined to exact pain in return, as her vengeful act indicates. Moreover, the speaker anticipates that she will be caught in this psychological and emotional suffering for an indeterminate amount of time and that her subsequent act will last and make its mark indefinitely, much as the violence enacted by a pack of dogs in their mauling of a fox is equated to "immortality" (56), that which does not end, in the speaker's extended simile (49–56). Metapoetically, "Burning the Letters" is a poem that immortalizes the drama of the situation depicted in the poem, which we know is domestic in nature and location because the speaker builds the fire in her "housedress" and in a kitchen garden that includes "yellow lettuces and the German cabbage" (29, 39). "Burning the Letters" is also a poem that profits by a biographical reading.[15]

"I made a fire" is the very first communication from the speaker (1), and she ensures that the letters she will burn will "have nothing to say to anybody"; they will not communicate to anyone except, ironically, the speaker, who wishes to rid herself of "the white fists of old / Letters and their death rattle" and secrets (2–3, 5). To the speaker, the letters signal aggression and/or anger, depending on how the "white fists" are interpreted, and while they are "dead" in the sense of old news or materials from the past, they contain information and have enabled future communication and developments that will have reverberations far into the future, especially in this case if we attend to the biographical context. Their "death rattle" suggests, too, that words can injure and can kill people and things. What the letters reveal is "a name with black edges" (42), which evokes the story of Assia's name fluttering to Plath's feet as she burned Hughes's papers. Moreover, the speaker elaborates upon this name, attaching a description to it after she details how it wilts: "Pale eyes, patent-leather gutturals!" (46). The allusions to pale eyes and gutturals gesture to Assia's striking light-colored eyes and her facility with the German language. The only exclamation point in the poem occurs in the line that offers details about Assia, and this punctuation mark creates emphasis and attaches emotional force to this line. The letters by Assia and/or about her are destroyed, as symbolized in the scrap of paper that bears her name and wilts like a "Sinuous orchis" at the speaker's foot (44); we may think, then, of the letters as a synecdoche for Assia as writer or addressee.[16] By implicating Assia as that which should be destroyed—in a poem about revenge and destruction—the speaker clearly communicates her attitude toward the Assia figure in the poem.

"THE FEARFUL"

For her part, Assia was stunned when she learned after Plath's death that Plath harbored an intense dislike for her, and she was taken aback by how much Hughes meant to Plath. Assia read Plath's last journals, and "she was shocked and hurt by Plath's savagery toward her. And nothing Hughes had told her about the marriage [to Plath] had prepared her for the depth of feeling and the passion for Hughes that she found in Plath's journals" (Middlebrook 220).[17] We encounter that passion in one of Plath's early journal entries, dated 4 March 1957. Plath confides: "My whole being has grown and interwound so completely with Ted's that if anything were to happen to him, I do not see how I could live. I would either go mad, or kill myself. I cannot conceive of life without him. After twenty-five years of searching in the best places, there is just no one like him. Who fits. Who fits so perfectly and is so perfectly the male being complement to me" (Plath, *Unabridged Journals* 274). This biographical context places an important lens on Plath's poem "The Fearful," a poem about Assia primarily and Hughes secondarily.

Channeling her resentment toward Assia into poetry, Plath animates gendered expectations of women in her short poem to shore up the speaker's animosity toward the Assia figure. Plath funnels aspects of her own life and details about Assia's into the poem, relying on stereotypes about desirable and undesirable women that are informed by gendered cultural scripts. For instance, the speaker derides the Assia figure in "The Fearful" as a supposed unnatural woman in that she thwarts conventional (read: desirable) femininity: she attempts to gender bend, and her biggest fear encompasses becoming pregnant, gaining weight, and becoming unattractive. The unnamed Assia figure in "The Fearful" is just that: fearful, specifically of no longer being viewed as desirable to men. She "would rather be dead" than pregnant, the speaker says (13). "The Fearful" shares with "Childless Woman" Plath's poetic theme that a woman who chooses not to have her own biological children—who actively prevents it, in fact, to attract or keep a man—is less noble, less attractive, and less worthy than a woman who makes a different choice. Such a "fearful," or childless, woman, according to Plath's poems on the theme, shows her to be selfish, shallow, vain, hateful, and figuratively more dead than alive.[18]

"Words heard, by accident, over the phone" and "Burning the Letters" are subtexts of "The Fearful" in that the earlier poems provide the backstories of the drama occurring in the later one. For example, according to the speaker in "The Fearful," "This woman on the telephone / Says she is a man, not a woman" (3–4).[19] The speaker continues: "The voice of the woman hollows— / More and more like a dead one, // Worms in the glottal stops" (7–9). These intertextual references reveal the identity of the historical woman behind the character figured in the poem: Assia, of course, is the woman on the other end of the phone, attempting to disguise her identity through gender bending and deceitfulness in the poem. Furthermore, Assia's familiarity with many different languages, including German with its glottal stops, lend biographical support that she is the primary person alluded to in "The Fearful." When Plath wishes to distance herself from a rival or a female other, she employs images and words associated with death, as she does here and in "The Munich Mannequins," also a poem about Assia. In similar fashion, desirable women in Plath's poems are fertile and productive, and unlikable or undesirable women are barren and unproductive, giving way to connotations of death, destruction, and/or hatefulness. Indeed, Plath belabors the point that the Assia character is associated with death in this short poem: her voice sounds "like a dead one" (8), and "She would rather be dead than fat, / Dead and perfect, like Nefertit" (13–14). The speaker declares that the Assia character "hates // The thought of a baby— / Stealer of cells, stealer of beauty" (10–12). To protect her physical appearance as a valuable commodity, the Assia figure abhors the idea of becoming a mother to biological children. Above all, the Assia character values her physical beauty inasmuch as it positions her to capture the man or men she sets her eyes on: "The silver limbo of each eye // Where the child can never swim, / Where there is only him and him" (16–18). In the cosmos of "The Fearful," women compete with each other for a man, and physical beauty is thought to be the coin of the realm. In shunning pregnancy and motherhood for superficial physical beauty that attracts the male gaze, the Assia figure is positioned to be thought of as a purported unnatural mother or woman in conventional and traditional discourses of desirable femininity. "The Fearful" attempts to position such a woman in contradistinction to the speaker, who strongly disapproves of the Assia figure to the extent that Luke Ferretter characterizes the speaker's tone as one of "undisguised contempt" (87). In "The Fearful," Assia, Plath, and Hughes (who is also referenced in the poem) are forever linked in a triangle and narrative that display the symptoms of a patriarchal society and an antifeminist culture.

"CHILDLESS WOMAN"

Christina Britzolakis argues, in considering Plath's poetry, that "the status of the reproductive female body as literary sign is highly unstable, announcing a crisis in femininity itself, as a social, psychic and literary-historical construct" (115). Plath's poem "Childless Woman" revels in the complicated dynamics Britzolakis outlines. The speaker in this poem considers the respective statuses of the nonreproductive female body overtly and the reproductive maternal body implicitly. The poem stages a crisis in femininity in the intense gaze on the female body that does not bear a child and the harsh symbolic judgment meted out to it by the speaker. Furthermore, "Childless Woman" showcases femininity for what it is: a construction that draws upon the discourses that Britzolakis gestures toward, namely the literary, the historical, the social and cultural, and the psychological. Additionally, through its poetic techniques, "Childless Woman" exhibits a bleeding, aberrant female body, a body that seems designed to elicit feelings of foreboding and dread from the reader.

As she expressed it in a journal entry, Plath's preferred identity pivots on "Books & Babies & Beef stews" (Plath, *Unabridged Journals* 269). In our parlance, we would classify her as a woman who wanted to have it all: who desired to be both traditional (i.e., occupying the conventionally feminine roles of mother and wife) and untraditional, or progressive (i.e., a woman working as a professional writer, literary author).[20] For Plath, Assia came to represent—in Plath's poems—all that Plath did not desire or want in terms of her own identity. The polarization we encounter in Plath's Assia poems between desirable and undesirable femininity, especially as superimposed on the (un) maternal bodies inhabiting the poems, is startling. Plath's strategy is to distance herself and/or her views as a presence in the poems from that of the Assia figure and her worldviews, which is certainly understandable when we reference Plath's biography. Plath reports to her mother, in a letter dated 23 September 1962, her understanding that Assia could not have children due to her many abortions. Fearing Hughes will want to take Frieda away from her as a result of Assia's purported inability to biologically have children, in her most vulnerable moments, Plath paints Assia and Hughes as the villains in her life story and in her poetry (*Letters of Sylvia Plath*, vol. 2, 834).

"Childless Woman" begins with the image of an empty womb, and this womb is meant to be pitied—setting the tone of the poem—as the womb rattles and discharges its unfertilized eggs. The poem grounds itself in the female body, as the opening stanza announces. Throughout its six stanzas, "Childless Woman" focuses intently on the beautiful but childless female body and its image. In an interesting development, the speaker in the poem is the Assia figure, making "Childless Woman" unique in the grouping of poems in which Assia is molded into a character. The speaker, however, elicits our pity, instead of our sympathy, because the speaker identifies herself as the problem: "My landscape is a hand with no lines, / The roads bunched to a knot, / The knot myself" (4–6). In these lines, the speaker views herself as the problem embodied by the symbol of a knot; everything that leads to her is "bunched to a knot," with the "knot"—the problem and catalyst that causes other problems—being herself. The metaphor of a hand without lines indicates that the speaker is associated with a landscape (of her own making, as the knot symbol insists in the lines immediately following) that is unnatural or inhuman. Destruction and death are certainly implied here, as the speaker sees her landscape, or world, as a mess without figurative lifelines.

The speaker's commodified body is presented as a trophy in the third stanza ("Myself the rose you achieve— / This body, / This ivory" [7–9]) to an addressee who is never fully developed but who may be understood to be a male character by default in the patriarchal world of "Childless Woman." Presumably, the speaker values herself insofar as her body is valued as a desirable (i.e., beautiful and sexy) object. The rose is a conventional poetic symbol of the female body, signaling feminine beauty and sexuality, and the fact that the speaker's body has to be "achieve[d]" points to the trophy status the speaker wields by virtue of the precious (and white) body she inhabits and maintains, in the image of "ivory" attached to her. Children do not belong to the speaker or in her world, as the speaker seemingly describes her body as "Ungodly as a child's shriek." The simile underscores the ungodly—not godly (or in metonymic fashion, not "good")—focus of the speaker: her image ("I spin mirrors, / Loyal to my image" [11–12]) and body. The commodification of the speaker's body continues as a theme in the fifth stanza as the speaker confides that she utters "nothing but blood—Taste it, dark red!" (13–14). In speaking and tasting blood, blood that connotes menstrual blood and, alternatively, injury, the childless woman reveals that she dies childless in the evocation of her funeral with attendant imagery ("My funeral, / And this hill and this / Gleaming with the mouths of corpses" [16–18]). The speaker personifies death and the destruction of lives and possibilities in "Childless Woman" in the funeral imagery; the poem ends with mounds of corpses, which may also be a poetic and biographical dig at Assia and the abortions she had.

"THE MUNICH MANNEQUINS"

Hughes believed that he had "never in his life found someone so physically attractive" as Assia, a sentiment he confided to Susan Alliston, one of his mistresses (Alliston 87).[21] Plath considered Assia to possess an exotic appearance and likens her to a "triumphant model" in a 9 October 1962 letter to her mother (*Letters of Sylvia Plath*, vol. 2, 850). Plath also confided that the prospect of Hughes marrying Assia would be one of the hardest challenges she would encounter in the same letter to her mother (Plath, "*Letters Home*—Part Seven"). Hughes never married Assia, but at the time her letter was written, Plath was apparently concerned that it was a possibility and that it could happen relatively soon. Assia's beauty galls Plath, as we see in her personal writing in the form of this letter but also in her poem "The Munich Mannequins." Physical attractiveness elevates a woman's status in a gendered and sexually charged marriage market, making the woman a trophy for a man to claim if she positions herself in that way in Plath's poems, as the Assia figure does in "The Fearful," "Childless Woman," and "The Munich Mannequins." For both Hughes and Plath, Assia's physical appearance was something to marvel at, but for Plath, in "The Munich Mannequins," Assia and her beauty are dismissed as selfish, shallow, and terrible, with attendant associations to death.[22]

The epigraph to this chapter, the first line of "The Munich Mannequins" ("Perfection is terrible, it cannot have children"), encapsulates the theme that braids the three later Assia poems together. Ironically, what the speaker calls perfect is anything but perfect: a glittering or beautiful surface or perfect facade cannot compensate for the womb that has "no purpose," resulting in the "absolute sacrifice" of no children for a woman dubbed a mannequin. Moreover, such a woman is "Intolerable, without mind," the speaker argues (15). The sacrifices the Assia-Munich mannequin characters make translates into "Voicelessness" and death (27). From the second line of the poem, when *womb* is associated with coldness and barrenness, to the last line, when we are told the snow has "no voice," we are faced with Plath's prophetic vision concerning Assia. Assia has been left voiceless in literary scholarship and in most biographies, although Plath was wrong in her assessment that Assia would forgo bearing and nurturing a biological child. But Plath was also correct in that

Assia cultivated her beauty and was concerned about what motherhood (and age) would do to her appearance and desirability.[23]

Ultimately, the mannequins of "The Munich Mannequins" give the observer an object to look at and maybe admire in their putative perfection, but the mannequins lack truly significant and meaningful attributes. The speaker assigns great value to maternity, viewing it as a natural and ideal condition for women. The first line shows us that an American or British traditional gendered script concerning women informs this poem because if we parse the logic of the first line, we see that if perfection could have children, then it would not be terrible. The speaker esteems motherhood above all else in the poem, as we see when she calls menstruation "the flood of love" because it is the "absolute sacrifice. / It means: no more idols but me, // Me and you" (6, 7–9). According to the speaker, in other words, forfeiting children in the pursuit of romance or personal appearance is the highest level of sacrifice one could make for a man. The Assia-mannequins come across as selfish ("no more idols but me") and shallow ("without mind" [15]). They also appear cold to the point of death: "These mannequins lean tonight / In Munich, morgue between Paris and Rome" (11–12). The mannequins are so cold and unnatural in the living world that the speaker figuratively places them in a morgue, where dead bodies are kept. And yet the mannequins emanate seduction and glamour: they are "Naked and bald in their furs" (13). These constitute the only redeeming qualities—if they can be called that—the speaker permits the Assia-mannequins.[24] Certainly, Plath had many reasons to feel animosity toward Assia, and the poems she penned about Assia exhibit that sentiment. Of especial significance, Plath's Assia poems are interesting in their mapping of and marshaling of traditional gender scripts and conventional gendered expectations. We can learn a lot about what we value and do not value culturally (and professionally and personally) when we examine our own approaches to the gendered dynamics in the literary texts we study, teach, or otherwise endorse.

Unlike Plath, who activates her voice in her Assia poems, Assia never speaks about herself, Plath, or Hughes publicly or in any text designed for public dissemination. This omission in the literary imagination should be noted by readers, scholars, and teachers because there are biographical contexts that frame the poems in enlightening ways and that may give us pause as we think about gender identity, gendered expectations and roles, and how gender is performed in literature and in the world outside the book. And poems are texts we need to attend to and carefully unpack; as Plath asserts, "The poet becomes an expert packer of suitcases," or poems ("A Comparison" 63). Plath possessed the ability "to transform mere human beings into characters in a myth," claims Middlebrook (280). Ted Hughes confided the following to a friend on 17 February 1968: "Sylvia had the power . . . to see their personal life objectively, to turn it into a myth" (Murphy, 266). And they are right. Whoever Assia may have been is transfigured into poetry—into something beautiful—but the actual person becomes the mythic Other: an archetypal femme fatale or dangerous and seductive woman, without mercy; an unnatural woman or (m)other; the scapegoated mistress; and a silenced woman. Plath is correct when she surmises that poems "go surprisingly far—among strangers, around the world, even. Farther than the words of a classroom teacher or the prescriptions of a doctor; if they are very lucky, farther than a lifetime" ("Context" 66). What is true today was true in 1965, when Hughes wrote to a friend and fellow poet about Plath as a "spectacular public figure" and how her poems "figure largely in school curricula." He refers to her poetry as "best-selling literature of despair & martyrdom, probably a permanent cultural treasure" (*Letters* 240). To Aurelia and Warren Plath in 1966, Hughes wrote, "I hear from friends of mine at various Universities in the States that Sylvia's poems are already a holy text among the students, and that in large groups she is the sole admired influence. I predict a future for ARIEL somewhat like the Catcher in the Rye, but broader and of course permanent" (253).

Correct in his early assessment of Plath's literary reputation, Hughes reminds us that Plath's body of work has long fascinated an academic audience and a general one simultaneously. Her literary texts provide the material we can use to become more aware of our cultural and literary values through our interpretations of the same (i.e., what we can find in the poems and what our interpretations look like). Plath's writing affects a significant number of her readers in powerful ways, as Hughes knew. Thus, the messages we identify in Plath's work and the manner in which we approach the same will resonate in a myriad of ways, especially if we write and teach about Plath or work in Plath studies more broadly. Plath's poetry is exceedingly influential, and so how women are depicted in her poems factors into what narratives and discourses are created, circulated, reinforced, contradicted, and/or reconfigured. In the next chapter, we will consider how Assia is featured in the work of the other influential poet in this relationship triangle: Ted Hughes.

CHAPTER 3

TED HUGHES'S TREATMENTS OF ASSIA WEVILL

Assia was my true wife and the best friend I ever had.
—from a 14 April 1969 letter from Ted Hughes to Celia Chaikin

Because Assia Wevill is not overtly addressed in Ted Hughes's poetry in the way that Sylvia Plath is, some critics and readers may overlook her influence on him and his work. It is the case that Hughes ruminated upon Assia and returned to her as a subject in his personal writing, such as his journal and drafts of poems that were never published, over the course of his lifetime. What will be explored here are Hughes's representations of Assia in his published poetry. While *Crow* (1970) is inscribed with a dedication to Assia and Shura, this is only a passing reference to the woman Hughes called "my true wife and the best friend I ever had" and to the daughter Hughes fathered with Assia (*Letters* 290).[1] More significantly, in terms of Assia's influence on Hughes, is *Capriccio: Poems* (1990), a poetry collection that was printed originally as an expensive limited edition art book; the poems were later included in the *Collected Poems* (2003) without the artwork. Also of interest to Hughes's reading public are "Dreamers" and "The Inscription," poems referencing Assia in the famous *Birthday Letters* (1998). The only other woman to whom Hughes dedicated an entire poetry collection is Plath, and she is the subject of both *Birthday Letters* and the art book *Howls & Whispers* (1998), which closes with the very poem (albeit carrying a different title) that opens *Capriccio*. In these ways—namely, publishing poems about Assia and emphasizing her importance to him—Hughes demonstrates the impact Assia had on his work (and his life), and he produced representations of her that need to be examined, analyzed, and discussed in systematic fashion because these portrayals continue to circulate and, thus, can effect discursive formations about Assia *and* harbor the potential to inform notions and ideologies about gender. As Rose Weitz has documented in her survey charting a history of women's bodies from women's legal status as property to voting citizen to legal battles over abortion, the "very real impact" that ideas about female bodies have made on female lives is astonishing (3–11).

Specifically, we see Hughes condemning and punishing Assia in *Capriccio* and *Birthday Letters* for her death, for Shura's death, for Plath's death, for his own despair and trauma, and for her beauty and sexuality. This lot is quite the (literary) burden for one woman to bear and contributes little in the way of recovering Assia's life and important artistic and literary contributions in all their complexity. In this chapter, we encounter narratives embedded in poems that exonerate Hughes (and Plath) from any responsibility in the miserable life and death of Assia and Shura after Assia became involved with Hughes and assumed Plath's place as his artistic partner, his romantic partner, and the caretaker of his children. More damaging, however, is the misogynistic rhetoric that we find in *Capriccio* and *Birthday Letters:* female victim blaming at the hands of a powerful man as well as recurring reproductions of the reductive and unproductive archetype of the beautiful but destructive woman who is without mercy. To deny Assia any redeeming qualities in his poetic record of his relationship with her is to shortchange her, especially as her life and work illustrate gendered dimensions of life and art then and now, in England and elsewhere.[2] Additionally, we are given a shortsighted version of who Assia was/might have been/might be, for those of us who wish to know more about her biography and the lives of Hughes and Plath. This chapter will briefly reflect on Assia and Hughes's relationship before moving on to literary analysis and feminist discussion. The bulk of the chapter features analyses of Hughes's poems, focusing on *Capriccio,* and showcases the issues addressed in chapter 1: bringing a literary, feminist perspective to bear on important texts allows and fosters a dialogue about gender, women's bodies, identity, and power in interpersonal relationships and their subsequent representation (and interpretation) in literature. This is a literary and cultural studies recovery project that pivots primarily on literary contributions, identity politics, and women. This approach forges new pathways into research on Assia as well as bolstering existing work and indicating new directions in Hughes studies, Plath studies, and literary studies more broadly. Ultimately, such scholarship is in service to examining and establishing Assia's significance in poetry and in according her a more proper place in the American and British literary and cultural imaginations.

ASSIA AND HUGHES'S RELATIONSHIP

Writing in her journal on 20 May 1963, Assia records her love for Hughes and her desire to be enough for him and for herself: "I should be pleased that [Ted] appears to love me, and love him back—wholly. Make it whole. Please make *me* whole" (qtd. in Koren and Negev 125). For Assia, Hughes was the key to her happiness and Shura's: a key to love and the good life. He was that which would make her whole and her life complete.

Assia's journal entries—and her suicide—suggest that the prospect of forfeiting her dream of establishing a home with Hughes and their daughter surpassed her threshold to cope. Combined with the stressors of her gendered situation, Assia's perceived loss of a life lived with Hughes was a psychological and emotional injury that engulfed her and which her death addresses, both in the act that mimics Plath and in her suicide letter and will. For his part, Hughes records that Assia's life was one characterized by trauma early in her life: in *Capriccio*, he returns repeatedly to her family's flight from Nazi Germany in the 1930s and establishes a motif in which her early escape from death and her identification with Plath marked her and groomed her for an early death. He suggests in his poetry that she is alive by accident, despite the fact that he states in letters that her death was preventable.[3] As Hughes's biographer Jonathan Bate notes,

Hughes "dreamed of Assia every night" and "castigated himself for their bitter misunderstandings" following her death, which we see in his personal journal, archived at Emory ("[Notebook 11]"). According to Bate, Hughes "blamed himself bitterly for the 'mistake' that 'cost two lives—three'" (277). Hughes, in his personal writing, "asked himself whether the 'momentary pleasure' of some stranger would one day 'pay' him for 'ruining' his own life 'and causing the deaths / of those I have loved best / and who loved me best, and who were my life.'" Hughes wrote in an attempt to "get out of the flames." The exercise in writing in his journals or in private notebooks allowed Hughes, in his words, to "bring me closer to my self. It does lock me in close conversation with my most conscientious self—and so it gives me energy, and ties me to my real feelings" (qtd. in Bate 277, 557). In short, we learn that Hughes loved Assia and Shura and mourned their deaths, but his public response in his poetry is as complex, when compared to his personal writings, as his relationship with Assia was.

The pain of mourning Assia and Shura caused Hughes to confide in Assia's sister, Celia Chaikin, on 11 March 1970, as the one-year anniversary of their deaths approached. Hughes writes Chaikin that the past year, in retrospect, was the wickedest he had ever experienced, underscoring the importance of Assia and Shura to him (and to others—he attributes the death of his mother and Assia's father to the news of Assia's suicide and Shura's untimely demise). He tells Chaikin that he associates everything in England with Assia, making London unbearable. These unguarded statements make Hughes a sympathetic figure, especially if one understands that his Assia poems served more than one function. As I maintain, Hughes's Assia poems served two primary functions: (1) to establish an official (poetic) narrative of Assia's life and death; and (2) to allow Hughes the opportunity to act out and work through trauma and make sense of the tragedies. While I find the content and slant of the official narrative to be a disservice to Assia and her legacy, as well as harmful to women more generally when we consider the power of discursive formations, I think the second function is just as important to consider as the first, and it is something that we would do well to acknowledge. Hughes struggled with surviving the traumatic experiences in his life and finding meaning in them, as his letters and poems show. If anything takes the sting out of the indictment of Assia in the Assia poems, it is this realization: working through trauma is no small feat, and finding meaning in trauma might be even more challenging. As Hughes himself declared to Chaikin shortly after the double deaths of his loved ones in 1969, "It's with me every minute of the day and night" (*Letters* 290).

Hughes was interpellated into a situation he never chose, as Butler phrases it (*Bodies That Matter* 123). Wounded by Assia's and Shura's deaths and knowing that Assia considered him the catalyst for her actions, Hughes acted out and worked through the traumatic injury by repeating it in poems and by reassigning the responsibility for their deaths, as I contend. Judith Butler observes, "The compulsion to repeat an injury is not necessarily the compulsion to repeat the injury in the same way or to stay fully within the traumatic orbit of that injury." We see Assia cast as the demon seductress because that is the only trope available for Hughes: he did not choose his situation exactly, nor did he choose his language exactly—both precede him. In this vein, Butler adds, "the force of repetition in language may be the paradoxical condition by which a certain agency [. . .] is derived from the *impossibility* of choice" (124). And yet language holds open the promise of liberation, transformation, or rebellion at the same time that it can sanction what Plath calls the "boot in the face" in her poem "Daddy" (line 49). Butler reminds us that "representation is the normative function of a language in which is said either to reveal or to distort what is assumed to be true about the category of women" (*Gender Trouble* 2). It is up to each of us to decide for ourselves whether Hughes's Assia poems reveal or distort what we assume to be true about women.

In Butler's *Precarious Life*, we see that what pertains to Assia in the realm of loss, grief, and violence also pertains to Hughes. Because they both claimed to be in a committed relationship with each other, as well as parents of their child, they understood themselves as being connected to each other. As we will see in the analytical discussions of *Capriccio* later in this chapter, Hughes grapples with memories of Assia, seemingly wanting to understand her life and her actions while insisting that he could not be the catalyst for her suicide. Butler posits, "Is there something to be gained from grieving, from tarrying with grief, from remaining exposed to its unbearability and not endeavoring to seek a resolution for grief through violence?" (*Precarious Life* 30). While we cannot answer this for Hughes, I would suggest that *Capriccio* provides us with the artifacts or texts of loss, grief, and trauma. In what looks like an attempt at working through the traumatic impact of Assia's and Shura's deaths on him, *Capriccio* emerges as a masterful narrative that seemingly interrogates its own narrative or its own history. Butler argues that we can be undone by grief because we have already been so with respect to desire. As Butler avers: "One does not always stay intact. One may want to, or manage to for a while, but despite one's best efforts, one is undone, in the face of the other, by the touch, by the scent, by the feel, by the prospect of the touch, by the memory of the feel" (*Precarious Life* 23–24). The memories of Assia permeate each poem in *Capriccio,* making the memories and the poems feel raw and insistent to the reader. As we know from Hughes's journal writing and his personal correspondence, keeping himself intact after Plath's death, followed by those of Assia, Shura, and his mother, required him to exert superhuman strength and resiliency. Perhaps this passage from *Precarious Life* captures the drama of *Capriccio* with Hughes as the focal point: "I am wounded, and I find that the wound itself testifies to the fact that I am impressionable, given over to the Other in ways that I cannot fully predict or control. I cannot think the question of responsibility alone, in isolation from the Other; if I do, I have taken myself out of the relational bind that frames the problem of responsibility from the start" (46). For Hughes could never separate himself from Assia in his poetry and thinking: she remained an unhealed wound in his poetic imagination, as the published Assia poems attest.

For Hughes as well as for his readers, Assia is a figure of abjection in his poetry. In *Capriccio,* she is positioned to be the ultimate abject totem; Assia fits Julia Kristeva's definition of the abject, "the corpse, the most sickening of wastes, [. . .] a border that has encroached upon everything" (3). Lynda Bundtzen believes Hughes wished to show that "he had nothing to do with Wevill's abjection, that it was a series of errors and choices made only by a willfully self-destructive and guilt-ridden woman" in poems such as "The Error" from *Capriccio* ("Traumatic Repetition" 138). When we read Hughes's Assia poems, we are surely startled at the vehement denunciation and the striking mythologizing that transpire; the angry and hostile undercurrents are related to the abject state associated with Assia, with the mythologizing marking an attempt at mitigating the effects of trauma or the pull of the abject. Kristeva's poetic description of the abject fits the dynamics of abjection that dominate the majority of poems about Assia by Hughes. Asserts Kristeva: "There looms, within abjection, one of those violent, dark revolts of being, directed against a threat that seems to emanate from an exorbitant outside or inside, ejected beyond the scope of the possible, the tolerable, the thinkable. It lies there, quite close, but it cannot be assimilated. It beseeches, worries, and fascinates desire, which, nevertheless, does not let itself be seduced. Apprehensive, desire turns aside; sickened, it rejects" (1). After Assia's suicide, which resulted in a literal and metaphorical corpse—one to be cremated and one to live on in Hughes's literary imagination—Hughes assumes a hostile stance toward Assia in the vast majority of his published poetry about her, most likely because of the effect her death had on him and the way in which it was bound up with abjection. Additionally, when considering Hughes's portrayal of Assia, we should bear in mind Iris Marion Young's reminder that "there are deep social divisions of masculine and feminine gendered dispositions and experience which have implications for the psychic lives of men and women, their interactions with one another, their dispositions to care for children or exercise authority" (14). In other words, Hughes absolutely would have experienced the world differently than Assia did: in exercising his authority and privilege to write about her and in referencing his experience of living in a masculine body in a gendered world, he was unable to understand what it meant to be her.

Because Assia served as a posthumous muse to Hughes, she is denied the opportunity to redress the ways in which she has been portrayed, and she suffers the further insult of unfavorable treatment. Luce Irigaray explores femininity in connection with the power of discourse and finds that women find themselves "in a situation of *specific exploitation* with respect to exchange operations: sexual exchanges, but also economic, social, and cultural exchanges in general." She clarifies that a woman's identity "is imposed upon her according to models that remain foreign to her." As Irigaray sees it, "The 'feminine' is never to be identified except by and for the masculine" (85). So the exchanges Hughes enacts in his literary transactions (read: poems about and poems that address Assia and that trade upon, claim, and/or invent her and her biography and personality) are imbued in a masculine prerogative that is already entrenched in exploitation and will always result in a one-sided exchange. Assia inspired Hughes as his muse, but she did not need to be deceased for Hughes to write *Capriccio;* he could have rewritten her, dead or alive, as he wished, as a femme fatale, the beautiful but dangerous and destructive woman without mercy, or the demon seductress. These are types of women we recognize, as archetypes. As it stands, in the role of Hughes's muse, Assia attracts more attention from a twenty-first-century public than she would have otherwise. (See chapter 5 for twenty-first-century representations and treatments of Assia.) Because of her association with Hughes and her significant influence on him, Hughes scholars and readers want to know more about Assia, as do Plath scholars and readers. Each of us, however, might keep in mind Irigaray's point about women, power, and discourse as we read this chapter: "The use, consumption, and circulation of [women's] sexualized bodies underwrite the organization and the reproduction of the social order, in which [women] have never taken part as 'subjects'" (84). In her own artistic products, Assia did not take the part of a speaking subject exactly; instead, she created and developed art that cloaked her as a subject. In the microcosmic world of *Capriccio* that correlates to the macrocosmic real world outside of the book, Hughes uses, consumes, and circulates a sexualized version of Assia's body that would not only maintain the status quo in a patriarchal, sexist society but that introduces, reinforces, and circulates stock representations of women that would harm them (and men) as a result. We will approach the gendered ways Hughes traded upon Assia through close readings of his poems about her later in this chapter.

In this study, I have selected only Hughes's published poems about Assia because of the potential power published words have. This book is invested in recuperating Assia and reconsidering her as a woman and artist, which makes it concerned with the propagation of injurious language and attendant concepts that create the conditions for interpellating women (and men) in deleterious ways. Although one is "derogated and demeaned" by injurious language, one becomes socially defined by it as well. This visibility, however, presents one with the possibility of producing an "unexpected and enabling response." Butler explains, "If to be addressed is to be interpellated, then the offensive call runs the risk of inaugurating a subject in speech who comes to use language to counter the offensive call" (*Excitable Speech* 2). To be clear, Butler is not claiming that it is inevitable that one will or can counter the injurious language/interpellation. Rather, she observes that the occasion for doing so—the potentiality—is activated. In advocating feminist readings of Hughes's poetry that interpret and discuss it within a feminist or trauma studies framework, I hope that we will activate a feminist consciousness in scholarship on his work, especially pertaining to Assia, because injurious speech can be placed in context and assessed and addressed in countless ways. My approach in this book is only one example of a revisionist, feminist track.

For Assia, a life without Hughes was unfathomable for gendered reasons, as I delineate in chapter 4. The good life, from Assia's perspective, involved institutionalized and structural commitments from Hughes: she desired marriage to him (to formalize his roles as her partner and the father of her child), which would alleviate her loneliness; provide a husband for herself; establish a permanent father figure for Shura; create more emotional support for her household; and secure more financial stability with two earners in the household. In the summer of 1968, Assia confided in a former coworker, Chris Wilkins, that as her biographers report, she "was worried about her insecurity, and wanted to marry again and settle, but things were not going right with Ted" (Koren and Negev 197). According to Wilkins, Assia envisioned no options for herself outside of a life with Hughes: "She couldn't stand the state of things as they were, and if it didn't change, she would kill herself" (qtd. in Koren and Negev 197). In her last letter to her father, Assia placed the responsibility for her demise on Hughes.[4]

CAPRICCIO: POEMS

As I interpret it, *Capriccio* shows itself to be a collection about trauma and the working through of Assia's and Shura's deaths. To be fair to Hughes, this undertaking is admirable: as Butler notes, there is "no way to work through trauma except through the arduous effort it takes to direct the course of its repetition" (*Excitable Speech* 38). And if nothing else, *Capriccio* pivots on repetitions of Assia's death and all that is related to it. If Assia's name has been repeatedly linked to beauty, death, and destruction in scholarship and the body poetic politic, then that story gains its momentum in *Capriccio*. As Butler asserts, "The force of the name depends not only on its iterability, but on a form of repetition that is linked to trauma, on what is, strictly speaking, not remembered, but relived, and relived in and through the linguistic substitution for the traumatic event" (36). In other words, we can dub the poems about Assia the "Assia poems" because they resonate with the force of her name, which is linked over and over again with trauma in both Plath's and Hughes's work. Her name becomes synonymous with the "other woman," a "bad woman," and the "demon seductress" in both cases, and she is implicitly linked to trauma in Hughes's *Capriccio* and his poem "Do Not Pick Up the Telephone" specifically. The iterability of Assia's name in poetry causes it to be recognizable to what are the traumatic triggers for Plath and Hughes: allusions to Hughes's affair with Assia for Plath and Hughes and, later, Assia's suicide and act of filicide for Hughes solely. In his Assia poems, Hughes neither adheres to a strict biographical account of Assia, nor does he concern himself with biographical accuracy:[5]

Capriccio serves a different purpose. Rather than remembering the good times or his love for her, Hughes's speaker in *Capriccio* ruminates on reliving the traumatic event and attempting to make sense of it by attributing blame to the deceased, a victim, too, but also the cause of Hughes's traumatic responses as they manifest in the twenty poems of *Capriccio.* As Hughes himself confided in 1996 to Eilat Negev, who would become one of a pair of Assia's biographers, "Every work of art stems from a wound in the soul of the artist. When a person is hurt, his immune system comes into operation, and a self-healing process takes place, mental and physical." He added that art plays the part of "a psychological component of the auto-immune system that gives expression to the healing process" (qtd. in Koren and Negev 166).[6] *Capriccio,* published seven years before this interview, is evidence of Hughes's praxis.

The nature of trauma is beautifully articulated by Hughes in an interview on 8 October 1996: "Being a writer, these things are chewed all the time, because you write about them and they disturb you, and they keep appearing and disappearing. They keep hanging on your neck and you deal with the emotions again and again, as if it's a broken record, stuck in the same monumental groove. And instead of letting go of the past and living for the future, you find your past in front of you. A monument, sitting on your head" (qtd. in Koren and Negev 227). In working with traumatized individuals, Dori Laub has observed that "trauma survivors live not with memories of the past, but with an event that could not and did not proceed through to its completion, had no ending, attained no closure, and therefore, as far as its survivors are concerned, continues into the present and is current in every respect" (Felman and Laub 69). We can easily discern the resonances and echoes between Hughes's account of what I have termed "trauma" and Laub's account of the same. Perhaps, with *Capriccio,* Hughes attempted to exorcise the demon (i.e., the traumatic event of Assia's death) by calling into being and casting Assia as the demon in the story through transference. In attempting to "work through" the trauma ushered in by Assia's and Shura's deaths, Hughes was embarking on a pathway toward healing, without being aware of it, perhaps. As Judith Herman outlines, "reconstructing the trauma story" is a necessary step in the three-part recovery and healing process that also includes "establishing safety" and "restoring the connection between survivors and their community" (3). Indeed, "working through" appears to be a necessary component of reconstructing the trauma story so that it makes sense to the survivor. While working through it may not necessarily lead to a cure, it is a desirable process because it begets critical distance and the ability to distinguish past, present, and future (LaCapra 143). According to Dominick LaCapra, working through allows one to say:

> "Yes, that happened to me back then. It was distressing, overwhelming, perhaps I can't entirely disengage myself from it, but I'm existing here and now, and this is different from back then. . . ." Working through does not mean avoidance, harmonization, simply forgetting the past, or submerging oneself in the present. It means coming to terms with the trauma, including its details, and critically engaging the tendency to act out the past and even to recognize why it may be necessary and even in certain respects desirable or at least compelling. . . . In any case certain wounds, both personal and historical, cannot simply heal without leaving scars or residues in the present; there may even be a sense in which they have to remain as open wounds even if one strives to counteract their tendency to swallow all of existence and incapacitate one as an agent in the present. (144)

In this conception of trauma as a wound, the victim's sense of safety, integrity, and wholeness is severely threatened and dismantled, putting into relief the devastation that trauma leaves in its wake—even when the survivor wants to move past it. As Cathy Caruth explains, the "history of the traumatized individual" hinges on "the determined repetition of the event of destruction" (63). And the evidence of traumatic devastation is everywhere evident in Hughes's poems about Assia.

In the wake of Assia's and Shura's deaths, Hughes retreated to

Ireland, where he recorded his grief over losing them in his journal. He laments, "Effect of A's [illegible word]—*Disastrous, yes*" (qtd. in Koren and Negev 216).[7] He immediately comments that he did not fight it, whatever "it" might be. From the timing, we know that he is referencing Assia's suicide: he recounts in the next entry, dated April [1969], that he feels a constant pain. He keenly marks the losses of Assia and Shura, reflecting on their deaths and what he has missed and will miss without them in his life. He acknowledges remorse in this private notebook (now held in his American archive). Among the painful revelations is one in which Hughes records that he dreams of Assia every night: she has not yet committed suicide, and Hughes states that the act could be prevented. His analysis of their last conversation and Assia's last act is that it was all a bitter misunderstanding ("[Notebook 11]"). Clearly, Hughes's conclusion was not Assia's: in this case, both become victims of misunderstanding. Almost a year after Assia's and Shura's deaths, Hughes confesses his traumatic responses to what has happened to his close friends Yehuda and Hana Amichai on 11 March 1970: "After Assia and Shura died I did not know how to write anybody." He continues: "I was just paralyzed, and I'm still not much improved. I've been swallowed up by this last year" (*Letters* 303). Hughes's traumatic responses to Assia's death further manifest themselves in his representations of her in *Capriccio*, a collection that takes Assia as its primary subject.[8]

In a journal entry following Assia's and Shura's deaths, Hughes reveals that he thinks Plath's poem "Gulliver" has become true: he feels tied down and unable to move. Indeed, he claims that instead of being focused on life, he is focused on what is holding him down ("[Notebook 11]"). In a 1970 letter to Peter Redgrove, Hughes confesses that he feels as if life has swallowed him whole and is in the process of digesting him: he does not feel in control of his life (paraphrased and qtd. in Feinstein 175). According to Hughes biographer Elaine Feinstein, Hughes thought that "he could spend the rest of his life trying to understand and come to terms with what had happened to him," especially in relation to the deaths of Assia, Shura, and (immediately following their deaths) that of his mother (175).

To his friend Lucas Myers, Hughes writes about the impact of Plath's and Assia's last actions on him in a letter from 29 September 1984, fifteen years after Assia's and Shura's deaths: "I wonder sometimes if things might have gone differently without the events of 63 [Plath's suicide] & 69 [Assia's suicide and Shura's death]. I have an idea that those two episodes as giant steel doors shutting down over great parts of myself, leaving me that much less, just what was left, to live on. No doubt a more resolute artist would have penetrated the steel doors—but I believe big physical changes happen at those times, big self-anaesthesias. Maybe life isn't long enough to wake up from them" (*Letters* 489). Here we see the admission of the traumatic impact of the suicides and the untimely death of his daughter. Those events rendered physical, as well as emotional, changes and challenges for Hughes, long after they happened. From my perspective, some of Hughes's most riveting writing is that which attempts to work through the trauma of Plath's and Assia's suicides.[9] Perhaps because of his difficulty in rendering his perceptions of and responses to those events in poetry, the poems display themselves as exceptional in their nature: they are unlike anything else he ever wrote, and they strike me as worked over and even polished, as if great care were taken in attempting to fix characters, their motivations, events, and the like into a tableau, pattern, or myth that makes sense.[10] In the Assia poems, in particular, Hughes grapples with powerful themes that are informed by the "real world," informed by the gendered aspects of his life and those of his female partners. *Capriccio* embodies Hughes's struggle to make sense of Assia and to represent her to a reading public ready to judge him, as well as, ostensibly, to make sense of her to himself. Because Hughes rendered *Capriccio* a deeply personal poetic sequence of poems, I will alternate between referring to Hughes's biography and Hughes as author and literary construct, the speaker of the poem, when appropriate to the argument and the literary interpretation that follows.

Capriccio is an impressive art book; it commands attention with its rough paper edges (well matched to the rough, raw emotion) that bespeak its high quality. Expensively bound and beautifully made, each poem invites us to read Hughes's horrific—and at times, it appears, traumatic—reflections about Assia. The frontispiece of the book prepares readers for what they will encounter: the personification of pure fright and horror is engendered. With its strange eyes, bone-white skull-like face, and hair standing on end like a porcupine, the figure (perhaps encased in a shroud) communicates *Capriccio*'s tenor in its appearance. The title page conveys the tenor of *Capriccio* even more powerfully: with wild blue hair standing dramatically on end, wild eyes, and hands placed in such a way to frame the title, this figure is imbued with fear and horror. As Carol Bere points out, while *capriccio* denotes an improvisational, joyful musical form (perhaps also suggesting capriciousness) in its modern usage, the archaic Italian definitions resonate more deeply with the collection: *capriccio* translates to "head with hair standing on end," denoting horror, and *raccapricciо* means "horror" or "shudder" (31). Rita Felski reminds us that "shock" is a "reaction to what is startling, painful, even horrifying" (105). From her perspective, "The literature of shock becomes truly disquieting not when it is shown to further social progress, but when it utterly fails to do so, when it slips through our frameworks of legitimation and resists our most heartfelt values. It is at that point that we are left floundering and speechless, casting about for words to make sense of our own response" (110). My goal for this project is to revisit the poems of *Capriccio*, this literature of shock that we have not managed to use to further social progress, and to call it to account: we will read *Capriccio* through frameworks of legitimation that reveal our heartfelt (feminist) values. We will not be left floundering and speechless, attempting to make sense of these difficult poems. From here, I offer analyses and contextual close readings of the poems in *Capriccio*, which will constitute the first extended literary examinations of them with a focus on Assia.[11]

"Capriccios"

"Capriccios" opens the collection, and this poem is renamed "Superstitions" and repositioned as the last poem in *Howls & Whispers*.

(*Howls & Whispers* revolves around Plath and contains, presumably, the outtakes of *Birthday Letters*). Because of its reappearance and repurposing in a later collection and because of its connection to both Assia and Plath, "Capriccios" retains special meaning. Rather than dismissing Assia here, Hughes acknowledges her status as his partner and the mother of his child by linking her to his first wife and the mother of his first two children. While much of the poem appears to allude to Plath (her American nationality and her status as his bride) in stanzas 1–7, which are printed as the first page of the poem in the art book, the rest of the poem addresses Plath and Assia equally. Ruing the bad luck of Friday the thirteenth, a day on which the speaker conflates the "unveiled perfumed / America" of Plath and presumably his unveiling (read: intimate relations) with Assia on the same day but in a different year (8–9), the speaker invokes "Frigga's / Two-faced gift" (15–16), which Bere interprets as birth and death (33).[12] This interpretation holds: both Plath and Assia brought life into the world in the form of children, and both took away their own lives, with Assia taking that of Shura also. The poem concludes with these lines, setting the stage for the characters and official narratives of *Capriccio* (and *Howls & Whispers*):

> (Even so,
> Remembering it: will make your palms sweat,
> The skin lift blistering, both your lifelines bleed.) (28–30)

Plath is the one who forgot death (22–23); Assia is the character in the poem (and throughout *Capriccio*) who forgot life (23–24); and Shura's life ends without a cry (24–25). Recognizing that his varied and complex mythological and occult references and framework(s) will be dismissed ("laughed at," 26–27), Hughes nevertheless insists on the price he paid for his love of Plath, Assia, and Shura, associating it with trauma: "Remembering it: will make your palms sweat, / The skin lift blistering." These details signal figurative and physical responses to the traumatic experience: the emotional injury presents itself physically, as if the traumatic injury has just happened and remains unhealed. The speaker insists on fate ("your lifelines bleed") or machinations out of his control (as gestured to by the Friday the thirteenth events) as the impetus behind the tragedies. As we know, Hughes was superstitious; he had an astrology chart drawn up for Shura ("Astrological Chart, '3rd March 1965, 9.55 p.m.'"), and he believed in portents.[13] This poem sets the stage for the poems to follow: it introduces the major characters and begins to treat what will emerge as important themes in *Capriccio.*

"The Locket"

In "The Locket," Hughes continues what has become the official party line of his poetry about Assia: her death was foretold and happened through no fault of his own. Indeed, as portrayed in "The Locket," Assia becomes an active agent of her own demise as well as a passive victim of trauma who has accidentally escaped death somehow, only to find it again. (This repetition of an earlier traumatic experience is a hallmark of trauma, and Cathy Caruth, in following Freud, understands the traumatic moment as the realization that one has survived only by accident [59, 62–63].) For his part, Hughes concludes, "While I juggled our futures, it kept up its whisper / To my deafened ear: *fait accompli*" (31–32).

We know that Hughes was assuring Assia of a joint future together as late as December 1968, three months before her death and at a stage in their relationship when she felt abandoned by him. In this excerpt from a late December 1968 letter to Assia, Hughes articulates the impact Plath's suicide has had on him: because he feels physically ill from the emotional and psychological trauma of her death, he wishes to start anew with Assia, without reminders of Plath:

> When I got back here Gerald & Joan had just arrived from Australia—they brought their holiday forward. Otherwise by now I would be with you. They leave this weekend. Your misunderstanding of me was as terrible as ever. But I felt I could not go on promising until I had actually cleared myself with

> some action. I saw that what I had done was probably what had been making you ill too.
>
> I have not put the children to school because I want them to start there. I am coming down to find a school and some temporary lodging for us, until we can find a place big enough for all of us.
>
> I know quite clearly what has been making me so ill. I want to start afresh with nothing whatsoever from earlier times—no furniture, place, mementos etc. I intend to get free of it and cut everybody but you out of my life completely. You'll see that I'll fulfill all my promises eventually. (*Letters* 286)

The promises went unfulfilled, as the temporary lodging for Hughes, Frieda, and Nicholas was never secured; Shura was not reunited with her father, half-sister, and half-brother as a blended family; Hughes, Frieda, and Nicholas remained in Devon; and a spacious home for Hughes, Assia, and the three children was not rented or purchased, much to Assia's great despair after the failure of the last house-hunting expedition with Hughes. The promises that Hughes offered to Assia, as seen in archived letters, kept her hoping for their fulfillment; such promises were common throughout the course of their relationship, from 1962 to 1969.[14]

For his part, Hughes may well have believed he would honor the promises he gave Assia. As he informed her sister, Celia Chaikin, Plath's traumatic death haunted Assia and him, but in his letter of 14 April 1969, he told Chaikin that he did not see that as an insurmountable barrier, even in immediate retrospect: "Our life together was so complicated with old ghosts, and dozens of near-separations over the years, but [Assia and I] belonged together so completely and so deeply, that her repeatedly testing me, saying that we'd better separate for good, were just like a bad habit, part of our old difficulties, and so when she repeated it on that last day over the phone, it was nothing new, nothing we hadn't got over dozens of times before" (*Letters* 290). "The Locket" plays upon this notion of Assia being haunted by old ghosts in the form of a symbolic locket, the keeper of her death. It also insists and concludes, by the penultimate stanza, that while Assia has beaten the odds—she has been living on borrowed time for "a quarter century" (30)—her untimely death is inevitable, ever since she escaped the Nazis: "You knew exactly / How your death looked. It was a long-cold oven / Locked with a swastika" (21–23). She was always going to be burned (i.e., her narrow escape from the Holocaust, as Hughes casts it; her actual cremation), and so the speaker associates her with the "brand of the burnt" (21). The locket, containing death, continually splits open as a result: "The clasp seemed to be faulty" (27), independent of what Assia herself or Hughes does in the poem.

And yet, confusingly, Hughes promotes another strand of argument in his poetic narrative about Assia's suicide. Addressing Assia, Hughes writes, "Your death / Was so utterly within your power / It was as if you had trapped it" (5–7). Hughes weaves a gendered story about Assia mothering, nurturing, and courting death. She nurses it, much to Hughes's disgust: "But who else would have nursed it / In a locket between her breasts!" (10–11). Assia is so abject that no one else would have done this, to Hughes's mind. Flirting with death, the woman who represents Assia gently bites the locket (16). She courts her own death, enjoying it ("Smiling, you'd hold it up. / You'd swing it on its chain, to tease life" (12–13), according to the speaker, even though the real-life Assia was miserably depressed. The reason for her depression and despair are skirted when the speaker mentions the "dreams of a spinster" (18). Morbidly afraid of being unmarried *and* of growing old, Assia was obsessed with her appearance and marital status, as I trace in the next chapter. Past the traditional age for marriage and facing the likelihood that she would not marry again (i.e., facing the life of a "spinster"), Assia ended her life. Hughes's portrayal of Assia is cutting in its gendered rendition: only a woman—and an abject woman at that—can do what she does in this poem and throughout the Assia poems.

The locket lends Assia "uncanny power" and a "Demonic flash" (14, 15); in other words, she is figured as rather demonic, as she is in "Dreamers" of *Birthday Letters* and as she is in the next poem of

Capriccio, "The Mythographers." Viewing her as a sexual and powerful woman, the speaker condemns those very qualities (and Assia) by associating Assia with evil forces throughout *Capriccio*, a rather unkind move in elegiac poems and a rhetorical move that asks us to consider how we treat women we deem to be sexual and powerful beings. Bundtzen views *Capriccio* as a failed "therapeutic strategy for dealing with his memories of Assia and Shura" for Hughes because it "does more to obscure their humanity than to transcend the autobiographical level as Hughes may have aspired to do. Instead of poetic transcendence for her, Assia Wevill is buried in myth" ("Traumatic Repetition" 132). And yet *Capriccio* remains a powerful collection of poems that treats gendered expectations of feminine and masculine performances. In studying the *Capriccio* poems as a group, we can reflect on how women and men are represented; interrogate how those discursive formations ameliorate or harm people in the world outside of the book; and consider how *Capriccio* puts into relief our own ideas and behaviors about gender.

"The Mythographers"

Hughes conflates Assia with Lilith and Nehama in "The Mythographers" and, later, in "Dreamers." Although Assia was perceived to be a "goddess" by those who knew her, including Jill Neville, the Australian novelist who worked with Assia in advertising and who wrote about her as a goddess to Hughes (Feinstein 173), Assia's beauty and power are conveyed in horrific details in "The Mythographers." Far from paying her a compliment, Hughes demonizes Assia by highlighting her sexuality and/or sexual desirability and her purported unnatural maternal instincts in associating her with Lilith and Nehama. (Nehama replaces or accompanies Lilith in her exploits, depending on the myth referenced [Bere 34]; she is also variously understood to be a sister to Lilith and a "charmer" [Bundtzen, "Traumatic Repetition" 132]). As Bere elucidates, Lilith, for Hughes, likely signifies the Jewish idea of a nocturnal, flying female demon. Lilith or Nehama (a stand-in for Lilith in "The Mythographers") plays two roles: "in the first," explains Bere, "she is the incarnation of lust, the seducer of men; and in the second, she attempts to strangle newborn babies. Occasionally, when she finds no children, she turns on her own" (34). By bringing Lilith/Nehama to bear on his poetic sequence about Assia, Hughes establishes Assia in the manner in which biographies and scholarship have depicted her: she is a demon seductress, bent on tempting men and destroying them in the process, in addition to destroying children and, by extension, families.

We learn that Lilith flies (flaps) into the bedroom with the "abortion of a laugh" (6–7): "Her abortions / (Freeing Woman for Man as Man for Woman) / Decompose to single-cell demons" (7–9), and these baby demons also roam the world (10–11). Initially, it might seem as if Hughes understands both men and women to be responsible for the sexual transgressions that occur, as well as for the abortions referenced on literal and metaphorical levels that result from unwholesome sexual activity, but that understanding is quickly undercut, as Lilith and, later, Nehama are roundly held responsible for tempting, bewitching, and leading the man astray from his preferred home life. Apparently, Hughes also viewed Assia in this way, if his poems and letters to Assia bespeak his views: in a letter, he commands Assia to get her witchcraft working on him (31 Aug. 1965), and more than once, he portrays her as Lilith (or Nehama): the demonic, powerful woman who seduces him and leaves him helpless and enthralled, all the while destroying his life and denying him agency in his poetry. That is the narrative of *Capriccio* at the thematic, macrocosmic level and also the narrative of "The Mythographers" at the microcosmic level.

In keeping with this theme, the unhappily married man (Lilith detects "the Mayday signal" under "his finger-ring" [11–12]) becomes infatuated with Lilith ("His fever shall be her, hallucinated" [13]), but his infatuation is staged in terms of sickness in the previous line and aberrant sex in later lines ("Flogging herself with her hair, phosphorescent, / Riding him upside down through the bed-head" [15–16]). While the first two stanzas introduce Lilith, the rest of the long poem (for *Capriccio*) explores Nehama's impact on the self-described "simpleton" (19), the speaker of the poem. Under Nehama's (read: Assia's) influence, the married man finds "instant amnesia. / The cries of his children: pangs / In a torn-off third arm" (24–26). While the speaker admits that he had already "quit his wife because television / Revealed all that her veil / Had hidden from him" (20–22), that *he* is the one who desires that Nehama "take" him and kiss him, and that he finds being with her "euphoric" (30), he presents Nehama as the pathetic villain. Disparaging her, the speaker dismisses demonic Nehama as "possessing / Some woman's divorced and desperate body" (31–32). Of course, this gendered belittling of Assia's real-life circumstances—as discussed in the next chapter—are galling, but what is more horrific is the virulent attack of the appearance and circumstances of a pregnant "Nehama"/Assia (lines 34–40). It is unclear whether the lines refer to Assia's first pregnancy carrying Hughes's child (she endured an abortion after finding herself pregnant with Hughes's child in the aftermath of Plath's suicide) or the second, which resulted in Shura.

Other personal details, directly relevant to Assia and Hughes, emerge in "The Mythographers." Their happy time in Ireland, living together as a family with their and Plath's children, is alluded to in the detail of an "Irish mirror," with a nod to Assia's preoccupation with and concern over her appearance (41). But the happiness is only passing and never fully rendered in this poem: death and horror, instead, reign. Although Hughes and Assia never married, despite her desperation to claim him as her husband, the speaker refers to himself as Nehama's "bridegroom" and to Nehama as "his bride" (42, 31), seemingly leaving behind references to Plath as the speaker concentrates on depicting Assia's horrific acts in broad strokes, including her supposed unnatural maternal instincts, her act of filicide, and her suicide. Here are the bitter lines:

> And the up-ogling skull
> That suckles her breast brings her screaming
> From the bedroom. She tries to kill
> This baby-skull properly dead and goes through

Death's oven door with it to make sure
It stays dead. She manages. Her last
Backward glance
Seals a star between his eyes.
"Let this,"
Said the Mythographers, "Be Nehama's fame." (43–52)

Nehama's fame is to be found in her abjectness, the horror she elicits. What Hughes has produced with *Capriccio* is a mythography of his relationship with Assia and of Assia herself in connection with Hughes and Plath. She has become a principal figure in their stories, and in setting down poetic narratives about her, Hughes both creates and propagates an "official" version of Assia and an archetype of a powerful but dangerous, beautiful but destructive, desirable but deadly, woman. Perhaps situating himself as a mythographer unawares, Hughes has crafted a legacy for Assia that defames her, rather than giving her fame. Assia is infamous rather than famous in literature, biographies, and scholarship. Her impact on him as a man and poet cannot be underestimated, the speaker implies: her last glance stays with him, sealing Assia's legacy (via a Jewish star of David?) on him. Just as the Mythographers pronounce that Lilith will be immortal, so, too, has Assia become immortal in *Capriccio*, *Birthday Letters*, and other Hughes poems as well as in Plath's poems and the stories and scholarship dedicated to their lives and work by biographers, literary critics, and less established writers of all persuasions and backgrounds on the internet and in the public sphere.

"Systole Diastole"

"Systole Diastole" shows itself to be an angry and bitter poem unequivocally, but it is also a poem that admits to Hughes's love for Assia, even after her death. The plot of the poem stems from Assia wanting more than Hughes could give, as this poem records their story. Featured as the "mother" (1), "lioness" (4, 26), and "ghost" with fangs of the poem (27, 28, 30), Assia drinks Hughes's lifeblood and spirit, if we read this poem as a thinly veiled autobiographical rendering. Not finding satiation, she sucks his heart with a "lockjaw grip" (5), seeking out his heart (after he has ripped it away from her and hidden it in a flower to repair it) even as a ghost in her afterlife. Locating his heart, she carries it back to her lair: "Where her ghost could gnaw it, lick at it, guard it" (30). Biographically, this poem lends support to Assia's conclusion that she and Hughes would never have married. Displaying a relationship in which he already felt stifled before her death, the speaker of "Systole Diastole" is quite clear that he finds the exacting or demanding love of the lioness to be too much to bear; he wants his heart back: "So he ripped it free he hid his heart" (19). This line belies the argument that Assia just needed to wait a little longer for commitment from Hughes. After more than six years with her, if "Systole Diastole" tells us anything from Hughes's retrospective assessment of his relationship with Assia, it is that further commitment was improbable: in the poem, the lioness drinks the speaker's very "life-blood" (13). One or the other—the speaker or the lioness—would have to die: it is the lioness/woman who "died of thirst," after the speaker's heart is taken away from her (27). Perhaps the lack of end-stopped lines and the relative lack of punctuation marks mirror the lack of both resolution and closure, as well as trauma, for the speaker/Hughes; everything is left open and cycling back, the force of which steers the narrative trajectory of the Assia poetry sequence. As Dianne Hunter comments, "In *Capriccio,* Assia [is] the destroyer," "a monstrous vampire with fangs in Hughes's grieving heart" (145). Each poem of *Capriccio* contributes to an overall master narrative about Assia (and himself) that Hughes created with this poetry collection.

"Descent"

Somewhat similar to "The Locket" and "The Mythographers," in which geographical locations associated with Assia in her actual life are associated with her in the world of *Capriccio,* "Descent" lists all the places she had previously lived: Germany, Israel, Canada (specifically British Columbia), and England. Addressing Assia, the speaker explains her life to her: from one locale to another, Assia strips herself from each home, removing herself and vestiges of her life from these places, and yet the speaker insists that each place harbored unhealed traumas, submerged in her personality and directing her life and behavior: she is forced to "go underground" (3); "go deeper" (6, 9, 18); "working deeper / As you moved deeper" (14–15). The poem indicates that Assia's traumatic past is the compass, directing her to her "descent"—the title of the poem and that which sets the stage for both the actions in the poem and the final location. Alluding to Shura's killing and Assia's own suicide, the speaker declares that the woman's

> own hands, stronger than your chocked outcry,
> Took your daughter from you. She was stripped from you
> . . . .
> Clinging round your neck[.] (26–29)

The language used in these lines reveals the speaker's understanding of these double deaths: positioned as the victim in these lines—the victim who loses her daughter—the woman is also the perpetrator. It is the trauma of her past that motivates the woman's actions, against her will: her own hands can do what she herself adamantly protests: "your chocked outcry"; "Took your daughter from you"; and "She was stripped from you" while "Clinging round your neck" all point to a loving mother whose daughter has been stolen from her in the vocabulary of the poem. Because her love for her daughter is all that keeps her from "the bed / In the underworld" (30–31), the mother perishes too. In its treatment of Assia as a loving mother—but whose actions are animated by trauma and embedded deep in her nature and history—"Descent" revises to some extent the earlier portrayal, in "The Mythographers," of Assia as an unnatural mother.

Interestingly, "Descent" highlights the gendered strictures Assia faced. As the woman who "had to strip off England / With your wedding rings" (16–17), Assia did indeed, as her correspondence indicates, feel "abandoned" (19). In the end, although she had previously been married three times and found herself as the partner to Hughes, ultimately and ironically, Assia was left without a husband for herself and a father for Shura, a situation that grieved her deeply. Moreover, this situation posed challenging and (for her) insurmountable obstacles and odds that left Assia bereft of social support and resiliency, as we see from her will, the suicide note to her father, and recollections from the people who knew her, as collected by her biographers. The speaker in "Descent" accuses the woman of hoarding "gem-stones" to shore up her future, but he and we know that the real-world counterpart of the woman addressed in the poem had not secured the right protection for her well-being or future in the way of a (fourth or final) marriage.

"Folktale"

Returning to the motif of a fated, dysfunctional romantic relationship that could never be successful, no matter how much the couple might wish for it to work, "Folktale" echoes the impression of inevitability emitting from "The Locket" and "Systole Diastole." Picking up on the title, the poem ends with a clock striking midnight, reminiscent of the Cinderella folktale in which Cinderella and the prince are separated because they are out of time. This overt allusion is the only obvious folktale reference, but the title leaves open the possibility that this poem relates or constructs a folktale about Assia and Hughes. (A gesture to her name, Assia, can be found in this line: "He wanted the seven treasures of Asia—" [12].) The poem suggests that Assia was always going to do what she did, and Hughes would always be helpless to prevent her from doing so because he did not fully know how trauma ("He did not know she had risen out of cinders" [1]) and persecution ("She wanted escape without a passport" [8]) marked her and animated her behavior.

In "Folktale," Hughes paints the relationship with Assia as one characterized by each wanting and seeking in the other what she or he cannot find. According to Bundtzen, "If there is a common theme to their desires [in "Folktale"], it is their impossibility. For him, she is less a woman than a repository for exotic, dangerous and foreign images that stir his imagination" ("Traumatic Repetition" 135). Echoing Assia's persistence in owning him, body and soul, in "Systole Diastole," "Folktale" declares, "She wanted only the runaway slave" (6), further stressing Hughes's desire *not* to be owned or captured by Assia and further clarifying that he was running away from her within the context of this poem. As the speaker asserts, "So they ransacked each other for everything / That could not be found" (27–28). As with most of the *Capriccio* poems, personal details are revealed, but they are only recognizable if one has read the materials, namely Hughes's correspondence to Assia, in Emory's archive. For example, "He wanted a mother of halva," writes Hughes in "Folktale" (24); Assia became a mother to his child and served as a caretaker of his children with Plath, and "halva" was a pet name Hughes employed both for Assia and for her writing (Hughes, letters to Wevill, 31 Jan. and 11 Feb. 1964).

"Fanaticism"

"Fanaticism" draws our attention to Assia's fanaticism for love, as the poem records it. The speaker believes that the "You" of the poem traded her future for Aphrodite's charms and intervention. Leaving her clothes folded at the door of Aphrodite's temple as a supplicant, the woman receives Aphrodite's benefits, or favors, among which includes exchanging her "face for the mask of Aphrodite" (4). However, the woman also exchanges marriage for "the manic depression / Of the ovaries" and her life for "those holy years" (5–6, 7–8). In this short poem, we understand that from Hughes's point of view, Assia valued love and beauty over "the plain security" of her "life-line" (7). Her demise is tabulated as that which is part of the exchange: for the years she was worshipped as beautiful and desirable, she gives up everything else, it seems:

> "After forty I'll end it," you laughed
> (You were serious) as you folded your future
> Into your empty clothes. Which Oxfam took. (10–12)

Personal details about Assia are presented here. Her sister, Celia Chaikin told Assia's biographers, for example, "[Assia] once said to me, 'I'll kill myself at 42'." After interviewing Chaikin, Koren and Negev explain Assia's declaration, "Assia was afraid of getting old and losing her beauty and wished to remain young forever" (180). Moreover, according to the biographers, Olwyn Hughes recounted that Assia's and Shura's clothes had been donated to the Oxfam establishment across the street from their home (210–11). As Feinstein comments: "Put it this way, [Assia's] story, like her beauty, is something from a fairy tale, and the end is inevitable. In some of the [*Capriccio*] poems she even prophesies it carelessly herself—not as a matter of anguish, but as a way of escaping the ugliness of middle age" (227). Assia herself comments that she finds middle age full of grotesque shapes and aspects, in a journal note dated 16 January 1969 (journal entries, 6 Sept. 1968, 16 Jan. 1969, and undated). What we can take away from this poem is a gendered dimension or a cautionary tale in the way of a fairy tale or master narrative. Assia valued that which she believed made her unique, worthy, important, and capable of being loved: apparently, she thought that beauty and youth made her desirable and lovable. Unfortunately for her, there were no other pathways—readily apparent to her—that provided alternatives in allowing her to accept her aging female body or in finding value in her life as a middle-aged, separated/unmarried woman.

"Snow"

The poem "Snow" appears to be about the last time Hughes saw Assia alive, when they parted ways at the Manchester station after a televised reading Hughes gave and a failed house hunting expedition (Koren and Negev 200–201). Feinstein identifies it as Hughes's "most affectionate" published poem for Assia (228). Stylish and elegant, the woman in the "sparkly black fox fur hat" and the "charcoal crimped black ponyskin / Coat" reminds the speaker of the Moscow Opera and of its "Soft chandeliers, ghostly wreckage" (2, 22–23, 3).

Associated with the snowy landscape, the woman is frozen, like the snow that continues to fall on her and around her, in the speaker's mind forever: it is a "short walk / That could never end was / Never ending" (8–10). For him, and now the reader, she is immortalized in her "unending / Walk" (4–5), one that expends what precious moments of her life are left ("Of a life / Burning out in the air" [789]). "Snow" shares the theme of an expiration of time with "Folktale." Also reminiscent of "Descent," in which Assia's past buries itself "deeper" with each escape from a home country and in which she embarks on a trajectory of descent, the speaker states, "You escaped / Deeper into the falling flakes" (21–22). "I watched you," the speaker quietly relates (30), in a line set apart from the other stanzas of the poem.[15] As Bundtzen remarks, this scene in "Snow" "is repeated endlessly in the memory-traces," and she notes that trauma, "the sudden wound unprepared for and doomed to unending recurrence," appears to be bound up in the "repetition-compulsion" of the language of this poem ("Traumatic Repetition" 131).

Addressing the beloved, the speaker sees her being erased: the snow is already at work, "burying your footprints, / Drawing its white sheet over everything, / Closing the air behind you" (31–33). Literary studies have erased Assia as a multidimensional woman, much as the snow erases Assia's footprints and any traces of her in the poem. Hughes himself seems to wish to recover Assia, too, in this poem and to render her again as the person he loved. In the poem, Assia's hat and coat are in sharp contrast to the snow that encases her, and the snow also puts into relief the conversation between Assia and Hughes that he characterizes as warm—so warm, in fact, that the words melt in their mouths (24–25). But the melting words dissolve "Whatever was trying to cling" and prevent any staying power (26): no sense of permanence remains in this conversation, and the conversation did not prevent Assia from leaving him. Instead, "Snow" recaptures that last face-to-face conversation and dwells on the setting and the beloved, with the hindsight that this scene is no more and can never happen again—while immortalizing it.

"Rules of the Game" and "The Other"

Titled "Rules of the Game" in *Capriccio* the art book and "The Other" in the *Capriccio* poems of *Collected Poems*, this poem castigates Assia for wanting what Plath had, for being a jealous rival. The speaker accuses Assia of stealing what belongs to Plath; Assia helped herself to what was Plath's because Plath "had too much," and Assia "had / Absolutely nothing" (1, 2–3). Furthermore, Hughes refers to Assia, within the context of Plath's ambition, as "a crossed-out page, tossed into a basket" (13). A cruel indictment of Assia's attitudes and abilities, Assia is faulted by the speaker in the poem for her situation: poetic justice has been served, the speaker implies. The implication is, of course, that Hughes was Plath's husband, and Assia took what was not hers to take, and this logic, then, denies Hughes culpability. What he actually asserts in the poem is that Assia's "nature abhorred" what it perceived to be her "vacuum" (6), her lack, compared to what Plath had, which is sketched variously as luck, ambition, and success (8, 11, 17). He emphasizes what becomes Assia's alleged selfishness: "You had redressed the balance, which meant / Now you had some, too, for yourself" (9–10). This statement follows three variations of "you took some," addressed to Assia in only a stanza and a half. Shockingly, Hughes compares his two love(r)s to each other and concludes that Assia was responsible for Plath's death ("Even her life was / Trapped in the heap you took. She had nothing" [21–23]), and so the speaker's attitude is that it is fitting that Assia will pay the price for moving in on and acquiring Plath's territory. After Assia has collected "Everything [Plath] had won, the happiness of it," and had gained "much too much" (17, 26), the ghostly Plath returns to take back what is hers ("It made no difference that she was dead // Only you / Saw her smile, as she took some. / At first, just a little" [24, 27–29]).

"Rules of the Game" / "The Other" is conceived within the metaphor of a game: in it, Assia becomes the competitor to the already competitive Plath. While Assia takes and takes from Plath, who is deemed the winner in the poem, until Plath has nothing left, it is ultimately Assia who has lost. Depicted as the loser throughout the game—much as she is in scholarship and stories we tell about her still—Assia comes across as selfish and excessive. Hughes decides who the winner and loser are in damning language.

In pitting Plath and Assia, woman against woman, against each other, Hughes establishes the story line for what became a deadly (literally) "game" of female rivalry that excludes him from consideration. Indeed, in "Rules of the Game" / "The Other," Hughes sacrifices Assia, the woman who was his partner and the woman he actively pursued, to ostensibly clear his conscience, pay respects to Plath, displace blame, and recast Assia in literature as the villainous seductress, the narrative that took hold and continues to hold our literary imagination. Concluding the poem, the speaker explains that now, in the afterlife, a ghostly Plath will exact revenge and take back what is hers from Assia, and the tone of the poem signals that this is not only poetic justice (pun intended) but poetic revenge, by both Plath and Hughes. In an interview with Assia's friend Fay Weldon, Feinstein records Weldon's take on the situation. According to Feinstein, "Fay thought that Assia left Court Green [her shared home with Hughes] not only because she felt that Ted's mother and father hated her, but even more because she came to feel that Ted himself blamed her for Sylvia's death: 'Ted would say[:] "You are the dark force. You are the dark destructive force that destroyed Sylvia"'" (166).

"Possession"

In "Possession," the speaker openly addresses a "you": a person whose dresses recall a séance, a mystical segue into the speaker's claim that the woman addressed is in "Possession / By ancestors become demons" (4–5). The effects of this possession are enumerated in widely arching arcane analogies and obscure allusions. However, the power of the poem rests in its opening and closing. Understanding that the woman is possessed, we learn, by the end, what power she has over the man, who remains in thrall to her demonic power. Such romantic or sexual "possession," replete with the man's "last swollen shame and wet fever / Of his infatuation" (32–33), will strip a man of his dignity and, as referenced earlier in the poem, his "future" (28). Accordingly, we read the last lines of this poem in horror when we realize that Hughes finds fault with Assia for his decision to pursue her romantically and sexually and that he faults her (not himself) for the breakup of his family:

> let him awake
> Copulating with the dust of the highway
> Stared at by his own children
> All still alive, as if resurrected
> (Days before, for her, he had thrown them
> To the dogs): (33–38)

Curiously, the poem ends precisely in this way with a colon, signaling something more to follow—but nothing does until the next poem, "The Coat." This stylistic decision indicates that the poem that follows it will explore or elaborate upon the situation set up in "Possession."

"The Coat"

As with "Possession," we approach the woman and her coat (a different one in both material and function than the one featured in "Snow," where it stands in as a beautiful memory). In this poem, the woman's coat functions as a receptacle for all the hatred and blame heaped upon the woman by the speaker-poet. The coat also is figured as the object that invokes the despair the speaker feels about the woman and his relationship with her. The speaker begins by pointing out that the woman's coat is not "natural tiger" (2); instead, it is "only dyed marmot" (1), and so it is not any help (presumably, to stave off what transpires). Fixated on the coat, the speaker explains that it soaks up nicotine in bars (implying that it is not wholesome), and it bedevils him with memories of "the perfume-dating / of that summer, like the imprinting shock / Noon-stench of a discovered corpse" (3–4, 9–11). This last line reminds us that the coat is left behind after the culmination of romantic interludes and the discovery of Assia's and Shura's bodies.

By the second stanza, the coat has been reduced to a "lining" (16), suggesting that the owner of it has already perished. To this end, the second stanza traces the impact on him of the speaker's involvement with the woman with the tiger-marmot coat: in cryptic fashion, the speaker tells us that faces are eaten; "the bed horror" involves "Screams that split bodies" (19, 21) and with "Roofs falling in, the morning empty" (22). Ultimately, the "sun itself is silenced" as the speaker encounters the "after-shock" of the horror that has taken place (23, 24). The most charitable line—and the most loving—occurs here, in the third to last line of the poem. Presumably for Hughes, the sunshine has disappeared in his life (the "sun itself is silenced") with the deaths of Assia and Shura; this line indicates to us the extent to which he loved the owner of the coat. When her voice becomes silenced, so, too, does his world; his external world appears darkened and deafened, a shadow—or similar to the coat, a semblance of itself in its lining—to him.

"Smell of Burning"

The speaker in "Smell of Burning" characterizes Assia's eventual suicide (and cremation) as inevitable: the woman was branded by fire and marked by death for the duration of her life. This poem is unusual in its place in the arc of *Capriccio* in that it considers that Assia may have been a "victim" and not a perpetrator after all (31). Tracking her from Germany to Israel, the speaker decides that the "smouldering / Conifer inside you" defines Assia's life (15–16); lightning, burning, smoke, and fire are operative images in the poem. And yet Hughes cannot miss the opportunity to sexualize Assia and to associate her with destruction (of herself and others), even in a poem purportedly about her victimizations and fear via her life circumstances before meeting Hughes: "Stretched out naked, on [her] bed" (19), Assia "watched [her] fear making the moon brown" (20). Even the moon is crisped or burned in its association with Assia. The mother in the poem "burst[s] from her room homesick weeping / With the smart of smothered embers" (21–22). The implication is that the fire, burning, destruction, and death associated with Assia follow her and engulf those closest to her, such as her mother. (The father in the poem assumes a fatalistic stance and takes the fire and burning in stride, though he has eluded death by burning earlier in the poem.) A later image in "Smell of Burning" features Assia burning from the inside, causing her to gulp and cough for oxygen. This poem gestures to Hughes's complicated thoughts and feelings about his perceptions of Assia's life and death—a life plagued by traumatic experiences and a death that ushered in trauma for Hughes.

"The Pit and the Stones"

"The Pit and the Stones" is fascinating in its treatment of Hughes's perceived victimization and the public condemnation of both him and Assia. The poem roundly faults Assia for Hughes's suffering in his relations with her and for his (and her) subsequent persecution in the sphere of public opinion. Addressing the woman point-blank, the speaker accuses her of collecting him as a trophy, one of many she has acquired. Her power and appeal lie in her physical attributes and her purported desirability: "the brimming power of [her] gaze" correlates to her romantic triumphs (of "trophies digested"), and her amusement is likened to "the movement / Of the most magnificent tigress" (2, 4, 10–11). Uncritically, the speaker places blind faith in the woman: "He made nothing / Of the hands that had held him, / Had led him, tethered him, left him" (14–16). The logic of the poem follows this line of thought: if the woman initiates and the man follows or accepts, then she is to blame as the instigator. In this poem,

Assia wields the power in the romantic relationship with Hughes, as Hughes frames it. And yet we know that this was decidedly not the case, as chapter 4 will demonstrate. Instead, Hughes is the one who made the formative decisions in the relationship, giving Assia the options to meekly submit to him or to leave him. Ultimately, she chose both; while alive, she deferred to him in all major life decisions, but she stated that she elected death as the better alternative to a life without him, thereby leaving him with memories of her castigations for his treatment of her.

Regardless of what Assia thought, this poem is Hughes's poetic record of the relationship as he experienced it and/or wanted to frame it. Thus, one line is cutting (to Assia and her memory or legacy) in its declaration that his relationship with her was cemented on weakness, from his perspective: "He saw / Absolutely no sense in his tether / But his own weakness" (19–21). Similarly, then, there is no sense in Assia's sacrifice of herself and him: "So you took him / With you in into the pit / Beneath him, where you were impaled" (22–24). Earlier in the poem, we are told that there are spikes in the pit, and we assume that Assia has been figuratively impaled by them as well as by the "eyes in the faces" that would condemn her from the top of the opening of the pit. The stanza break between this last line of the penultimate stanza and the first line of the last stanza builds to the climax in the poem: the public condemnation—the metaphorical stoning—of Assia.

Conventionally, Assia has been thought of as Hughes's mistress, who, the public believed, stole Hughes from Plath, thereby causing Plath's eventual suicide. The last two stanzas of "The Pit and the Stones" read thus:

So you took him
With you into the pit
Beneath him, where you were impaled

By the eyes in the faces, incomprehensible
To you as to him. They crowded

The hatch of dawning sky, their jubilation
Like tin cans wildly shaken:
Each with a stone in it. (22–29)

To some extent, the two lovers share a fate beyond their making, as they understand it. For Assia did not understand herself to be the reason for Plath's suicide, as Koren and Negev document (115). And Hughes indicates that for the real-life counterparts of the woman and man in "The Pit and the Stones," public censure affected their reputations for "incomprehensible" reasons: the speaker relates that neither he nor the woman can read the eyes of those who would throw stones, and so they cannot understand them. Ultimately, Hughes fared much better than Assia in the public eye, as he acknowledges in a careful reading of the poem. It is Assia, the woman, who is impaled by the scrutiny and opinion of others and who is mortally injured by their "jubilation" at her state at the bottom of the metaphorical pit.

"Shibboleth"

"Shibboleth" provides further details about Assia for the readers of *Capriccio.* In this poem, Assia's German and English backgrounds are referenced, as is her command of Hebrew. Interestingly, Hughes writes, "Your Hebrew / Survived on bats and spiders" (4–5), which makes Assia's celebrated English translations of Amichai's Hebrew poems all the more impressive. (Further discussion of her translations of these poems takes place in the next chapter.) Also, Assia's interest in Russian literature is alluded to in the last lines of the poem, which underscores her foreign tastes and presence in the poem.[16] In "Shibboleth," as signaled by the title, Hughes ties Assia to a way of speaking and behaving that were persecuted: even the dogs in the poem are startled in her presence, sensing something dangerous or someone in danger. While this poem is somewhat similar to "The Pit and the Stones" in its acknowledgment of Assia's supposed persecution—ethnic persecution in "Shibboleth" and social persecution by public opinion in "The Pit and the Stones"—it offers little sympathy for Assia and refuses to flesh her out more than by her cultural boundary crossings.

"The Roof"

Following in the poetic vein of "Shibboleth," "The Roof" considers Assia's mixed cultural heritages. Although Hughes wished for her to present herself as German and, especially, Jewish ("Draft Constitution"), Assia was not, in fact, Jewish. Because Jewish lineage is matrilineal—Assia's German mother identified as a Christian—and Assia was not a converted or practicing Jew, Assia could best be described as someone who was familiar with Judaism culturally, in that her father was Jewish, and she could read and write Hebrew. And yet Hughes is right in what he implies in "Shibboleth": what was considered a mixed marriage between Assia's Christian mother and Jewish father would have indicted Assia's family from a Nazi point of view; she and her family would have been persecuted, with their lives at stake, had they stayed in Nazi Germany. Likewise, her German background does not provide any refuge for her in the poem either. The speaker of the poem posits that Assia's safety is contingent on her living "incognito" (12). And yet the speaker concludes, "Either way you lived / Waiting for the knock on the door" (13–14). These last lines of the poem present Assia as someone who lived with apprehension and fear as well as instability and insecurity. The latter two qualities persisted throughout her life, and they characterize her relationship with Hughes and her life at large, as I will explore in the next chapter.

"The Error"

From its first lines, "The Error" reproaches Assia for her death; it places the responsibility and the blame on her, naming the influence of Plath's suicide and the censure of Assia following it as contributing causes. The speaker assumes that the woman addressed had the ability to stand outside of the tragedy of Plath's suicide and its aftermath, despite her eventual internalization of what may be described as the trauma of the situation. "When," Hughes accuses Assia in the poem, "[Plath's] grave opened its ugly mouth / Why didn't you just fly?" (1–2). He continues, "Why did you kneel down at her grave's edge / To be identified / Accused and convicted" (4–6). Although Assia blamed Hughes for her death in her suicide note to her father, Hughes is careful to extricate himself from such a charge, especially in connection with Assia's decision to commit suicide and filicide immediately following an argument with him over the telephone:

> You must have misheard a sentence.
> You were always mishearing
> Into Hebrew or German
> What was muttered in English.
> Her grave mouthed its riddle right enough.
> But maybe you heard in the air somewhere
> An answer to one of your own
> Unspoken enigmas. Misheard,
> Mistook, and kneeled meekly [at Plath's grave].
>
> Maybe they wouldn't stone you
> If you became a nun
> And fearlessly incinerated yourself
> In the shrine of her death. (10–18)

In these lines, he also shifts the blame onto Plath, Assia, and the public (the people who would stone Assia for her role in the story about Plath-Hughes's dysfunctional marriage), respectively. Everyone but he is at fault, with Hughes returning in the final two stanzas of the poem to Assia's death as her own mistake. She gave up her life and everything he associates with her: "Shops, jobs, baby daughter, the German au pair" (24). He asks why she did not commit herself to a hospital—perhaps thinking about their last argument on that fateful day, which he does not acknowledge except for the repeated reference to a translation error. If she had sought out medical help, the speaker muses, it might have been possible to "Drop the whole mistake: simply call it / An error in translation?" (32–33). She misunderstood him, Hughes wishes to plead in apostrophe to Assia. And yet the penultimate stanza fully condemns her for giving in to the despair of life in the shadow of Plath's suicide over the course of their six-year relationship.

Hughes does concede that Assia has been "strong" during those six years with him: "All you were doing was being strong" (41). But he undercuts this compliment and nod to Assia's six-year resilience by commenting that she was simply cultivating death in the meantime ("Waiting for your ashes / To be complete and cool" [42–43]). The poem ends with an acknowledgment of Assia's death (not Shura's) in a reserved and objective tone.

All in all, this poem is not one that will endear Hughes to a readership invested in recovering Assia because the poem functions as exculpation instead of being a poem of contrition. To clarify, I am not advocating that we hold Hughes responsible for Assia's death or that the poem would be better if Hughes claimed a part in the tragedy, but I think that it is ingenious of the poem (and *Capriccio* as a whole) to set an unsympathetic narrative that excludes completely Assia's point of view, of which Hughes would have known from her correspondence (some of it archived), if nothing else. I believe this marked exclusion of Assia's perspective as well as a decidedly harsh treatment of her throughout the collection constitutes an injustice, to some extent, especially as *Capriccio* is a collection about Assia exclusively, and it divulges personal details about her. And of course, she cannot respond in turn, and the legacy created for her in *Capriccio* is not useful in empowering women in discursive formations.

"Opus 131"

"Opus 131" contains a bit of a lament for Assia as it seemingly reflects on her last days. (Assia writes in her journal about listening to Beethoven's String Quartet No. 13, Op. 130, on the last weekend of her life [Koren and Negev 201]). The speaker queries: "Where was the lifeline music? What had happened / To consolation, prayer, transcendence—" (11–12); he recounts that Beethoven (a favorite composer of Hughes) had "broken down" (18). There is no lifeline to be had for Assia.

As the speaker explains: "[. . .] You strained listening / Maybe for divorce to be resolved" (18–19). But it is too late; the musical notes take the woman away with them as we see in these last lines of the poem: "Were already carrying you off / Each with a different bit, into the corners / Of the universe" (28–30). Several aspects of this poem are noteworthy in terms of Assia's biography and Hughes's literary treatment of her. One is that Hughes equates Assia with beautiful music, with an art form and a composer he cherished. Artistic herself and someone Hughes loved, Assia emerges as an important figure in Hughes's life here; the conflation of Opus 131 with Assia's life signals the importance of Assia to Hughes. Another noteworthy aspect of this poem is the admission that her marital status meant a lot to Assia: she desperately wished to be married to Hughes, and Olwyn Hughes speculated that Assia received paperwork related to the finalization of her divorce from David Wevill upon returning to her home from her weekend house hunting expedition with Hughes. The trip was a spectacular failure, as Hughes admitted he could not marry Assia because of the shadow of Plath's suicide, and so a joint home for them was not secured. The failure of the trip combined with the divorce decree spurred Assia's frantic call to Hughes.[17] "Opus 131" ends with the inferred conclusion that the addressee is already gone and presumably beyond reach of the speaker.

"Familiar"

Compared to the other powerful poems in *Capriccio*, "Familiar," from my perspective, is the weakest one in literary execution. It features a white horse as Assia's "familiar," a horse associated with "massacre and pogrom" (11), harking back to Assia's family's emigration from Nazi Germany in the 1930s. It follows the theme set by the other poems in *Capriccio* in reflecting on Assia as a wanderer, a possible "migrant" in this poem (25). As a whole, the *Capriccio* poems suggest that Assia is spurred on to suicide by Plath's ghostly influence, the public's censure of her, and/or some personal attribute (i.e., impact of trauma and defect in personality) that she herself possesses. "Familiar" takes its cue from the latter theme, but it renders its message obliquely. In harboring her familiar, Assia cannot disassociate herself from a legacy of trauma and death.

"Flame"

A startling amount of biographical details concerning Hughes and Assia's last weekend together—up to her last day—are embedded in "Flame." It is appropriately placed at the end of the collection, the penultimate poem. (Hughes closes *Capriccio* with "Chlorophyl," which contains reminisces of the start of their romantic affair, rounding out the collection in such a way that the end meets the beginning.) From it—and Koren and Negev's and Bate's biographies of Assia and Hughes, respectively—we see Hughes confirming what the biographers have also argued: that for Assia, everything hinged on a joint home with Hughes. Cohabiting with him, sharing their family, and formalizing (in a way) their partnership were her desperate dreams. Hughes acknowledges Assia's desires: for Assia, he writes, house hunting was her "oxygen mask" (1). The hope that she and Hughes would live together as committed partners kept her persevering in the relationship and in her life. The importance for Assia of having a home with Hughes is underscored by the amount of space Hughes dedicates to actual places they toured and to his impressions of them in the poem: Green Farm, near Hexham; Dower House, at Park End; and homes in Manchester. And yet Hughes avoids the explosive details of their conversations together during that fateful weekend in March 1969; instead, he focuses on Assia boarding the train at Manchester Central—the last time he saw her alive—and what awaits her upon her return to her London flat.

Unsurprisingly, following the other eighteen poems of *Capriccio,* the speaker declares, "You did not know how history had already / Cast you to repeat itself" (25–26). It is not because of him that Assia detonates (a bomb figures as an implied metaphor in the poem) but because of mail she has received, likely notification of the finalization of her divorce from David Wevill. As the speaker informs us:

> You had no idea
> What signed bit of paper had found you at last
> After so many years, what detonator
> Waited in your flat
> To include even your wildest hopes
> . . . .
> You barely had time to open the envelope
> And grab for the telephone
> Before it was all over. (27–31, 35–37)

Haunting in its revelations and in its merciless denouement, we realize that we are given a firsthand personal account about Assia (and Hughes) in this poem. Her "wildest hopes" dashed—what I call the "good life" in chapter 4—Assia despaired of securing Hughes for herself and living with him in a blended family situation, as she had previously done and as Hughes had led her to believe would happen again (hence the residences toured and recounted in "Flame"). Perhaps realizing that she was legally unattached to David Wevill and feeling abandoned by Hughes, Assia's franticness and panic resonate in the last three lines of "Flame." Engulfed by the metaphorical flame of the bomb that has triggered her realization of her precarious situation and (what appeared to her) unrealistic life plans with Hughes, Assia was decimated by both personal tragedy and structural forces outside of her control.

"Chlorophyl"

"Chlorophyl" closes *Capriccio,* and it presents us with the now infamous start of the Hughes-Assia affair. For Bundtzen, the placement of

"Chlorophyl" at the end of *Capriccio* signals the "traumatic and recurring" wound of the material that is *Capriccio* ("Traumatic Repetition" 142). What Hughes leaves out in "Chlorophyl" is that he was the instigator of the affair: he pursued Assia, arriving at her workplace and leaving her a note that indicated his willingness to see her despite their marriages to others. (We know this to be the case because Assia's coworkers have verified it to her biographers Koren and Negev.)[18] "Chlorophyl" opens with Assia's response: she sent a blade of grass, soaked in her Dior perfume, via mail to him at his home in Court Green.[19] (Likely this gesture was a play on Court Green: sending him something green, Assia affirmed he could "court" her in response to the note he had left for her.) However, Hughes dubs the blade of grass a "witchy doll" (3): invoking the now traditional, and misogynistic, interpretations of Assia as a demon who wields magic, Hughes relates that their future was foretold in that bewitched communication. He sees (in retrospect) a portent, in relation to Assia specifically:

> The gravestone. Inside it
> A sample of her own ashes. Inside it
> Her only daughter's
> Otherwise non-existent smile. (5–8)

Here we have a puzzling combination. On one hand, it looks as if Hughes is acknowledging that the affair with him will destroy Assia and Shura. On the other hand, he removes himself from the scenario: Shura is described as Assia's daughter (her only daughter), not "their" daughter. Assia's and Shura's deaths are foretold in something Assia has created, the perfume-soaked communication and artifact. Indeed, the receiver of the communication is elided altogether, except in the admission that he has received the communication. Thus, the way I read this poem is as a final statement about responsibility for the affair for the literary record, as *Capriccio* records it and immortalizes it. Instead of giving life, Assia and her grass blade with chlorophyll and Dior take away her own and Shura's lives. Hughes appears very circumspect in "Chlorophyl" as to his role in the affair and his impact on Assia's life when we recognize that a masculine pronoun is used only once in this short poem, but female ones are used three times. Moreover, Hughes attributes death to Assia and her behavior, not to himself or his behavior. For the closing poem in a collection remembering his deceased partner and, to a lesser extent, their daughter, it is a poem that does little to commemorate and recuperate memories of Assia's life in loving ways. Instead, it gives Assia to us as the archetypal beautiful-but-deadly, powerful-but-destructive woman, whose badness is captured in Hughes's motif of Assia as the demonic seductress, the villain of his (and Plath's) life story and of *Capriccio.*

BIRTHDAY LETTERS

"Dreamers," from *Birthday Letters* (1998), is far unkinder to Assia than anything in *Capriccio.* While there are moments of anger, bitterness, and resentment in *Capriccio,* "Dreamers" is the one poem among the eighty-eight of *Birthday Letters* that does the most damage to Assia and her legacy in Hughes's oeuvre. Far more recognized than *Capriccio,* Hughes's poetry collection *Birthday Letters* became a best seller and won the Forward Poetry Prize, the T. S. Eliot Prize for Poetry, the Whitbread Poetry Prize, and the Whitbread British Book of the Year Prize. Due to its overt treatment of Plath, *Birthday Letters* generated extraordinary attention upon its publication. Readily identifiable in "Dreamers," Assia is represented in the collection in damaging ways (to her and, I would maintain, women more generally). Ostensibly, *Birthday Letters* purports to set the record straight about Hughes's marriage to Plath, from his point of view. Unfortunately, Assia is a casualty in the narrative of *Birthday Letters,* which is all the more unfortunate given the exceptional popularity of the collection. As such, Assia is best known in poetry through the hostile lens of "Dreamers." She appears as a predatory German-Russian-Jewish-Israeli wolf / witch's daughter, whose Jewishness and dangerousness become almost hyperbolic, resulting in an ironic effect for readers who know that Assia was not, in fact, Jewish or, as the poem admits toward the end, in control of the situation either. "Dreamers" opens with Hughes siding with Plath from the first lines: "We didn't find her—she found us. / She sniffed us out. The Fate she carried / Sniffed us out" (1–3). Concerning an official or truthful recounting, the opening of the poem is quite bold and audacious in its positioning Assia as the scapegoat. We know—and no one contests this—that Plath and Hughes invited Assia and David Wevill to their home in Devon for the weekend.[20] Assia did not invite herself, nor was she attempting to get closer to the Hugheses in 1962, prior to the invitation extended to her and her husband to visit Devon. And yet in the first stanza, Hughes addresses Plath in apostrophe, commenting that the "Fable [Assia] carried / Requisitioned you and me and her, / Puppets for its performance" (5–7). In other words, Fate governs the lives of the people in the poem, and yet it is Assia who holds the Fable that makes puppets of them all.

The longest stanzas in the poem, plus an additional shorter one, portray and discuss Assia's beauty, but her beauty is denigrated in "Dreamers" too; nothing about Assia emerges as a positive attribute or creates a favorable impression, which seems to me to be quite a disservice to the woman whom Hughes pursued, led to believe he would marry, set up a home with over the course of six years, and whom he called his best friend and true wife and the mother of his second daughter. That woman does not appear in this poem.[21] Instead, we see Assia as a destructive force who is associated with death, darkness, and, in one word, horror. Nothing about her seems redeemable because, in no small part, she is the result of "Hitler's mutilations" (30); her "slightly unnatural" eyes give her away (19). While she fascinates Plath, we come to fear for Plath in the poem because Plath is being watched closely by Assia, who is a "Black Forest wolf, a witch's daughter / Out of Grimm" (20–21). The speaker relates that "When she suddenly rounded her eyeballs, / Popped them, strangled, she shocked you. / It was her mock surprise" (14–16). Assia's uncanny and/or remarkable eyes become a focus of the poem, and while she fascinates Plath to the extent that Plath cultivates her warily in "Dreamers," the

Plath figure in the poem sees only death in Assia, as the speaker asserts: "But you saw hanged women choke, dumb, through her" (17).

Jillian Becker has argued that "Dreamers" is anti-Semitic (59, 65).[22] Dianne Hunter also indicates that such is the case in her exploration of the poem (144). The hostility aimed at Assia in the poem certainly fuels such an interpretation, especially when Assia's supposed Jewishness is highlighted ("Her Jewishness, her many-blooded beauty" [23]) and coupled with evocative details in the same stanza:

> Who was this Lilith of abortions
> Touching the hair of your children
> With tiger-painted nails?
> Her speech Harrod's, Hitler's mutilations
> Kept you company, weeding the onions.
> An ex-Nazi Youth Sabra. Her father
> Doctor to the Bolshoi Ballet. (27–33)

As a person purportedly affected by Hitler, Assia is dubbed a former Nazi supporter in childhood by Hughes, a venomous charge, and yet this "ex-Nazi" identity is connected to that of a "Sabra," a Jewish person born in Israel. An unbelievable juxtaposition and tension reside in that characterization, one that is ultimately false when we consider the historical person in question. Assia was born in Germany, not Israel; was not a practicing Jew; and did not support Nazi ideology or belong to a Nazi youth group. In fact, her family escaped Germany in the 1930s to avoid persecution of her Jewish father. Her father told others he had served as a doctor to the Bolshoi Ballet, and so Hughes mingles fact and fiction together in a poem that denounces Assia and her presence in his family's home. Hatred surfaces in the speaker's accusatory denunciation of the "Lilith of abortions" who runs her "tiger-painted" fingernails through the hair of Plath's children: the choice of the possessive ("your children") renders Assia as a possessive and unwholesome woman who has no business being affectionate to or being proprietary of what belongs to Plath—and by extension, Hughes.

During the fateful May 1962 weekend in Devon that Hughes recounts in "Dreamers," Assia reportedly did weed onions with Plath. And her cultivated English accent—also described in the poem as "her Kensington jeweller's elocution" (11)—is rendered by others, including Hughes's friend Lucas Myers, as an upper-crust accent that may have galled Hughes as a reminder of social class distinction: as it appears in "Dreamers," Assia's acquired English accent is referenced twice, second only in importance to her unusual eyes, here represented as eliciting the "gaze of a demon" (41).

Assia's appearance is addressed as if the speaker is fixated on her, though he despises her, apparently:

> She sat there, in her soot-wet mascara,
> In flame-orange silks, in gold bracelets,
>
> Slightly filthy with erotic mystery. (37–39)

Finding fault with Assia's appearance—she is too erotic, so he is not responsible for being infatuated with her—Hughes prevents readers from seeing Assia in a light other than as a demonic seductress. His "Dreamers" perpetuates the bias, sexism, and misogyny in poetry that the literary scholarship has long embraced in relation to Assia. Becker argues Hughes "must have meant the reader to be awed and appalled that with this slightly filthy demonic creature—who was also 'beautiful'—he fell in love. It was love of Evil itself" (62). The poem ends with Hughes admitting that he fell in love with Assia, as she had with him, but by the end of "Dreamers," we cannot understand how anyone could fall in love with the "German / Russian Israeli with the gaze of a demon / Between curtains of black Mongolian hair" (40–42).

"The Inscription" is another *Birthday Letters* poem that pertains to Assia, although it does so rather tangentially and obliquely. Those familiar with Plath's and Hughes's biographies and with this poem know that Plath succeeded in gaining admittance to Hughes's bachelor flat and had a face-to-face meeting with him there during their separation. Looking around with great curiosity as well as pleading with Hughes for assurance that he had faith in her and that they would be reunited in Devon by summer, as Hughes describes the scene in the poem, Plath discovers a copy of the "red Oxford Shakespeare" (39). This book appears to be the very volume "Resurrected" after she had destroyed it (41), the volume she had "ripped to rags" while angry with Hughes (40). Startled,

> She opened it. She read the inscription. She closed it
> Like the running animal that receives
> The fatal bullet[.] (43–45)

We never learn what Assia had penned in the replacement volume, but we learn that the speaker believes that Assia's inscription provides the mortal blow to Plath in its indicting simile. The responsibility for the "fatal bullet" Plath receives in this poem is not attributed to Hughes's having allowed Plath entry into his flat, where she "got what she wanted—to see / The islet or reef or rock he'd ended up on" (12–13), greedily soaking up all the details ("Her eyes went over the walls and into / Every corner, like a dog in a new home. Like a dog / That had seen a rat vanish, that smelt a rat" [14–16]). In this poem, Plath is likened to a dog ferreting out Assia the rat, and she succeeds in finding evidence of Assia in Hughes's new home; her presence in his literary life; and her usurpation of Plath's role as Hughes's partner, as epitomized by Assia's inscription in the Shakespeare volume that has replaced the former one in Hughes's domestic life. Neither depiction of either woman is sympathetic, but what is especially noticeable in this poem is Hughes's obliviousness to his role in Plath's despair. Not only is Assia faulted indirectly for Plath's actions and responses to Hughes, but the poem finds fault with Plath too: "she hid from him / The wound she had given herself" (51–52). Hughes suggests that he did not know how Plath had harmed herself (and would again as a result of a self-inflicted wound). Other than the inscription, Assia is not referenced in this poem, despite the fact that she is positioned as the catalyst for Plath's death. Much like "Dreamers," Hughes attributes responsibility for tragic outcomes to Assia, making her a scapegoat of *Birthday Letters.*

"DO NOT PICK UP THE TELEPHONE"

Hughes's poem "Do Not Pick Up the Telephone," in the "Uncollected (1980–81)" section of his *Collected Poems,* views the telephone as an instrument of death. This poem alludes to both Plath and Assia. In a literary allusion to Plath's "Daddy," in which we learn the "black telephone's off at the root, / The voices just can't worm through" (69–70), Hughes describes the telephone as that which can "screech at the root of the house" (37). As we also know from Plath's "Words heard, by accident, over the phone," Plath learned about Hughes's relationship with Assia—at its very beginning—from Assia's call to Hughes at Plath and Hughes's Devon residence. To this end, the phone is associated with death in "Do Not Pick Up the Telephone": "A dead body will fall out of the telephone" (40), the speaker asserts. And in symbolic fashion, he is correct. The fated telephone call that Plath intercepted in July 1962 detonated a series of events that ended in the death of Plath in February 1963 by gas, and the troubled telephone call that Assia placed to Hughes on 23 March 1969 prompted her to end her life and Shura's by gas the same day. Indeed, the lines that precede "A dead body will fall out of the telephone" suggest the responsibility of the telephone as the very instrument in the deaths of those whom Hughes loved: "Do not pick up the detonator of the telephone / A flame from the last day will come lashing out of the telephone" (38–39).

Similar to "Dreamers," this poem discounts Hughes's important role in Plath's and Assia's lives. Instead, it engages in victim blaming:

Death invented the phone it looks like the altar of death
Do not worship the telephone
It drags its worshippers into actual graves
With a variety of devices, through a variety of disguised voices[.] (4–7)

Those who "worship" the telephone (seemingly a synecdoche or a metonym for death) are worshipping their own deaths. Moreover, as lore has it, Assia disguised her voice to mimic that of a man when Plath answered her call to Hughes. To some extent, then, Assia is subtly punished again for her relationship with Hughes in his poetry; she causes death (Plath's, Shura's, and her own) with her disguised voice over the telephone. The speaker is clear that what has occurred in his life and what harm has been done to "beautiful people" are out of his control (20). He has no agency: "Do not think your house is a hide-out it is a telephone / Do not think you walk your own road, you walk down a telephone // Do not think your future is yours it waits upon a telephone" (9–10, 12). The telephone can "tremble with the sudden appetite to see somebody undone" (32). As it stands, this poem radiates anger at an entity or force that can hurt, "undo," and kill those the speaker apparently loves. This poem stands as a marker of grief for Plath, Assia, and Shura, although due to its slight barb at Assia in its allusion to disguised voices, it does not ameliorate or counteract the more negative portrayals and damaging representations of Assia in *Capriccio* or *Birthday Letters.*

The next chapter will focus on Assia's life and work. It will highlight her accomplishments and reposition her within the contexts of feminist theory, the social conditions and expectations of her day, and her unique contributions to literature and other media. Primarily, the chapter provides analyses of and discussions about how Assia represented herself and her world while paying particular attention to texts that she authored or collaborated on in some way. This approach is noteworthy in its reliance upon the Assia Wevill materials housed within the Ted Hughes papers at the Stuart A. Rose Manuscript, Archives, and Rare Book Library at Emory University. Additionally, the investment in feminist recovery of an important woman and her important contributions to literary studies and cultural studies is a distinctive feature of the following chapter. In short, we have seen the impact Assia had on Plath's and Hughes's poetry in chapters 2 and 3, and next, in chapter 4, we will turn our attention to Assia herself.

CHAPTER 4

ASSIA WEVILL AS AUTHOR, ARTIST, AND TRANSLATOR

I think that even Newton discovered
Whatever he discovered
In the lull between
One pain and another.

—from "The Heart Is a Corrupt Director," by Yehuda Amichai, translated by Assia Gutmann [Wevill]

Presenting Assia in her own words, when possible, is a daunting and ambitious feat; this chapter is the first attempt at analyzing and assessing her artistic products and texts in literary scholarship. Among the materials considered are her letters, her journal entries, her English literary translations of Yehuda Amichai's poetry, her Sea Witch commercial, and photos of her as well as photos she kept in her personal collection until the end of her life. Because Assia's life and contributions have been backgrounded historically, now, with the momentum begun by Yehuda Koren and Eilat Negev's biography of her and the acquisition of Assia-related artifacts in the Ted Hughes archive at Emory University, we can construct a panoramic picture of her contributions to the literary and artistic world. This type of recovery work on Assia can fuel feminist conversations and reflections about power in heterosexual relationships; femininity and its challenges, dangers, and pleasures; and gendered representations or manifestations of a woman's life in literary studies, art, and cultural studies.

The epigraph to this chapter derives from lines in "The Heart Is a Corrupt Director," an Amichai poem that Assia translated for *Poems* (1969).[1] The speaker of these lines muses that great discoveries and achievements can occur even in a life punctuated by pain. The speaker indicates greater respect for Newton's resilience (and by extension, that of other human beings) than she or he does for success. Newton is simply alluded to as an example; his specific successes—"Whatever he discovered" (8)—are glossed over in favor of his heroic persistence. More to the point, I think, is the emphasis on the effects of great pain: the speaker suggests that it was only during the reprieve from pain that the brilliant scientist could work and achieve success. In many ways, this poem and these Amichai-turned-Assia lines via translation remind us of Assia's own life and the startling successes of her own achievements. For Assia's heart must have been "a corrupt director" (3), as she terms it in Amichai's poem. Regarding her love for Hughes, she writes in her journal: "I refuse to sink my teeth into T[ed]. If I'm not claimed, I can't claim. Only David [my husband] can claim me morally." She continues: "Reality is David, my own income. T is a long list of nightmares. Whatever the consequences for me, T is unconcerned" (qtd. in Koren and Negev 127–28). From Assia's perspective, to be "claimed" (i.e., married) meant the promises and realization of love, security, and the foundation for a good life. Knowing what she did about Hughes's attitudes and behaviors, Assia chose him to be her partner, despite, as she acknowledges in various documents, reason and logic.

In a handwritten letter, decorated by Shura's colorful scribblings, Assia informs Hughes that she is writing to his body, not his brains, from her body, not her brains. The letter is one of passion and despair. Assia tells Hughes she is full of love for him, so much so that she is frightened at the power he has over her; never has any man possessed such power over her. She mentions in passing what she loves about him: his hands, his wrists, his eyes, himself at his sweet best, and the qualities that make her admire him (undated, MSS 1058, Box 1, FF 71). The letter is painful to read from the start: Shura's cheerful yellow crayon markings on Assia's heartbreaking letter to the man she wished to fashion as her husband and the father of her child are brought into relief against the material reality of Assia's situation. As a single mother, separated from David Wevill and romantically involved with Hughes, she wished to claim Hughes and have him claim her so that they could form a traditional family unit.[2] Her heart served as a corrupt director: unwavering in her love for Hughes once she committed to being with him and bearing his child, she gambled everything (i.e., the security of her third marriage and the love of David Wevill; her life and that of her child) for the pursuit of what she deemed the love of her life. In her last letter to her father explaining her suicide and her decision to take Shura with her, she writes: "I have lived on the dream of living with Ted—and this has gone kaput. [. . .] There could never be another man. Never" (qtd. in Koren and Negev 204). As Richard Murphy reports in hindsight, "Of Assia herself [Ted Hughes] said, 'If I'd put a ring on her finger she'd still be alive'" (*Kick* 279). Assia explains in her suicide letter to her father that her life is intolerable without a husband for herself and a father for Shura, that such a life breeds loneliness and insecurity for her family of two, and that she "couldn't leave little Shura by herself. She's too old to be adopted" (qtd. in Koren and Negev 205). She wished the epitaph on her gravestone to read, "Here lies a lover of unreason and an exile" (Assia qtd. in Koren and Negev 178).[3]

Rarely has Assia's life been treated as grievable. Judith Butler contends that some lives are deemed ungrievable, and she points to the importance of the obituary as that which "functions as the instrument by which grievability is publicly distributed. It is the means by which a life becomes, or fails to become, a publicly grievable life" and "the means by which a life becomes noteworthy" (*Precarious Life* 34). Without an obituary, Butler implies, the deceased is considered unimportant and not positioned to be publicly grieved. As it turned out, no obituary ran for Assia or Shura.[4] Although Assia requested burial and a headstone in her unsigned will, the two were cremated, preventing them from having physical memorial spaces where people could pay respects. As Jonathan Bate notes, Hughes assumed leadership of Assia's funeral arrangements (275), and he would not have been inclined to commission an obituary for her or Shura.[5] Instead, he directed his attention to minimizing the public exposure of the deaths of his mistress-partner and daughter. Butler poses the following questions, and we could ask them of Assia's and Shura's situation: "What is the relation between the violence by which these ungrievable lives were lost and the prohibition on their public grievability? Are the violence and the prohibition both permutations of the same violence?" (36). For Assia and Shura, the answers revolve around gendered structures and dynamics, and the violence and prohibition are, indeed, permutations of the same gendered violence. While Butler is invested in international politics and deaths related to war activities in *Precarious Life,* her queries as to whose lives constitute lives worthy of grieving are relevant to this project because she is unpacking the mechanics of dehumanization. Unsupported in life as she was following her death, Assia's life displays the hallmarks of vulnerability and loss, as I will discuss in the next section of this chapter. Associated with vulnerability and loss are mourning and violence, and these qualities, too, feature in Assia's life and work in particularly gendered ways.

As a result of the interest in both her fabled beautiful body and affair with Hughes while he was married to Plath, Assia's suicide and act of filicide have always overridden the accomplishments of her life. Likely the horror of her abject acts captures and holds our attention: How could someone do what she did? Because we cannot truly fathom the answer to this question, we fixate on the terrible acts that led to two dead bodies, that of a mother and her child. Julia Kristeva observes, "The corpse, seen without God and outside of science, is the utmost of abjection" (4). She elucidates this statement: the corpse is the ultimate symbol of abjection, when it cannot be redeemed by religion or science, because it signifies death in engulfment. A corpse proves that death does not observe boundaries or borders (Kristeva 3–4). Intimating a threatening promise—that we will all become corpses someday—the corpse is something that we typically want to shun. Considering, too, the untimely and preventable demise of Assia and Shura, we have a formula for ultimate abjection. While we cannot rewrite the terrible distress and desperation of Assia's final act, we can turn our attention in new directions and focus on her successes as well as the gendered elements of her situation.

Assia's accomplishments—in the lull between one pain and another, to allude to one of the poetic lines she translated for publication—contribute to a professional body of work by important women who lived and worked before the gains made by second wave feminism could be felt. I suspect that we underestimate how difficult and challenging Assia's life was—making her achievements all the more impressive—as a separated or single (in actuality or practice, though not legally) working mother in England. She would have come up against far more daunting structural biases in the 1960s than in the twenty-first century. For example, the majority of women did not participate in the labor force in her day: less than half of all women, 40 percent of those aged twenty-five to forty-four, worked for pay in Great Britain in 1961. Indeed, from 1960 to 1969, approximately 40 percent of females fifteen years of age or older participated in the labor force in Great Britain, with the lowest percentage (39.5 percent) occurring in 1960 and the highest for the decade (42 percent) occurring in 1966. In 1969, the year Assia died, females (fifteen years or older) constituted 41.8 percent of the labor force (Sorrentino 33, 25). Married women in Britain in the 1960s were even less likely to participate in the labor force: only 32 percent of married women were a part of it in 1961. The reason for married women's decreased participation in work outside the home is due to the "prevailing ideology of the 'home.' If you married you had children, and women of course were presumed to bear the weight of care" (McCloskey 168). So, Assia's situation was even more unusual when we consider that she not only worked outside of the home but she would have been considered a lone parent with a dependent child after she separated from David Wevill and lived apart from Hughes. For instance, we know that in Great Britain in 1961, only 2 percent of households contained a lone parent with dependent children. This astoundingly small number suggests the highly unusual nature of Assia's situation, especially when we take into account that the Office for National Statistics includes individuals who are not family members as part of a household. Unfortunately for Assia, she really was a "lone parent," living with her daughter, with no household support other than her au pair, during the last years she lived with Shura in 1960s London.[6] By 1971, two years after Assia's death, only 2 percent of "lone mother families with dependent children," with mothers who were separated or divorced, existed in Great Britain, comprising an almost nonexistent group, comparatively speaking, in the social mix (Office for National Statistics 15, 17).

As we might recall, Assia was separated from her third husband; her divorce was finalized shortly before her death. This status also placed her in an unusual position, especially given that she was divorced three times. Although Assia was technically married to David Wevill, she bore Hughes's child outside of marriage to him. Shura was born in 1965 in England; only 7 to 8 percent of births happened outside of marriage in 1965 in England and Wales (Office for National Statistics 24). Taken together, we see that Assia's life proved to be unusually marginalized—and stigmatized. As we might recall, her life also served (in negative capacities) those of others who were, and are, far more famous than she, notably Plath and Hughes.

Iris Marion Young's concept of the "body-in-situation," or the "lived body," serves as a reminder to us that Assia's experiences and behavior stem from her inhabiting a specific physical body that was formed and conditioned in its living in a specific sociocultural context with operative social norms and expectations (16, 18). Additionally, the social structures that she came up against and the lack of social support available to her would have necessarily affected the way that she would have thought about herself and experienced the world (21). I argue that this acknowledgment of the particularity of female subjectivity and embodiment should give us pause if we are tempted to engage in victim blaming with Assia. We cannot know exactly what we would have done because it is impossible for us to know what it meant to be Assia, as removed as we are from her by time, space, and place(s)—and the formalist idea of a stable, original, knowable presence. Instead, we can only approach her textually and interpretively. The metaphor Young employs in her scholarship on the body-in-situation is that of an actor: within the facticity of her physical and social environment, Assia could play her part with some license. As Young clarifies, "The human actor has specific projects, things she aims to accomplish, ways she aims to express herself, make her mark on the world, transform her surroundings and relationships" (16). This metaphor is useful in allowing us to contextualize Assia as we approach her in letters, journal entries, and her artistic products.

Assia's life and work allow us, in the twenty-first century, to reflect and interrogate what it means—then and now—for women to be agents of their lives, especially in light of what it means to be successful and desirable in a gendered world. Rose Weitz pinpoints for us three recurring ideas about women's bodies in the Western world: one, society regards women's bodies as mentally and physically inferior to men's bodies; two, society considers women's bodies as men's property; and three, society assumes that women's bodies transform women into sexual seductresses who pose a threat to men's bodies and souls (3). These are the ideas that informed the expectations about female bodies that Assia encountered and confronted or embraced. What we know about her is that she both worked within and against the sexist system. Impressively, she became a translator-poet, more than simply the muse to other poets. In her professional career, she worked outside of the home in a creative capacity, earning accolades for her copywriting and supporting her household as the breadwinner. While her copywriting and poetry translation work will not be valued in the same ways as Plath's and Hughes's poetry, Assia's creative writing and translations of poems are noteworthy; in fact, they were heralded as achievements in her time. Clearly, her mind was not inferior to her male (or female) counterparts, as the rhetoric Weitz highlights would have us believe. Assia also collaborated with her male partners who were successful poets, but with Hughes, she left her profession and assumed child-rearing and homemaking duties more than once in order to meet his expectations of her through the various attempts she made to cohabit with Hughes in different locales. Living with Hughes required that she follow a gendered sociocultural script, as Hughes articulated in his "Draft Constitution," a suggested list of house rules for her to follow.[7] In this regard, she did defer to Hughes and acquiesced to his wishes, but it should be noted that Assia found pleasure in caring for Hughes's two children with Plath and her own daughter with Hughes while that domestic arrangement lasted. Finally, Assia's self-styling in photographs demystifies and may discredit the notion that she was an evil seductress who threatened men's bodies and souls. In moving past traditional and sexist ideas about women's bodies, we can focus on the opportunity to recover Assia's contributions to literature and artistic circles while reflecting on her achievements within the context of the body-in-situation.

ASSIA'S LETTERS, OTHER DOCUMENTS, AND CONTEXT: GENDER AND IDENTITY POLITICS

Assia's letters present a place for us to begin, with respect to analyzing and discussing artifacts related to her, because they give us access to her voice as she recorded it, unmediated or unredacted by others. Six letters from Assia to Hughes are archived, along with letters to other correspondents. Her letters depict her as a woman suffering for love. They also show her to be a complex and intelligent individual who was very self-critical, self-aware, and literary. What we do not find in Assia's letters is the oversexed demon or rival who was bent on destroying Plath or Hughes. We also do not see someone who is building herself up to be the victor. Instead, in most cases, she paints her love life as anything but glamorous and as anything but happy. She also addresses the power dynamics in her life, and we are able to evaluate her literary products and artistic contributions within the context of her life as a result of these letters.

In her letters, Assia exposes the gendered facets of her life while actively interrogating and problematizing her thoughts, her options, and her own life situations. Through a sample of her extant letters and diary entries, we discern her working over gendered issues and literary matters and analyzing her interpersonal experiences, especially her romantic relationship with Hughes. Assia's archived letters and selected journal entries permit insight into the woman who influenced Plath and Hughes, and more important, they humanize her. In her representations of herself, she does not resemble the barren demon-goddess she has been made out to be in Plath's and Hughes's poetry or in traditional scholarship, to the detriment of feminist research on Plath, Hughes, or Assia.

From here, I will discuss the gendered identity politics of Assia's life and, later on, her work. In a March 1965 letter, Assia highlights her maternal side, causing us to revise traditional representations that painted her otherwise. In three archived letters to Hughes's close friend Lucas Myers, Assia confides her feelings concerning the birth of her daughter, Shura, as well as developments (or the lack thereof) in her relationship with Hughes. She asks solicitously about Myers's writing and expresses her views about other literary people, clearly thinking he will find such descriptions interesting. In the March 1965 letter, Myers is addressed possessively in the salutation, subtly emphasizing the relationship between Hughes and Assia herself to Myers. Assia tells Myers that she has been ecstatic for the last ten days, due to the birth of her beloved daughter, and she describes the pretty baby, closing her descriptions by reiterating that she is very moved by Shura emotionally. This letter, in particular, counters the harshness of both Plath and Hughes and their characterization of Assia as an unnatural mother and, by association, a bad woman. We encounter Assia as someone who is sweetly maternal in her 29 November 1966 journal entry in her catalog of the close of what appears to be a typical day for Hughes's children, including their daughter, and herself: dinner will be served at six or seven, followed by a bath, a story, and a cup of milk. Love is included in her list of what comprises her bedtime ritual for Frieda, Nicholas, and Shura (journal entries, 29–31 Nov. 1966).

Unaware of how Hughes would represent her in print decades after her traumatic death, Assia's letter to Myers becomes even more startling as a reminder that no story or narrative is one-dimensional, an important lesson we can impart when reading, researching, or teaching Assia in Hughes's *Capriccio* and Plath's Assia poems. For his part, Myers remembers Assia in his memoir: Assia "dressed with taste but a good deal of panache, had striking looks, spoke with great articulation and a kind of bejeweled accent, and was fundamentally a very vulnerable person and capable of authentic human affection" (127–28). Becoming the partner of Hughes and the mother of their daughter positioned Assia to be even more vulnerable and affectionate: these were two of the great loves of her life, as Koren and Negev's published biography about her makes clear. Her September 1965 letter to Myers acknowledges that her relationship with Hughes had either plateaued or reached an impasse: nothing has changed since he last saw them, which is in keeping with the trajectory of her letters concerning Hughes and their relationship as a whole.

The July 1965 letter to Myers divulges Assia's preference for literary language and talk.[8] Informing Myers that her father prefers Myers to all the other friends she and Hughes share, Assia establishes a friendly tone and depicts herself in an active relationship with Hughes. She delivers the highlights of the trip to the Festival dei Due Mondi in Spoleto, Italy, that she took with Hughes, explaining that she put in a good word for Myers with Allen Tate. Of Tate, Assia comments that she is impressed with his poetry. In two sentences she dispatches Ezra Pound, who also attended the festival, as silent, hand-dressed, and old, but her spotlighting of him and Tate show she was informed about who the important poets were. I share these details because, in reading letters by Assia and to her (notably from Ted Hughes and David Wevill), one sees that Assia was a literary woman who expected to review her poet-partner's drafts of poems, who was well informed about the literary scene, and who appeared eager to collaborate, whether by providing visual illustrations of poems or translations of poems and other literary work. More than her good looks, Assia interacted with her male partners as an intellectual equal. And yet she was a mass of contradictions. She doubted herself, despite the fact that her male partners recognized her talent and invited collaborations. While she confides in her journal, on 29 November 1966, that she can play a typewriter like a piano—insisting on authorship, she declares she stamps the documents with her name—she despairs of her abilities two days later. On 31 November, she employs a mixed metaphor of her writing as the equivalent of spangles that drop into her lap but then blow away and burst as (soap) bubbles will. It is her obvious fault, she declares to herself, that she cannot harness her writing in the way that Plath could; she invokes Plath and moves on to reflect on Plath's own journal writing. She finds herself lacking when she considers what she describes as Plath's muscular brain and splendid brilliance. On 6 September 1968, Assia records in her journal that she feels that she possesses too many minor qualities without either the will or the brilliance to do them justice (journal entries, 6 Sept. 1968, 16 Jan. 1969, and undated). With respect to her literary and artistic abilities, Assia was far harder and more critical of herself than is warranted; both Ted Hughes and David Wevill warmly encouraged her writing and drawing in their letters to her. But she did not have the time to pursue artistic endeavors to the same degree as Hughes could, for instance. When she did share a home with Hughes, she assumed the bulk of the caregiving and domestic work, a very gendered arrangement, at his request. While Assia minded the home and cared for the children, Hughes wrote. She became the partner, the muse, and the helpmate minding the genius when she lived with him. When she lived on her own with her daughter, she worked full time as a copywriter—not as a poet, translator, or artist—in part, perhaps, because copywriting provided steady paychecks.

In a September 1968 letter, Assia acknowledges a gift from Richard Gilbertson, a publisher of Hughes's work. She thanks him for a charming book he sent her and requests a catalog, presumably a book catalog. Closing the short letter, she invites him to visit her when he is in London. The respect that other literary-minded people accord her, as we can infer from the letters of people such as Myers and Gilbertson, was not the norm for Assia because she was roundly blamed for Plath's suicide. Myers recalls that she experienced scapegoating to a terrible degree, so much so that he declares that Assia's situation was torturous for her. Cast as a villainous seductress, Assia was singled out as the person responsible for Plath's death by a public that desired to take sides in the Plath-Hughes scandal. Reports Myers: "The gossip of London was a rack for Assia. It was hard at first to make a villain of Ted, at least until the dirigible of publicity gained some altitude, but the emblematic model for the evil seductress was very much at hand, exotic, her beauty just beginning to fade. Sylvia herself had identified the rival. Right-thinking people did not want the villain of the psychodrama with the prescriptive given name to be comfortable" (130). In the documentary *Ted Hughes: Stronger than Death,* Ruth Fainlight recalls: "To me, Assia was the evil demon incarnate. In fact, [she and I] became very close because I became more and more sorry for [Assia]." With her exotic looks and qualities, it must have been relatively easy to fault the other (read: foreign, bad, beautiful but destructive) woman for Plath's and Hughes's marital problems.[9] Elaine Feinstein summarizes the situation: "By [. . .] 1965, Sylvia was the most famous poet in the Anglo Saxon world. And suddenly Assia was the woman who was responsible for Sylvia's death. [Assia] really felt quite lonely and hated in the literary world" (*Ted Hughes: Stronger than Death*). For her part, Assia did not believe that she was the reason for Plath's suicide, which would have made the blame directed at her and the scapegoating she experienced feel unjust, from her perspective.[10]

Assia certainly experienced blame through ostracism within Hughes's family circle: Myers remembers Assia telling him that Hughes's father blatantly ignored her, refusing to look at her or speak to her, even when she would set a plate full of food in front of him. Explains Myers: "[I wondered,] Why this animosity? Ted told me, 'Her accent is his enemy.' The plainspoken Yorkshireman [that was Hughes's father] could not tolerate [Assia's] Versailles inflections and international elocution" (132).[11] As for Hughes's mother, she took the more common gendered approach that Assia had married too many times and was still married to David Wevill, making her behavior "unheard of" and, therefore, reproachable, as Olwyn Hughes, Hughes's sister, informed Myers (133). Royston Taylor, a friend and colleague of Assia, recalls, "Assia told me that she felt his parents were blaming her for Sylvia's suicide" (qtd. in Koren and Negev 169). Fay Weldon recounts that "Assia looked after [Plath's children] as well as the new baby [Shura]. Then Ted's parents joined the family. Assia felt they disliked her and that they blamed her for Sylvia's death, as indeed, increasingly, did Ted: that they used her as a servant, punished her perpetually, and that her situation in the household was untenable" (qtd. in Hayman 203). Murphy adds: "Privately Assia told me that she had left Court Green to resume work in advertising, but hated being alone, except for her child, in London. She had lost in the conflict waged by Ted's mother from her bed in a Devon hospital, and by his father, who hadn't spoken to her for the past year, though he had lived in the same house and had eaten at the same table the food she had cooked and served. She asked me if I felt the same 'atmosphere' existed today between herself and Ted as the one I had felt between him and Sylvia three months before Sylvia's suicide, and I replied, to give her hope, that it was altogether different" (260).

Add to all this the structural challenges Assia faced—namely, her lack of a social support system—and the challenges almost become obstacles. With her own family living in Canada, Assia was bereft of family support in England, especially as Hughes did not provide the support she needed; to illustrate this point, Hughes asked Assia to move out on her own and secure a job to support herself and their child because it was too complicated and unpleasant having his partner, their child, his children with Plath, and his parents living with him under the same roof.[12] I interpret Assia's metaphor of emerging aboveground and asking if anyone is there (and if so, who?) in her 29 November 1966 journal entry as further evidence of her vulnerability in connection with missing social support structures (journal entries, 29–31 Nov. 1966).

Hughes urged Assia to destroy his letters to her and to stop keeping a journal (although he initially recommended that she keep one and send it to him), thereby destroying a written record of their relationship.[13] While she did not destroy his letters, she apparently did send a telegram in code in May 1968, almost six years into their relationship. Using her middle name, Esther, Assia signs an *A* in the "From" field of the telegram. In the "To" field, she writes, in her distinctive handwriting, that Thursday morning would be manageable, likely for them to meet for her forty-first birthday, because she had reorganized her workload. She asks him to confirm the plans (telegram; Koren and Negev 178). It seems likely and in keeping with Hughes's concern over prying eyes that he would have asked Assia to code their correspondence. In a 11 February 1964 letter, Hughes advises Assia to be careful with her telegrams to him: he explains that the postmaster and his wife are gossipy, and Hughes suspects that they read his mail because they are curious about his relationship with Assia.

The telegram demonstrates two characteristics about Assia and Hughes late into their romantic relationship with each other that is indicative of the type of gendered, uneven playing field Assia encountered. One, Assia was still willing to reorganize her life for Hughes in ways that he would not do for her, even though she depended on her job to support herself and their child. She explains to her father, in her last letter to him, that she was employed by an agency that would fire her should she become sick and miss work (Koren and Negev 204). (Assia did not receive financial support from Hughes; when she asked for money, he loaned it to her, expecting repayment.) The second characteristic that becomes readily apparent with this telegram, read within the context of the other documents and artifacts in the 109 file folders in the same materials box in the Emory archive, is that Assia still cannot claim Hughes in any formal way in public, other than as his occasional date to literary events, even at the end of their relationship. He can claim her if he so chooses: as a man, he wields all the power in their relationship. While their friends and associates knew they were involved romantically, official sanction was withheld—and marriage to Hughes was what Assia desperately wanted. She urged him to commit to her.[14] In significant ways, Assia was a product of her time: the gendered expectations that governed her life are revealing of the institutions and structures that dictate what we should want and what we should be, and these desires appear natural and self-chosen when, really, they are indebted to our socialization. As a result, we cannot underestimate Assia's love for Hughes or the importance of marriage, to her mind, as an institution that would have brought stability, security, and happiness to her life and that of their daughter.

Gender is a force that defined Assia's life and work. Although addressed in chapter 1, I would like to take a moment to revisit the manner in which I am theoretically framing my analyses and discussions of gender before analyzing Assia's thinking about gender in one of her journal entries. Every person, man or woman, "experiences aspects of gender structures as facticity, as sociohistorical givens with which she or he must deal" (Young 25). What emerges from the structures that locate us in terms of identity and power are identity categories, such as gender (18). Because it is impossible to refuse representational politics, we can work toward critiques of them and engage in examinations of how gender is structured, as Butler recommends (*Gender Trouble* 7). When we allow that gender is "an ongoing discursive practice" that is "open to intervention and resignification," then we understand that we can deconstruct or dismantle that which seems natural or original (45). For instance, one learns to become a feminine woman through socialization, and the performative facets of identity beckon us to inspect, interrogate, and problematize gender if we wish to work from a feminist approach.

Concerning gender, Assia delivers a startling disclosure in her 29 November 1966 journal entry. After recording what she remembers of a childhood trip to a family friend's home in Germany, she declares that she identifies as one of the boys in that memory, not one of the serving girls. To be a serving girl, Assia declares, is a brutal punishment: their work sets traps for them, she writes, and the same traps await her (journal entries, 29–31 Nov. 1966). We see in this passage that Assia understands the different gendered scripts assigned to people based on their sex, and she is revolted by the systematic molding of, in this illustration, working-class women—she discloses that she weeps over their situation. Instead of bright futures, these serving girls encounter traps or dangers, which are left unexplained. In the 31 November 1966 journal entry, Assia muses over Plath's writing abilities and femininity compared to her own and concludes the paragraph underscoring the importance of books. For her, books and what she has learned from them, along with what she has been told and deemed desirable, have shaped her world, to paraphrase Assia. In writing to Hughes about a film she saw by herself, she offhandedly compares the atmosphere of the film to pages from Kafka's diaries, explaining that it is all spare and excellent, while making an additional reference to Kierkegaard (2 Feb. 1968). Moving on to a new topic in the same letter, she relates what she observed of two women discussing marriage on the bus, on her way home from the film. Assia found the conversation interesting and summarily tells Hughes that the women congratulated themselves for being sweet, even though the men they attract are bastards. The two women resemble Assia in the details she provides: they are beautifully dressed and sad, with indeterminate ages. Assia guesses they are in their thirties. Closing her letter, Assia laments that there is not a safe anniversary between Hughes and her. In her archived letters, Assia frequently addresses the status of her relationship with Hughes, sometimes imploring him to commit to her. In one letter she declares that she will flourish with him, care for him, and give him everything she has (undated, MSS 1058, Box 1, FF 71). Taken together, her letters point to her vulnerability, which is principally informed by gendered dynamics.

According to Butler, vulnerability depends on existing norms (*Precarious Life* 43). The norms, or unwritten social "rules," underwriting a "good life" for a woman and the expectations for femininity likely contributed greatly to Assia's distress. But fundamentally, her attachment to Hughes as her partner and father of her child exceeded every other attachment or desire of her life, according to Assia, as we see in her last letter to her father and in her archived will. Butler argues that attachment is critical for one's survival and that loss is bound up in one's sense of self (45, 20). This scenario rings true, even when the relationship is not especially healthy or nurturing. As Butler comments, "The bind of radically inadequate care consists of this, namely, that attachment is crucial to survival and that, when attachment takes place, it does so in relation to persons and institutional conditions that may well be violent, impoverishing, and inadequate" (45). Despite Hughes's lack of adequate care for her and Shura, as

Assia purportedly perceived it, her attachment to him was crucial for her survival, as she plainly informs her father. Fearing that she had lost Hughes after their last house hunting trip, when he could not commit to securing a home with her and following his revelation that Plath's death prevented him from marrying her—implying that Plath's death would forever be between them and perhaps insinuating that Assia was responsible for it—Assia experienced great loss: she could not fathom a life without her love, the partner upon whom she had staked all her hopes for happiness. In recounting Assia's and Hughes's last trip together, Bate records: "In a small notebook, [Assia] wrote down [Hughes's] words: 'It was no good thinking they could live together in a house—it's because of Sylvia.' Then she wrote, 'I have no answer to that, so die soon . . . execute yourself and your little self [Shura] efficiently'" (274). Years earlier, in a 1964 letter to Hughes, she intimates how vulnerable she was and what damage had been inflicted upon her from the instability of her relationship with Hughes. "My future is blanked with you," she writes. "I'm convinced you have mayhemed my life. You've left me with a rubbishy life, with nothing to salvage. Absolutely nothing" (letter, 22 Jan. 1964; Assia qtd. in Koren and Negev 138).

To my mind, Butler articulates what Assia expresses: without Hughes, Assia could not envision a future, and this realization seems to have been an overwhelming, perhaps traumatic, loss. "It is not," writes Butler, "as if an 'I' exists independently over here and then simply loses a 'you' over there, especially if the attachment to 'you' is part of what composes who 'I' am. If I love you, under these conditions, then I not only mourn the loss, but I become inscrutable to myself. Who 'am' I, without you? When we lose some of these ties by which we are constituted, we do not know who we are or what to do" (*Precarious Life* 22). We would do well to remember that Hughes was the only "family" Assia had in England, other than her daughter, and that all her decisions were based on him after she left David Wevill. Further clarifying the dynamics of grief, desire, and sexuality, Butler explains that one may want to be in control and "stay intact" and "manage for a while, but despite one's best efforts, one is undone." Explaining that gender or sexuality is "a mode of being dispossessed," of "being *for* another or *by virtue of* another," Butler inadvertently echoes Assia (23–24). In an undated letter to Hughes, Assia states that he has "dispossessed" her and that he is in complete possession of her (MSS 1058, Box 1, Folder 72). Her phrasing is the same as Butler's, underscoring the powerful dynamics of her gendered, sexual, and romantic attachment to Hughes. This is all to say that Assia had little to no support system or structures—and perceived none—outside of Hughes in England proper; there was nothing to replace what he represented to her. She would have understood that her life was circumscribed in ways that Hughes himself could not have fathomed, by virtue of his masculinity.

Ironically, Myers comes to the conclusion that very few people supported Hughes in helpful ways; rather, they looked to Hughes to help them (133). Not incidentally, Assia typed documents for Hughes, in addition to working full-time and pursuing her own artistic projects (Hughes, letter to Assia Wevill, undated, MSS 1058, Box 1, Folder 55); Koren and Negev observe that she proved herself to be an "integral part of her men's artistic work" (141). With respect to institutional structures and norms, I submit that Myers's is an ironic conclusion in light of Assia's situation. Assia needed far more help than Hughes did. According to Weldon: "Being a single mother in the late 1960s was difficult on all levels, and Assia found it hard to support Shura and herself. She felt that time was working against her, she was getting older, and it was her last chance. For a woman as striking as she was, it was humiliating to revert to dating services, and it showed her degree of despair" (qtd. in Koren and Negev 192). We should note several sharp observations Weldon makes: age and beauty are valuable commodities that could be traded in marriage, with the greater the beauty, the more valuable the trade. Culturally, a woman's looks are a valuable commodity, purportedly the source of her feminine power, which is an ideology we can identify firsthand today. Facing abandonment and the single life as a middle-aged mother, Assia feared her looks were fading. And so marital status was not a small matter to Assia; she always had her sights set on the next husband before she would leave her current partner. That gendered pattern—a woman needs a man (and marriage) to acquire and live the good life—ended when she left her third husband to partner with and support Hughes.

In fact, Olwyn Hughes believed that Assia received a document finalizing the divorce from David Wevill on the day Assia returned from house hunting with Hughes: Assia called Hughes in an agitated state, questioning his commitment to her (Koren and Negev 201). As Bate explains, in his recounting of Assia's last day and mind-set, Hughes had fatally misjudged Assia's vulnerability. Bate elaborates on this vulnerability: Assia "had always been conscious that her body was not nearly so beautiful as her ravishing face; now she felt that she was losing her looks altogether, running to fat. She no longer walked into a room and turned every head. If Ted was not going to give her hope, there was no future" (274). Assia's boss, Angela Landels, remembers that Assia wanted to die young "because growing old, with one's skin wrinkled and hanging down, losing one's feminine potency, was ghastly" (qtd. in Koren and Negev 84). To Assia, a certain standard of beauty needed to be maintained to justify her self-worth, and her appearance gave her status (or potency, power) in the marriage market. Unfortunately for Assia, she wanted to marry Hughes only. Olwyn Hughes, who was at Court Green when Assia made her last phone call there to Hughes, expresses her horror over Assia's and Shura's deaths in a letter written on 24 April 1969 to Dido and Bill Merwin. She attributes what she calls Assia's depression to Ted Hughes's inability to set up a home with Assia and live with her; she thought Assia assumed Hughes did not care about living with her very much. Olwyn Hughes writes that she, too, thinks Assia felt she was losing her beauty, which contributed to Assia's decision to kill herself. Clearly, this overriding concern about the attractiveness of one's body is a problem women face to an extraordinarily greater degree than men do: nowhere does Hughes write about his appearance, and his contemporaries do not report his thoughts about it, which is in stark contrast to what their contemporaries tell us about Assia.[15]

ASSIA AS LITERARY COLLABORATOR

Her role as muse aside, Assia actively contributed to literary projects with Hughes and others. Christopher Reid, the editor of *Letters of Ted Hughes,* writes that Assia likely gave Hughes ideas for his version of *Gaudete* in 1964 (Hughes, *Letters* 230). Indeed, as early as 1962, Hughes and Assia traded ideas for a film script they thought they might cowrite, a project Hughes revisited with Assia in 1964 (Koren and Negev 107, 140). Assia's artistic abilities appealed to Hughes, as we see in his unpublished letters to her, and she provided illustrations of his poems, often at his request. At least two projects were in progress before she died. One was a book that would feature Assia's drawings of brilliantly colored plants and animals; Michael Hamburger remembers Assia showing him Hughes's poems with her accompanying illustrations (Koren and Negev 149). Probably related to that project, Hughes asks, in an archived letter, about a triptych Assia was creating; he inquires whether she has become sidetracked with work on drawing animals (MSS 1058, Box 1, Folder 57). A different project was entitled "Full House," which involved Hughes writing poems and Assia creating illustrations of the kings, queens, and jacks of playing cards.[16] Neither of these projects was published, and it is likely that Assia's contributions no longer exist. In the next section, I will focus on Assia's celebrated literary translations of Yehuda Amichai's poems, but I will mention here that Assia was involved in significant translation work, including for Reuters in the 1950s. Over two weeks in 1968, she also wrote and directed a play (meant for television), which is no longer extant, and translated Eda Zoritte-Megged's Hebrew play *Last Game* into English before she died (Koren and Negev, 61–63, 179–80, 208). Because Assia's work in these media and collaborations, with the notable exceptions of the translated Amichai poems, is inaccessible or no longer extant, we will turn our attention to her

BBC poetry reading collaboration with Hughes before moving on to her published achievements.

Assia embarked on the literary translation project of Amichai's poems at Hughes's recommendation and with his encouragement. According to Koren and Negev, "Assia was eager to comply" (166): she wanted to pursue literary work. For his part, Hughes extolled Assia's literary language abilities. In a letter to Amichai in late 1967, he writes enthusiastically about Assia and her translations of Amichai's poems: "As soon as she'd gone over them for the last time, I felt I must write to you straight off to tell you how good they were—they're excellent, in fact. I think they are the best of all I've seen, of translations of your poems, Yehuda" (*Letters* 277). Hughes himself read over Assia's translations and offered editorial suggestions. The credit, he maintained, belonged to Assia, whose name, at Hughes's suggestion, was displayed prominently on the cover (Koren and Negev 172). For this project, Assia assumed her maiden name of Gutmann.

Professionally, Assia's most public collaboration with Hughes took the form of a BBC radio program that introduced her translations of the Amichai poems. The program was prerecorded on 28 June 1968 and aired on BBC Radio 3 on 12 December 1968. The complete typescript of the program exists in Hughes's American archive at Emory ("'Yehuda Amichai'"). Assia is credited with translating and introducing the poems in the typescript of the program, and Hughes is credited with reading the poems that are interspersed among the discussions of the poems. As the translator and the person who worked most closely with the Amichai poems, Assia likely wrote the portions of the typescript that she read on air, rendering her the poetry expert of the program. The typescript shows that Assia and Hughes traded off reading: she read the literary-critical portions that contextualized, explained, or led into the poems that Hughes subsequently read. In this rare instance, their voices and names—although Assia was using her unfamiliar maiden name in this circumstance—were interlaced and linked professionally, with Hughes's approval.

The poems Assia selected to introduce to her audience cover a variety of subjects. Of interest to the readers of this book are her comments about the qualities of Amichai's poems: in them, she reveals what, to her, are the striking aspects and the quintessential features of them. From Assia's perspective, Amichai is first and foremost a poet who writes about love. To me, this is quite revealing of how she approached the poems: I would not have characterized Amichai in this way, even after studying the book of poems Assia translated. She points out he is fundamentally sad and elegiac, always lamenting that which is separated, lost, or foredoomed, to use her words. According to Assia, in Amichai's poems, love comes across as the most valuable part of life. But love appears vulnerable and doomed, she claims, in Amichai's poems. To this end, the poems she translates and which Hughes reads on the BBC broadcast offer ironic metacommentary on the romantic situation of their translator and reader. From here, I will analyze Assia's translations of select Amichai poems—poems that became hers, in a sense, through translation—and I will suggest ways that the poems resonate with her personal situation. I will tease out the gendered implications of the identity politics embedded therein while reflecting on the literary merits of Assia's literary contributions.

ASSIA AS AUTHOR

In the two letters penned by David Wevill to Assia in the archive at Emory, we see a writer who would enjoy a successful career as a poet encouraging his estranged wife to nurture her own writing abilities. To him, Assia was a muse but also a talented writer. He addresses her as "Mrs. Hughes," though Assia, of course, was not married to Hughes. Technically, she was still married to David Wevill. But we see the proprieties of the time, which underscore the complicated and difficult situation in which Assia lived and worked. In a 19 April 1968 letter, David Wevill informs Assia that she is a good writer, underlining *good*. Cautioning her that good writers burn out in advertising, he inquires about her writing, wanting to know if she has finished a film script based on Turgenev's *First Love* that she had wanted to pursue (Koren and Negev 140). He encourages her to trust her thoughts about her writing.

Although translation may be understood as a kind of collaborative process, Assia's English translations of Amichai's poems were viewed as excellent products independent of their Hebrew versions. A poetry critic in *The Guardian* praised the book heartily upon its publication: "The translations of [Amichai's] *Selected Poems* by Assia Gutmann are so stunning, such good poems in English, that it seems absurd to treat them as translations at all" (Kavanagh 6). Assia put together an impressive collection of English poems, and I will treat the ones that stand out as particularly relevant to Assia and to our approach to her.

Three of the poems Assia introduced on the BBC broadcast of her translations of the Amichai poems are very moving within the context of her life and relationship with Hughes. "A Pity. We Were Such a Good Invention," "It Was Summer, or the End of Summer," and "In the Middle of This Century" showcase her literary, and language, abilities and address the dynamics (i.e., the pleasures, dangers, and power) of heterosexual romantic love, with content that bespeaks her own situation as a woman in the mid-twentieth century in England.

Perhaps what drew Assia to Amichai's poetry, other than Hughes's suggestion that she translate his work, is his remarkable use of imagery: Assia highlights Amichai's imagery as his crowning achievement as a poet ("'Yehuda Amichai'"). With this in mind, I will attend to explicating the images embedded in the poems she introduced on air as well as analyzing and discussing "Eye Examination," "Indian Summer in Princeton," and "The Heart Is a Corrupt Director," also from Assia's and Amichai's *Poems*.

"A Pity. We Were Such a Good Invention" makes spectacular use of caesuras, to the effect of emphatic pronouncements about the lost potential of a foreshortened romantic relationship, in spite of the couple's capabilities and the promise of their love. Ultimately, the speaker shows us that it is a relationship that cannot last, due to the interference of others outside the relationship. One of the most striking poems in the collection, it serves as metacommentary or metacriticism on Assia and Hughes's actual romantic relationship, whether intentional on the part of Assia in selecting it for her translation work or not. In retrospect, we see how fitting this poem is in its representation of Assia and Hughes's love and its circumstances. This realization becomes more poignant when we know that they elected to partner together to introduce and read the poem on the BBC airwaves. The title underscores the primary emotion—the objective correlative, as T. S. Eliot would call it—evoked through a series of images, tailored to produce the emotional affect. Pity reigns as the primary emotion, from the title to the last, aberrant line, which forms a unique stanza.

An explication of the first two stanzas provides the context of the couple's fraught relationship. The first stanza features figurative forced bodily separation, which results in injuries inflicted on the couple. "They amputated / Your thighs off my hips," declares the speaker (1–2). The first (unpunctuated) caesura heralds what follows by inserting a natural pause after *amputated*: this couple was intertwined in a sexual embrace that is couched as loving. The speaker calls those who have torn the couple apart "surgeons" and dismisses them in emphatic tones, with the help of caesuras (4). The second stanza extends what transpires in the first: those outside the relationship are responsible for its dismantling. This time, the culprits are dubbed "engineers" (8); they have engineered the breakup and are responsible for the destruction of the love that is the "good / And loving invention" and the focus of this poem (9–10). Both the first and the second stanzas address the separation of the lovers and people who love against the odds, two themes that run through poems Assia chose to translate.

From the beginning to the end of "A Pity. We Were Such a Good Invention," we are reminded that this relationship could have lasted, under different conditions. Signaling the importance of the figure announced in the title, the speaker transforms the image of an invention into a metaphor:

> A pity. We were such a good
> And loving invention.

An airplane made from a man and a wife.
Wings and everything.
We hovered a little above the earth.

We even flew a little. (9–14)

As a couple, the man and wife fit perfectly together: they are so well constructed, so well suited, that they can metaphorically fly (their relationship succeeds, soars "a little") through mutual efforts. Theirs, on the surface, appears to be a relationship of equality, a feminist undertaking. Interestingly, Assia identifies the couple as "a man and a wife," not a husband and a wife or a man and a woman. Tellingly, perhaps, this positioning mirrors her own: Hughes was a single man in a seemingly committed relationship with Assia, and she was technically still married to David Wevill, although she was romantically involved with and loyal to Hughes by this time.

The caesura following "A pity" asks us to pause to reflect on the injustice that has been meted out to the couple in the previous two stanzas of this four-stanza poem, as does the concentration of end-stopped lines that make up the last five lines of the poem. Nowhere else in this text do we find such emphatic declarations, as effected by the end-stopped lines, with the exception of the powerful caesuras in lines 1, 4, 5, 8, and 9. Against their wishes, the couple has been figuratively "amputated," (1), "dismantled" (5), and otherwise separated from each other and broken down. That they succeeded at all—the last line of the poem informs us that the airplane "flew a little"—comes across as miraculous when we analyze and take into consideration the first half of the poem. In their personal lives, both Assia and Hughes fault others for their relationship troubles. According to Assia, in an undated letter to Hughes, everyone has dictated how they should live their lives, except themselves; she emphasizes that she and Hughes need to be alone together so that they might heal from what she terms their "Intolerable" (MSS 1058. Box 1, Folder 71).[17] For his part, Hughes writes Yehuda and Hana Amichai, explaining that he and Assia must live apart, due to his parents' incivility toward her. Their poor behavior caused stress for Assia and Hughes, making their living situation untenable. He writes: "We've been having upheavals. [. . .] Assia has gone to London. Situation here too intolerable. She'll work there—get a well paid job—till I can pull out of here with the kids etc. A straggling act of migration" (*Letters* 277).

"It Was Summer, or the End of Summer" suggests another parting and intimates the forlornness felt by the speaker in its sentiments and the images. Literal and figurative endings emerge throughout the poem. On the literal level, the poem is set in summer, and the speaker acknowledges that the season will soon end. On a more symbolic level, the happiness or figurative sunshine has been drained out of the relationship between two people, the speaker and an addressee. The addressee of the poem roams "from east to west" (2), and the speaker listens to the footsteps and remarks, "And in the world / Handkerchiefs were lost, and books, and people" (3–4). The catalog of lost objects ranges from insignificant to significant, but this is the last line of the stanza. Nothing more is said by the speaker in this regard. We might assume that she or he is one of the people lost, given the privileging of the sentiment in the two-stanza poem. Alternatively, she or he may simply recognize that the world is a place where people lose objects, possessions, and people they love. Perhaps, too, the poem suggests that a person may fail to notice how another, even someone whom one loves, can be lost.

A theme concerning the impermanence of the things of this world is underscored in "It Was Summer, or the End of Summer" and is carried into the second, and final, stanza. It is unclear whether the person addressed by the speaker is present or whether she or he is addressed in apostrophe, but the second stanza prefigures either the literal death of the addressee or the death-in-life situation she or he is facing. As a whole, "It Was Summer, or the End of Summer" is a poem that mourns the transitory nature of human life. If we think about this poem as a means to reflect on Assia's life for the purposes of this study, we could consider the many displacements, losses, and transitory states that she faced. Indeed, Assia called herself "a displaced person" in 1968, toward the end of her life, according to her friend William Trevor (qtd. in Koren and Negev 191). To her third husband, Assia writes an endearing letter, one in which she laments the state of their relationship. The affair with Hughes brought about displacements, losses, and transitory states in every aspect of her life, most obviously in the demise of her relationship to David Wevill and the permanent instability and uncertainty of her relationship with Hughes. In her undated letter to him, Assia tells David Wevill that she wants to be with *David*, even though she acknowledges that he may hate her. If he still wants her, she writes, they can start again. This archived letter is in keeping with what Wevill recalls about his relationship at this time with Assia. In an interview with Carl Rollyson via email in 2010, Wevill writes, "[I did not] plead with Assia to stay (rather, the other way around) [she pleaded with me to stay]" (278).

Hughes pressures Assia to choose between himself and Wevill in his 27 March 1963 letter to her, all the while gesturing to the displacements and losses that he, Assia, and David Wevill would experience as a result of various choices. Writes Hughes: "As things are, it is bad for all of us. If you come to me, David suffers. If you go to him, you suffer, and does he stop suffering? [. . .] If [David] refuses to accept it, what hope is there for you, or for him, or for me. If what you've said really happens, then you'll go to pieces. He'll go to pieces in the mess. And I add one mistake to my other one. [Plath committed suicide the month prior to this letter, on 11 February 1963.] I've concentrated all my life on these two children & on what you and I might do." He ends his letter by proposing that Assia live with him in a transitory arrangement, which led, ultimately, to Assia experiencing life as a transitory state for the next six years. Urging her to consider a liminal situation, Hughes queries, "Will David let you live away from him, and with me, for six months? Anything shorter is silly. You say you want to leave him now. If you still want to live away from him then after 6 months, how can he claim you, except by law, which he must feel is as meaningless as you do" (*Letters* 217). As we know, Assia remained married to Wevill but estranged from him while, simultaneously, entreating Hughes to marry her and establish a permanent home with her during the remaining years of her life. (In her previous relationships, Assia would have another man in place for a new relationship before she ended the current relationship. She possessed a strong fear of and aversion to loneliness, and being in a committed relationship made her feel secure. Wevill composed a dialogue for Assia after she died, imagining what she would say: "A woman can't live alone. She's only half herself, by herself" [qtd. in Koren and Negev 198]).

"In the Middle of This Century" is another poem on which Assia and Hughes collaborated in their joint radio program. Again, this poem pivots on a couple and their relationship, and it is bittersweet, even heartbreaking, in its conclusion. In the vein of the other poems examined here, this one also provides us the opportunity to reflect metacritically on the real-life dynamics in Assia and Hughes's partnership. True to the setting of the poem, Assia and Hughes's own relationship ran its course during the middle of the twentieth century. The speaker of the poem showers affection on the beloved, wishing to keep the beloved with him or her. As it turns out, this, too, is a poem about the beloved going on a journey, away from the speaker—she or he "stroked your hair / In the opposite direction to your journey" (5–6). She or he takes pleasure in the physical intimacy of the relationship, despite the evil, sin, and pity present in the world: "In the mingling of ourselves, you and I, / Lovely is the world" (13–14). Their love makes the world better than it would be otherwise. And yet theirs is a companionship that is plagued by leave-taking and strife: "We shall never find peace" (20). This line would be distressing if it were not positioned within the poem to read in a dignified and controlled manner. Moving on, the speaker praises the beauty of the beloved, noting the "mortal hips" (25), in much the same way that Assia herself lovingly documented what she perceived as Hughes's physical perfections.[18] In reciprocal fashion, the speaker tells us that the beloved "spoke in praise of my passing face" (26), and Hughes and others certainly lauded Assia's beautiful face. Assia and Hughes each admired the other's appearance, and in fact, they were heralded as a glamorous couple.[19] In many ways, "In the Middle of This Century" is relevant to Assia. Outside of the historical grounding, we can identify a physical passion in the poem ("I stroked your hair" [27]; "I touched your flesh" [28]; "I touched your hand" [29]; and "I touched your mouth" [30]) of the type that ignited Assia and Hughes's relationship and was a hallmark of it. We see the value they placed on their physical as well as the emotional and psychological connections in their letters and other writing. To them, intimacy—physical but also a more cerebral attachment—was important to the health of the relationship.[20] Also, almost as a nod to Hughes, the beloved in the poem is associated with the potential of the gift of song ("I touched your mouth which may yet sing" [30]), suggestive, perhaps, of poetry and the lover's role as muse.

"In the Middle of This Century" ends with the speaker recording the name of her love, who is unidentified literally in the poem, in the dust of a tabletop. This is an act of claiming and insisting on the physical reality of the speaker's love. The last line of the poem references the "letters of your name" (34). We conclude, from the details and development of the poem, that the speaker's love for the beloved is passionate, fulfilling, and loyal. The pleasures of her own relationship were not lost on Assia, but the dangers of it were not lost on her either. As a woman who needed her man to commit to her, Assia despaired of finding another narrative that would give her life meaning; in this way, she was very much a woman of her time. As Fay Weldon remembers: "The times were against Assia, as against Sylvia. Both talented women died of love, not depression, let alone suicidal tendencies. In those pre-Feminist days, women saw their lives in terms of being loved or not loved by a man. It was terrible to be abandoned, death was better than rejection" (qtd. in Koren and Negev 218). Mira Hamermesh recalls that Assia discussed killing herself more than once, but her female friends dismissed her humiliation (and desperation) as similar to what they, too, had experienced by the social virtue of being female. According to Hamermesh, "We had all been through the humiliation of waiting for a man to ring, so we didn't take it seriously, especially as Assia always said it with a smile, out of the blue, in the middle of dinner" (qtd. in Koren and Negev 196). Her nonchalance about ending her life suggested to her friends that she must not have meant what she said, but she was considering it as an option to what appeared, to her, to be an unfathomable situation.

But "In the Middle of This Century" is more than an example of how literature can supply a scaffold upon which we analyze real-world dynamics. The artistry of the poem is noteworthy. For example, the speaker tells us that the couple possesses "half faces and full eyes"; they "turned to each other" for "a short while" (18). The half-faces may already be turned in opposite directions in anticipation of the journey, while at the same time, the speaker "stroked your hair / In the opposite direction to your journey" because she or he does not want the beloved to depart (5–6). (Later in the poem, the speaker is resolved to let the lover go and so "stroked your hair in the direction of your journey" [27].) The full eyes carry a multitude of meanings: words that cannot be said; words or emotions that overwhelm; and eyes that communicate privately and in ways that make sense to the lovers but not to us as readers. Here is another example of the privacy cloaking the couple in the poem:

> We called to each other,
> Like calling out the names of towns
> Where nobody stops
> Along the route. (7–10)

The actual words are hidden from us, but the tenor is offered. In a casual manner, the lovers call one another, but the simile alerts us that the act is one tinged with a rarity—this is a love that will become more distanced and rarefied. Indeed, the couple is prepared to part, as we see here:

> In the middle of this century we turned to each other,
> I saw your body, throwing shade, waiting for me,
> The leather straps for a long journey
> Already tightening across my chest. (21–24)

Here is also the first instance in which the speaker indicates that she or he may be preparing for a long journey (without the beloved); earlier in the poem, it is only the beloved who is singled out as the one embarking on a journey. The sweetness of the love depicted is mixed with pathos: no homecoming or return trip is signaled. The stanza is moving in its tension between the coming together ("we turned to each other") of the lovers and the passion ("I saw your body, throwing shade, waiting for me") that brings them closer and invites intimacy. Juxtaposed with this image is a jarring one: the speaker is dressed for a journey, and the straps of the pack constrict his or her body, reminding the reader that this is not a joyful moment. Memorably, the poem closes with the speaker tracing the name of the beloved in dust: we sense that the speaker has been imprinted by this love, just as she or he leaves an imprint of the lover's name, to record it and announce it. The speaker is a lover who is proud to love, and the imagery conveys the bitterness and the sweetness of parting with a lover for an indefinite amount of time.

Turning to poems that Assia and Hughes did not present together, "Eye Examination" picks up on the ideas and themes contained in other Assia-Amichai poems. This poem forces the speaker (and its readers) to face the reality of her or his situation, which is unclear. It is unclear also who is speaking a line at any given time, although we can determine there are two speakers in some sort of relationship. To me, this poem captures qualities of Assia and Hughes's relationship. Uncertainty permeates "Eye Examination": the figurative eye exam that sets up the poem does not place anything into focus for the reader. Instead, one of the characters, presumably the one with "sad" eyes, asserts: "I can see now. // And nothing else" (18–19). With the last line, the poem closes on a disillusioned note. Full of questions—eight question marks appear in the nineteen-line poem—we never learn what the speaker sees specifically or what she or he understands about the given situation.

The depressing atmosphere of the poem reaches a climax in the middle. In panic, one character begs: "Don't leave me. Please. Please. / You're not leaving / I'm not" (9–11). While the addressee assures the other that she or he is not leaving, the line is not attributed or tagged, as in keeping with the practice of this poem. And so the line could be spoken by either character. What we do learn is that one of the characters is at a remove: "I can't hear—I'm already far away" (13). We can surmise that the speaker is troubled about her situation, brought into perspective by her interlocutor. Both Assia and Hughes sought assurance from each other about the health and status of their relationship. Asking Hughes to reassure her about his love for her in an undated letter, Assia then urges, "Love me back—and if you can't, then say so, and let me go with whatever peace I can salvage" (qtd. in Koren and Negev 176).[21] She inquires about her status in the same letter, asking whether Hughes only wants her as his child keeper or whether he wants to mend their romantic relationship. In a second letter, Assia asks him whether he has forgotten her (MSS 1058, Box 1, Folder 72). Hughes, too, attempts to evaluate the status and health of his relationship with Assia in his letters to her.[22]

"Indian Summer in Princeton" introduces a speaker and a person addressed, the latter depicted as imbued in a sadness brought about by "the weight of remembering" (6). But it is also a poem about love: "Time to sit down and ask ourselves / Whom we really love" (11–12). The speaker observes that in "the house lives someone whose name is not the same as the name on the gate" (13). This puzzling line is followed by the declaration that a woman has confided in the speaker that "she does not love her life" (14). After reading Hughes's sixty-one archived letters to Assia and Assia's six to him, it seems to me that art mirrors life in many of the poems Assia translated. It is quite likely that she was drawn to what she could identify with: what clarified, complicated, interrogated, or in some way validated her experiences. Addressed variously in the 1960s as Mrs. Hughes (she was never Mrs. Hughes legally), Mrs. Wevill (a name she retained after her separation from David Wevill), and Assia Gutmann (though it was no longer her legal name), Assia would have understood the situation of a decentered identity alluded to in the poem, as she might understand the woman's inability to love life. For Assia could not value her life without Hughes, though she put forward a strong effort to do so. Tellingly, "Indian Summer in Princeton" references what is frequently a metaphor for trauma: falling. According to the speaker: "The ground beneath us moves further away— / This falling away will go on, / And go on" (7–9). This figure of a couple falling away from each other and falling apart appears throughout Assia and Amichai's *Poems.* What we know from trauma studies is that falling is a metaphor used to portray the experience of trauma and to indicate what it feels like. The pain (and possibly trauma) of displacement, separation, and loss manifests in the most powerful poems translated by Assia.

I will end my analysis and discussion of her poems by referencing briefly "The Heart Is a Corrupt Director," the poem that opened this chapter. Similar to "Indian Summer in Princeton," the speaker of "The Heart Is a Corrupt Director," which is printed on the backside of the page containing "Indian Summer in Princeton" in the first edition of *Poems,* so that the two poems appear to be two sides of the same coin, investigates links between unhappiness and love. And unhappiness and love are the underlying currents in Assia's artistic work and her life. For the speaker of "The Heart Is a Corrupt Director," love is that which troubles the speaker: "It is terrible to battle against love / With sleeping pills. What have we come to!" (18–19). Assia's decision to commit suicide, with gas and sleeping pills, was a result of how she felt about Hughes and her present and future prospects for happiness, as we know from the last letter she wrote her father:

> The prospect before me is so bleak, that to have lived my full life-span would have entailed more misery than I could possibly endure.
>
> [. . .]
>
> What I have done was necessary—you wouldn't have wished another 30 years of hell for me—would you?
>
> Life was very exciting at the beginning—but this living death was too much to pay for it.

> [. . .]
>
> Please don't think I'm insane, or that I have done this in a moment of insanity. It was simple accountancy. (Qtd. in Koren and Negev 204–5)

I quote these passages not to sensationalize the tragedy but to display and expose Assia's thoughts and feelings about love, loss, and her future prospects as she chose to express them. As Koren and Negev echo, "For her, it was living with Ted, or nothing" (163).

From Assia's perspective, love was the grand prize, and she staked everything on the dream of Hughes sharing a home with her and their daughter. This dream was built on her love for him and on traditional expectations of what a good life looked like for women, as Weldon observes. The good life was inflected with heterosexual and sexist norms and expectations, but they did not detract from how compelling and desirable it must have appeared: indeed, because what struck Assia as the good life was so grounded in gendered scripts, the good life would have appeared as the natural and best way to live one's life. Accordingly, Assia conformed to traditional roles and responsibilities, as Hughes expected her to do; we know what some of them are, as a result of the "Draft Constitution" Hughes drew up for her and from tidbits of information he relays in his letters. Assia demonstrated her willingness to shape her life around Hughes: moving and relocating when and where he told her to do so as well as quitting and securing high-profile professional jobs when she needed to do so, at his request. The tragedy of the situation is not Assia's conforming to gender roles. The tragedy lies in her conviction that her life and that of her daughter were ruined if Hughes did not commit to her romantically and set up a home with her and Shura, all contextualized by the norms and expectations of a precarious society that disadvantaged women.[23] Assia could not see any pathways to a good life without Hughes. From my perspective, I view this shortcoming as a structural and gendered one, not a personal fault of Assia. Koren and Negev point out that police records of the time show that single, separated, divorced, and widowed women constituted the largest group of suicides in 1969; the modal age was forty-two years old. As they note, "On all counts, Assia fell into the typical category [of suicides]" (214). Because she was achieving success and a living as a professional writer *and* she was successfully raising her child as a single parent, we cannot expect more of her professionally and personally—other than wishing she had more resilience, borne out of future feminist structural changes, future feminist revised expectations, and a better social support system.

As with her successful literary translations, Assia's professional success in advertising is uncontested. In fact, Koren and Negev point to her writing of "Lost Island," a 1965 cinema and television advertisement for Sea Witch hair color, as a major highlight of her career. Strikingly original, Assia's copywriting alludes to both Greek mythology and James Bond; it was a complete turn in a new direction from what had preceded it in its expense, epic qualities in filming, and literariness. It appeared in movie theaters and on television: audiences in cinemas relished and applauded it (Koren and Negev 150–51). Assia's ad campaign on behalf of her employer, J. Walter Thompson (JWT), established her as a star in the advertising world. In addition, explain Koren and Negev, she also earned the respect of her colleagues: "Assia got a standing ovation from her colleagues, as well as a nice salary raise and became known in the business as the Sea Witch Lady." Her colleagues remember that she was known for her "unconventional" triumphs in advertising (Koren and Negev 151). In his research on the historic Sea Witch commercial, Richard Farmer chronicles the public reaction to "Lost Island," which was overwhelmingly positive: "In mid-July, internal JWT correspondence recorded that the film was 'being received with riotous applause and laughter in every cinema in which it is shown': We keep hearing stories about how people [are] discussing the commercial[,] which appeared to overshadow the feature film, and today I was told about a class of sixth form girls who spent the whole morning discussing [it] and describing it in great detail" (9–10). It was praised by *Tele-*

vision Mail as "a terrifically courageous and effective commercial" (Farmer 12).

The targeted demographic was young women who used hair dye for cosmetic, fashionable purposes because it was believed that growth in the market would be a result of young women, who had money to spend, buying hair dye; thus, the Sea Witch commercial needed to appeal to young women (Farmer 4). Furthermore, JWT strove to present a glamorous approach to Sea Witch (5); Assia would have been tasked with envisioning and delivering glamour in her copy for the advertisement. Fortunately, she had quite the budget: historical records indicate that Assia's Sea Witch spot was one of the most expensive commercials ever produced. The ninety-second advertisement cost more than sixteen thousand pounds to create and produce, in contrast to a sixty-second spot with a purported unlimited budget that cost two thousand pounds in 1965. JWT was proud that "Lost Island" equaled the film *Ben Hur* in its cost-per-second. Unfortunately for Assia and feminist scholars who wish to build up women, their achievements, and legacies, Assia is credited in a 2016 article, funded by the UK Arts and Humanities Research Council, as the JWT copywriter who wrote the Sea Witch script—and as the woman "who is now perhaps better known for having an affair with Ted Hughes, a relationship that may have driven Sylvia Plath to suicide" (6). As we can see, Assia's notable achievement with Sea Witch is overshadowed by her notorious personal life involving Hughes and Plath: the scandalous love story is the last word the author writes about Assia, and the responsibility for Plath's death is attributed to her by suggestion. She is the active agent, the one "having an affair with Ted Hughes," not the other way around, and that affair is speculated as the reason for Plath's demise in an article about the history of film and television.

The Sea Witch commercial is extant and available for viewing online. In it, seven men traverse the Aegean Sea on a motorboat, headed to the island inhabited by three sea witches: a blonde, a brunette, and a redhead. In mock epic fashion, the narrator informs us that thousands of men have made the journey to the sea witches' island, only to perish at their hands. Six of the men become victims of the sea witches, after trying to steal their hair dye; the hair color renders their hair legendary, we are told. One man escapes with a briefcase of twelve boxes of the sea witches' hair color. The commercial closes on a box of Sea Witch hair dye placed on the counter of a pharmacy, with the narrator stating the price. The commercial balances mock seriousness with humor, and its success lies in its sophisticated humor. According to Farmer: "The [commercial], as its overblown, portentous script makes very clear, is intentionally comic. A mock-heroic mini-epic, the [commercial] is wildly, joyously ridiculous. Much of the humour in 'Lost Island' is dependent on the audience recognising and enjoying the juxtaposition of a bombastic yet ostensibly sincere tone" (7). While the expedition the men embark on could be considered glamorous, the glamour is most evident in the styling of the sea witches and in the gorgeous waterscape. Altogether, the components of the commercial—the script and the cinematography—make it glamorous and intelligently interesting.

The issue of whether the glamorous sea witches are depicted in a feminist way is debatable. Approaching the ad in this fashion, however, makes it relevant to our own day, for we are still occupied with teasing out feminist (or sexist) implications and messages and determining what is feminist and what is not. "Lost Island" is feminist in its depiction of powerful and empowered women: they manage their own island and treasure (in the form of Sea Witch hair color). The veiled feminist critique emerges in that the sea witches do not need saving by the men; the men need saving *from* them, and the sea witches successfully defend themselves and their treasure, with the exception of the twelve stolen boxes of hair dye. This critique is surprisingly and discerningly feminist for its time. But the commercial embeds mixed messages. The sea witches are monsters who turn violent, and what they value is tied to cosmetic beauty: these are traditional, rather sexist, expectations of powerful women, women who are powerful only because they are monsters or are beautiful. Thus, "Lost Island" mirrors symbolically Assia's own situation.[24] On one hand, she appears empowered; for a time, she thrived professionally and personally. On the other hand, she needed a man to feel fulfilled, and she has become the beautiful monster in the Plath-Hughes mythology.

A feminist takeaway message from the Sea Witch commercial may be that it asks us to consider what we condone and condemn in femininity. As Judith Barry and Sandy Flitterman-Lewis posit, a "feminist art evolves from a theoretical reflection on representations: how the representation of women is produced, the way it is understood, and the social conditions in which it is situated" (71). They identify a type of art that plays with contradictions in a patriarchal society; the objective of such art "is the critical awareness (both on the part of the spectator, and informing the work) of the construction of femininity. For it is only through a critical understanding of 'representation' that a *re*presentation of 'women' can occur" (72). What I have endeavored to do with my analysis and discussion of "Lost Island"—and with Assia's artistic products at large—is to interrogate representations of women, their lives, and their femininity in order to reflect on them from a literary studies and feminist perspective so that we may understand such treatments and perhaps work to change, expand, or augment our thinking, our conversations, our activism, and our work in the classroom and in scholarship for feminist ends.

ASSIA'S SELF-REPRESENTATION AND HER IMAGE(S)

Photographs indicate how Assia styled herself, but I would venture to say that our interpretations of Assia are more revealing of our assumptions about the female body and our values in terms of its desirability.[25] As we know from Koren and Negev's biography of Assia, she internalized the cultural valuation of feminine beauty, and having been deemed extraordinarily beautiful by people who knew her, she became concerned when she thought her looks were fading with age. Assia's beauty constituted her cultural capital, fostering heterosexual admiration and, as she believed, the opportunities for a good love match. Thus, for some time, she was fearful of becoming pregnant; that, in itself, is not surprising considering that the maternal body can be denounced as abject, that which is excessively feminine and, therefore, m/other. Koren and Negev remark, "It was never clear whether it was the pregnancy, labor, delivery, or motherhood that Assia abhorred so much" prior to her daughter's birth (59). In her clinging to beauty as that which makes women valuable, Assia was a product of her culture and age—not so removed from our own time in this respect. Culturally, a message we are sold is that feminine beauty is power.

We are privy to the way Assia saw herself in her extant self-portrait from 1967–68, which forms a fascinating part of the Olwyn Hughes collection in the archive at Emory.[26] In it, she appears beautiful and vulnerable. Granted, this is my interpretation of the portrait, informed by what else I have seen in the archive. But in the self-portrait, her expression is one that is open and searching; she is not smiling, but she looks approachable. It is not a glamorous self-portrait; if anything, Assia's exotic glamour is missing in it. She depicts herself as looking more Anglo-British than German Israeli, though her beauty traditionally has hinged on the latter. Giving herself a rather lank light-brown bob (which is in stark contrast to the black hair, cut and styled in fashionable ways that she is featured with in photographs of her prior to 1965, available on the internet), blue-gray eyes, and natural-looking eyebrows, Assia further depicts herself in muted colors without makeup. Her image wears no jewelry and displays a bare neck area, which could be a gesture to her reputation as a seductive woman (suggesting nudity) as well as to her willingness to make herself vulnerable by producing an image of herself as she sees herself without cosmetics, enhancements, or ornamentation (though she loved stylish clothes). The naturalness of this image renders Assia as *wholesome* and organic. Her famed dark beauty has been figuratively redrawn—I would suggest this is a problematic move but revealing of societal influences. Her searching expression, confronting the viewer steadily as if to show she has nothing to hide, is memorable. For my part, I would not have recognized Assia in this self-portrait, and I have viewed more than one hundred different images of her. What is striking to me about this self-portrait is Assia's re-presentation of herself, and the simplicity and vulnerability that emerges from the portrait is poignant, especially when we are familiar with Assia's backstory.

Assia's coworker Martin Baker remembers that, in 1968, Assia "was very critical of her looks, edgy when people looked at her, and uptight when complimented on her beauty." As we might recall, Assia's sister, Celia Chaikin, details how Assia was afraid of aging and losing her beautiful appearance: "She once said to me, 'I'll kill myself at 42'" (both qtd. in Koren and Negev 180). Koren and Negev assert, Assia "abhorred a lined face and a baggy body," and she wanted to maintain "her forever-young Aphrodite image" (180–81). Chris Wilkins, who at the time was a twenty-three-year-old coworker of Assia, avers that she "was one of the most beautiful human beings I have ever encountered, she wore her beauty innocently, even clumsily, as though she herself were unsure what to do with it" (qtd. in Koren and Negev 181). These observations and remembrances, combined with Assia's self-image and concerns about the same, are all in keeping with what John Berger identifies as the special problem of female body image. Berger maintains: "[A woman] has to survey everything she is and everything she does because how she appears to others, and ultimately how she appears to men, is of crucial importance for what is normally thought of as the success of her life. Her own sense of being in herself is supplanted by a sense of being appreciated as herself by another" (49). He explains that women participate in this process, which turns them into objects (50). Participating in her own objectification, Assia became a perpetrator in her own victimization when it came to her self-worth. What Berger argues clarifies Assia's relationship with her body image; he published his theoretical scholarship only three years after Assia's death. And not much has changed. According to Iris Marion Young in 2005, "Contexts of discourse and interaction position persons in systems of evaluation and expectations which often implicate their embodied being; the person experiences herself as looked at in certain ways, described in her physical being in certain ways, she experiences the bodily reactions of others to her, and she reacts to them"

(17). To be a woman means to be fully enmeshed in her embodiment and the reactions to her body.

Assia's surveying of her appearance is most evident in the fact that she kept photographs of herself over the years. In April 2013, Bonhams announced the auction of seventy photographs of Assia; these were photographs from Assia's personal collection that had become property of the Ted Hughes estate. From this lot for sale, we learned that Assia kept the photographs of herself and herself with others. What we also learned was that Assia's "stunning beauty and allure" are marketable commodities in the twenty-first century: three photographs of Assia in a sarong are highlighted in the promotional textual material of the lot to be auctioned (Bonhams, "Lot 239"). This commodification of her appearance both displays and reinforces our cultural expectations of women in general. According to Luce Irigaray, "The use, consumption, and circulation of [women's] sexualized bodies underwrite the organization and the reproduction of the social order." She explains that women's status is that of merchandise or the commodity. As a result, women find that, in their daily lives, they cannot find pleasure unless they relish being chosen "as an object of consumption or of desire by masculine 'subjects'" (Irigaray 84). In other words, women will always experience exploitation unless they can divorce themselves from femininity, a model imposed upon them in a patriarchal system that, in Irigaray's analysis, only favors masculinity (85). I would add that the compelling aspect of femininity is the promise that adhering to its cultural script appears to promise success and pleasure. From Assia's own life, we can see that her beauty and femininity brought her admiration and love for a time, but they did not make her content or happy. The images of her body (versus her accomplishments) continue to matter and be important because they factor into traditional narratives and expectations of Assia—and women at large—in the literary imagination and the public sphere. The collection of photographs featuring her sold for five thousand pounds, indicating the significant interest in Assia (Bonhams, "Lot 239"). The rare photographs are now owned by Emory University, further bolstering its important holdings related to

Assia Wevill in Sarong in Mandalay, Burma (summer 1959). Courtesy of the Stuart Rose Literary Collection, 1821–2012, Stuart A. Rose Manuscript, Archives, and Rare Book Library, Emory University, Atlanta. © David Wevill.

Assia Wevill and allowing privileged access to previously unavailable concrete images of her.

While the three sarong photographs are suggested as important parts of the collection, they are not racy or seductive images. However, I need to temper my observation by quoting Berger: "She is not naked as she is. She is naked as the spectator sees her" (50). From my perspective, the sarong images are modest. In one sarong photograph, Assia is kneeling on a riverbank: she is viewed mostly in profile with her arms and shoulders exposed in a strapless, floor-length sarong. In another, she faces the camera in a full-body shot and wears a maxi sarong with a conservative button-up white sleeveless blouse.

Her arms, neck, and one foot, clad in a sandal, are exposed in this photograph. Standing in front of windows and French doors that let in much light, she appears politely accommodating as she poses casually for the camera. The last sarong photograph features Assia seated with legs crossed in a chair. Arguably the most interesting of the three photographs for those looking for a seductive image, Assia wears a sarong that allows her arms, shoulders, ankles, and feet to show. The maxi sarong is tied securely over her chest; no cleavage can be seen. But she sits with one hand touching her bare shoulder in a caress. The other arm rests on the armrest of the chair. Her attitude seems to be one of seriousness; her head is tilted slightly to the left, while her eyes look off to the right side of the room. In the end, though, she remains inscrutable as far as how she intends her image to be interpreted in this instance or how she felt about herself as the photograph was taken. What we can take away from these sarong photographs is that the traditional expectations of Assia as an overblown seductress are thwarted. If anything, she strikes me as dignified and serious in most of the seventy photographs from the Bonhams auction and in the additional nine restricted photographs of her in the Ted Hughes Papers. The photographs of her, available in the archive and on the internet, circulate messages about Assia that are more revealing of our attitudes and expectations of beautiful women and of Assia, in particular, than they are of her own attitude toward herself. In other words, to some extent, they are mirrors that put into relief our own attitudes about the female body.

With this in mind, I will introduce two of the nine restricted archived photographs that I find most moving.[27] These two color images support the argument put forward in these pages, which may be why I am drawn to them. One of the images captures Christmas 1966. Assia is wearing a white lacy top, which comes across as festive but modest. She looks directly and calmly into the camera and appears content. Shura is standing in front of her with a finger in her mouth, also gazing into the camera. Assia's hands are resting sweetly and protectively on Shura's shoulders. Frieda Hughes stands next to Shura, wearing a holiday dress and headband and looking into the camera with a slight smile; she is holding a red-wrapped present. Nicholas Hughes is wearing a beige V-neck sweater, a white button-up shirt, black pants, and a black bowtie; he stands on the other side of Shura and hugs a green-wrapped present. It is a family photograph of all Hughes's immediate family members (Assia Wevill, et al., photograph, Dec. 1966). To me, this photograph counters the anti-family sentiment that informs representations of Assia; she was a woman who very much loved Shura, Frieda, and Nicholas (and Hughes), and this photograph captures her role as a mother and maternal figure in their lives.[28]

The second image supports my interpretation of the previous one: Assia is featured with Shura. With the date inscribed on the back of the photograph, we know that we are encountering another photograph from 1966. In this one, Shura is smiling, and Assia's head rests sweetly on her daughter's as she stands and holds her. Assia might be wearing pigtails, but because she is in profile, it is difficult to determine. She wears a knee-length dress and a lightweight coat as long as her dress. Draped on her left arm is a decorative floral scarf. Her hair is black, and she wears black flats. Shura is barefoot, wearing a ruffled dress and capri leggings. The setting resembles Court Green, and indeed, that may be where the photograph was taken. As my favorite image of Assia, this photograph evidences the love and happiness of Assia and Shura, together. This mother-daughter image stands in stark contrast to the charge that Assia was not a loving mother and/or was an unnatural m/other in affective responses. Assia adored Shura, as we see in these photographs. Upon asking her sister to serve as Shura's caregiver, should something happen to her, Assia told Chaikin: "I couldn't bear some [other] bloody woman looking after Shura. She is all I have. I adore her, as I only adored [Mother]" (qtd. in Koren and Negev 164).

ON ASSIA'S ACHIEVEMENTS

As we know, Assia's life in the 1960s was not an easy one, and yet this was the decade of her best achievements and the realization of her greatest loves in the forms of her daughter and partner. It also was the decade that would immortalize her in Plath's poetry and provide the experiences and memories for Hughes to draw upon in his later poems about Assia. Impressively, Assia produced important translations of poems that proved her literary abilities in spite of structural challenges and personal obstacles to her well-being. The poems she worked over are brilliant in their execution: they capture reflections and presentations of love and its pleasures and dangers, and many of them resonate with her own gendered experiences as a heterosexual woman. Assia's translated version of Amichai's *Poems* allows us to revel in a significant contribution to literary studies.

Additionally, we are fortunate in that we can access an artifact from Assia's time as a star in advertising. Having made a name for herself as the copywriter of the Sea Witch "Lost Island" commercial, Assia's contributions put women on the artistic map in advertising in the 1960s while providing us material with which we can problematize and discuss gender roles and expectations. The photographs and self-portraits that remain of Assia further hold up to us our own expectations of her—and of other women more broadly—as we interpret them and process what we value concerning femininity and female bodies.

Altogether, her writing, in the forms of letters and journal entries, contextualize her other artistic products as well as her life. We learn that Assia's ideologies and gendered concerns are not so different from our own in many important respects. She was convinced that feminine beauty and sexuality are powerful; as a result, she worried about losing her looks with age and motherhood. She displayed her insecurity about managing a household on her own in tandem with managing her professional career and caring for her daughter, all the while forgoing long-standing spousal support. Her writing about her life corresponds to the instability of her life in a world that does not take very good care of its women and girls. Instead of dismissing successful women as "hangers on" when it comes to men, especially male partners, or less than ("not real writers"), we can recalibrate our thinking by affirming and sanctioning the accomplished body of women's work and contributions, thereby readjusting women's status in our worldview.

One way that we can redress misogynistic or sexist wrongs is to seek out, validate, and celebrate significant women and their work. Literary scholars and the literary public find that they can champion Ted Hughes, despite his flaws—likewise with the exceptional Plath, exceptional in both her following and her importance. While Assia's own contributions to literary and cultural studies are not of the same caliber as those by Plath and Hughes, her life and work are significant in their quality and in what they show us. Indeed, her life and her texts illustrate various gendered dimensions of art and the real world. In other words, we are presented with the opportunity to (re) consider why and how Assia has continued to matter to this day. With Assia, we find that her legacy in the twenty-first century is gathering momentum, as I will examine in the next chapter. This book hopes to contribute to that momentum and catapult Assia to new (re)presentations, ones that signal and sanction our feminist commitment to women and their lives and achievements. Surely new work will follow this project because it is, after all, impossible to definitively know Assia or any other person: if we can only access others via identitarian categories—and those categories always fail to capture who a person is—then we are left with recognizing the open-endedness of the other and approaching her as best we can. As Butler asserts, "As we ask to know the other, or ask that the other say, finally or definitively, who he or she is, it will be important not to expect an answer that will ever satisfy" (*Giving an Account of Oneself* 42–43). In other words, we should not expect a single definitive interpretation, analysis, or presentation of Assia's life and work. In the chapter that follows, then, we will survey new approaches to Assia and consider why Assia still matters to the literary imagination today.

CHAPTER 5

ASSIA WEVILL IN THE TWENTY-FIRST CENTURY

Have I denied you a father
As your mother
Denied me mine?
—from "For Shura," by Frieda Hughes

We will encounter many texts in this chapter that portray Assia Wevill in the twenty-first century. Many of these texts continue or elaborate upon the complementary narratives about Assia authored by Sylvia Plath and Ted Hughes presented in chapters 2 and 3. Other texts, however, strike out on new terrain and carve out space for new representations in the Plath-Hughes literary and cultural landscape. What we will discover is that regardless of whether she is portrayed positively, negatively, or neutrally, Assia continues to matter to the literary imagination and to American and European culture now more than ever, as literature and creative work, a major motion picture film, a BBC documentary, and websites or blog posts dedicated to Assia demonstrate. With the exception of the film *Sylvia*, all of the other pieces I examine here follow the 2006 publication of Yehuda Koren and Eilat Negev's *Lover of Unreason: Assia Wevill, Sylvia Plath's Rival and Ted Hughes's Doomed Love* in order to capture the most recent developments in treatments of Assia. It is that book, in fact, that made this project possible. Assia's biography needed to be established before critical literary and/or women's studies scholarship could scaffold upon it.

What follows are analyses and discussions of how Assia's legacy has manifested in the representations of what she has come to mean to different people working in different artistic or literary genres a half-century and more after her death. It is what Assia represents—how she signifies and how we interpret her or women purportedly like her—that has attracted such fascination and has molded her into a symbolic figure in transatlantic literature and culture. In many ways, Assia still fascinates us, as she did Plath, and attracts and repels us, as she did Hughes.

THE FILM *SYLVIA*

Sylvia is an art film that was screened in theaters in both the United States and England—in 2003 and 2004, respectively—and it brings Assia to a commercial, mass audience. Perhaps the major difference between Plath's and Hughes's literary texts, on one hand, and this cinematic representation of Assia, on the other, lies in the elision of an acknowledgment or understanding of Assia's role as the exotic but dangerous muse to Plath and Hughes. Instead, she becomes a foreigner who has far less brashness and glamour than the accounts of her by her contemporaries in Koren and Negev's biography or the BBC documentary *Ted Hughes: Stronger than Death* (2015) would have it.

The Assia in *Sylvia* is pleasant and polite—in contrast to the depiction of Plath in the film—and circumspect (until the steamy and provocative assignation with Hughes, but he is the one who appears to be in charge in that scene and throughout the film with respect to both Plath and Assia). Assia's legendary charisma and charm are missing in *Sylvia,* as is the depiction of her as a willful seductress. If anything, she seems to be a fan of Plath in the film: in chapter 9 of the film's scenes, she is very forthcoming in her admiration of Plath's *Colossus.* It is Hughes who is portrayed as having designs on Assia: in chapter 9, he looks her up and down and fixes his intense gaze on her while an oblivious Plath tenders an invitation for a stay in Devon to Assia and David Wevill. While Assia is courteous toward Plath during their weekend in Devon, Hughes is overly solicitous about Assia's comfort in apparent bids for her attention in chapters 10 and 11, and the Plath character in the film notices, much to her displeasure. Instead of taking her resentment out on Hughes, however, in *Sylvia*, Plath unleashes it on Assia. When Assia compliments Plath on the "extraordinary" soup at dinner, Plath responds by insisting rudely and aggressively that Assia must eat more, implying that Assia takes what is not hers or that she takes too much (which is a theme associated with Assia in Hughes's *Capriccio*). The Plath in the film wants Assia to know that she is unwelcome by this point, and anything Hughes does in relation to Assia infuriates Plath. Finally, Assia ventures to say to Plath, "You shouldn't have gone to all this trouble," as a way to appease her and indirectly thank her for her hospitality. Plath retorts, "I'm beginning to think the same thing myself," which makes each character in the scene visibly uncomfortable because, at this point, nothing untoward has happened between Assia and Hughes and Assia has not done anything to incur Plath's wrath.

The story line communicated in *Sylvia* of the fated weekend in Devon sticks to the basic plot lines (the four have dinner and listen to a record of Robert Lowell reading poetry, and Assia and Ted remove themselves to the kitchen, ostensibly to clean up after dinner), but it presents all four characters—Plath, Hughes, Assia, and David Wevill—as cardboard, one-dimensional figures. Plath is the overworked mother who tries to have it all; she breaks down in chapter 11 and begs David Wevill to leave with Assia, claiming that she is tired and has two small children and her life is one that neither Wevill nor Assia can understand. Hosting friends over the weekend is too much for the Plath character, who is suspicious of her husband's attention to their friend. The Hughes character makes his attraction to Assia known in small ways, and he is positioned to be the initiator of the affair. The Wevill character simply plays the role of a naive husband and friend. And Assia appears blameless until chapter 12, when Plath seemingly finds incriminating documents at Hughes's desk after he departs for London and when the camera cuts to Hughes kissing Assia during a sexual encounter. The affair is officially detected by Plath in chapter 13, when Plath finds Assia's name and telephone number on a scrap of paper and intercepts Assia's legendary call to Hughes at his home with Plath. Until chapter 16, the mainstream story about Assia and her role in Plath and Hughes's lives is a relatively diluted or tame version of what we have come to expect.[1]

What sets *Sylvia* and its account of Assia, Plath, and Hughes apart from other popular, twenty-first-century texts are two big story line developments in the Plath-Hughes-Assia saga. One is the Plath character's admission: "That woman [Assia]—I invented her; I conjured her." Clearly, what Plath in *Sylvia* fears most is losing Hughes, and the film indicates that Plath herself made it happen by being a difficult personality. But the film also posits the idea that Plath created ("invented") Assia or called her into being ("conjured"). In this line of thinking, then, Plath projected the fears and desires that were core to how she saw herself and her place in the world onto Assia. Assia becomes less a real person than a manifestation of Plath's desires and fears of what it means to be a desirable woman (e.g., physically attractive and socially engaging) or an undesirable one (e.g., a difficult personality, a person who has difficulty in juggling the multitude of obligations expected of a wife, mother, and professional writer).

The second big story line development is tragic and shocking. In chapter 16, after being sexually intimate with Hughes, despite the fact that they have separated due to Hughes's affair with Assia, Plath apprises Hughes that he will never have with Assia what he has with her. The Hughes character affirms this observation. This scene fuels the rhetoric of Plath as Hughes's true partner and Assia as less special. Most strikingly, it also undercuts Assia's importance to Hughes: she was Hughes's romantic partner for nearly the same amount of time as Plath, and she also had a child with him. This part of the scene is the tragic development; we are reminded here that neither Plath nor Assia will feel fulfilled and that neither will survive or thrive, regardless of their beauty, talents, and successes. The film takes up the aspect of Hughes's blended family situation in a stunning way when Plath asks Hughes to leave Assia. He replies: "I can't. She's pregnant." Other than one speculative account, we do not have recorded evidence that this scene occurred.[2] To introduce this story line into an already tragic story is, of course, sensational and generates interest and garners attention, but ultimately, it further condemns Assia as having had a part in Plath's demise when factored into the overall trajectory of the film and the basic Plath-Hughes-Assia master plot. Overall, *Sylvia* endorses the traditional narratives in the Plath-Hughes mythos.

FOLLOWING THE PUBLICATION OF KOREN AND NEGEV'S *LOVER OF UNREASON*: ASSIA IN PRINT AND ONLINE

Before I offer a survey and analyses of how Assia has been represented since the biography about her was published, in 2007, we will examine a book that folds her in as a character and which was published at roughly the same time as *Lover of Unreason* so we can see how representations of Assia have stayed the same in some cases and have changed in others. It is fascinating to track how Assia manifests in conventional forms in the twenty-first century *and* how some twenty-first-century representations have diverged from what I term the more traditional approach to her. What we will find is that conventional images and rhetoric of Assia still have a firm hold on the literary and cultural transatlantic imagination. And yet there are significant inroads and changes in how she is presented and treated, which suggest that conventional expectations for women and femininity may be modified or eroded eventually by other media. Differing approaches and representations of who Assia was or might have been (or could be!) can only enrich the gendered discourses in our scholarship and teaching, and those have the power to shape expectations and norms for women in the future.

A book that shows us that twenty-first-century texts are not so removed from works produced decades earlier is *Your Own, Sylvia: A Verse Portrait of Sylvia Plath* (2007) by Stephanie Hemphill. It relies on the most salacious depictions of Assia, as informed by the first biographies of Plath, which were reviewed in chapter 1. The book is dedicated, in part, to "all those who love or come to love Sylvia Plath," and the dedication is revealing of Hemphill's embedded message: to love Plath, one must abhor Assia. Hemphill embraces the traditional, antifeminist discourse that has swirled around Assia, essentially pitting Plath and Assia against each other in a no-win battle. In her first appearance in Hemphill's book, Assia is the persona of the poem titled "Sylvia," a poem in which the Assia character derides the Plath one, dubbing Plath a "watchdog" (read: a bitch) who even "snarls." Unkind to herself as well, Assia self-identifies here as a "Gypsy, / wandering, thieving what I fancy." Of course, these lines continue the narratives about Plath and Assia as constructed by Ted Hughes, painting Plath as too difficult for Hughes to remain married to and Assia as a heartless, calculating, and murdering thief. Further, Hemphill promotes Assia as a hypersexual woman (i.e., not a "nice girl") when Assia states: "I am experienced. / I have thrown my nightgown / over more than one man's head" (176).[3] As examined in chapter 1, this scene involving the nightgown likely never happened, though it certainly makes for salacious storytelling.[4] Adding to the image of Assia as a hypersexual aggressor, Hemphill imagines Assia running through a garden, with Hughes chasing her in sexual pursuit until he figuratively "rolls down the hill / and into [Assia's] bed" (177), after he cuts ties (the "fraying rope" of the poem) with Plath. This poem effectively erases Hughes from sharing in any responsibility for the problematic love triangle; if anything, he is to be pitied as the "fading husband" of the poem (176). Assia is primed to bear the brunt of our disgust and, perhaps for some, hatred.

"All the Bitter Things," another poem in Hemphill's book, continues the themes that "Sylvia" makes explicit. For instance, the Hughes character in the poem actually calls Plath a "bitch" while he details "how nightmarish / living with her was" (198). For her second appearance in the book, Assia is invoked by the Hughes persona as callously thinking that Plath will perhaps commit suicide as a result of their affair:

> Assia and I think perhaps
> Sylvia will kill herself;
> David, Assia's husband,
> attempted suicide when Assia left him,
> and he was strong. (199)

In this stanza, Hemphill attributes Plath's suspicions that Hughes and Assia wish her dead to the characters of Hughes and Assia, making them out to be monsters.[5] What stands out about this stanza is its fabrication of the lives and characters of Hughes, Assia, David Wevill, and Plath. In contrast to how Hemphill portrays him, Hughes was devastated over Plath's, Assia's, and Shura's deaths, as we know from his poetry.[6] From the Plath archive at Indiana University's Lilly Library, we learn from Plath, in a 16 October 1962 letter to her mother, that she believes Hughes and Assia wonder at the fact that she has not attempted suicide again and that Hughes does not like her and thinks it would be convenient if she died (Plath, "*Letters Home*—Part Seven"). By her own admission, Hemphill did not visit the Lilly Library; she resorts to furnishing details cribbed from old biographies of Plath—namely, Edward Butscher's *Sylvia Plath: Method and Madness* (1976, reissued 2003), Anne Stevenson's *Bitter Fame* (1989), and Paul Alexander's *Rough Magic* (1991) (Hemphill 249–50). As we know from chapter 1, these are also problematic biographies in terms of Assia's treatment. From *Lover of Unreason,* we learn that Assia was taken aback that anyone, including Plath, would have held her responsible in any way for Plath's suicide (Koren and Negev 115, 117). And we know from letters in the Hughes archive at Emory University that Assia did not immediately leave David Wevill, as *Lover of Unreason* also makes clear; in fact, the opposite scenario took place.[7] As for Plath, it seems cruel to infer that she was not "strong," as compared to David Wevill, when Plath arguably demonstrated remarkable strength, as did Assia, to persevere and succeed in many ways despite the stigma attached to being a single mother and an "abandoned" woman in the 1960s.[8] The details in Hemphill's reimagining of Hughes, Assia, and Plath become twisted and are employed in such fashion as to make the reader feel that she is privy to gossip and information only an insider would have. *Your Own, Sylvia* maintains the status quo and rehashes old, faulty stories for a new audience.[9]

Now we will turn to online media that responded to a newfound interest in Assia following the publication of *Lover of Unreason,* and I will touch upon examples of how Assia has been taken up as a figure to investigate and recover in the twenty-first century. Perhaps the most symbolic online development in recuperating Assia and Shura, her daughter with Hughes, confronts us when we search for them online. While it is uncontested that they have been virtually erased from literary scholarship and from Hughes's documented public life, their lives are just beginning to be publicly reclaimed and grieved, as a result of the publication of *Lover of Unreason*. For example, both Assia and Shura are listed on the *Find a Grave* website, and the entry for Shura, in particular, is noteworthy ("Alexandra Tatiana Elise 'Shura' Wevill"). The online presence of this entry amounts to an incredible development when we consider that Assia's and Shura's lives have been what we think of as "ungrievable," as noted in chapter 1. With attention to detail, the various contributors to the site construct a public site of mourning: they have posted photos of Assia and Shura as well as a photo of their last home, 3 Okeover Manor, Clapham Common, in London, which is also the place where they died. The site offers informed speculation that their ashes may have been scattered at Saint Mary the Virgin Church in Ashford, Kent, while taking care to cite *Lover of Unreason* and the interview with Brenda Hedden therein as the key to identifying the churchyard. Shura's *Find a Grave* site is more detailed than Assia's, but both are examples of how people who never knew Assia or Shura have come together to commemorate them and mark their deaths with symbolic virtual gravestones. Of interest, however, are the differences between Assia's and Shura's *Find a Grave* sites; Shura's contains more details and evidence of detective work than Assia's, and Shura's site boasts four times more "notes" left in the section of the web page that serves as the equivalent of an online guestbook than Assia's at the time of the writing of this book ("Assia Esther Gutmann Wevill").[10] Perhaps guests who visit these sites may feel more moved to leave a token of recognition on Shura's site, being as her death was so untimely, and they may be less inclined to leave a note for Assia because she took her own life and that of her daughter. Visitors may also be less inclined to mourn Assia to the same extent they might mourn Shura because of the ways in which Assia has historically been represented.

Less morbid—and more impressive in its detective work—is another example of how Assia has been commemorated online: the sixteen-page blog post "Assia's Dior: A Mystery." The post opens with Hughes's "Chlorophyl" from *Capriccio,* the poem that alludes to the allure of Assia's Dior perfume. This fragrance is closely associated with her, and so the author of the blog, a perfume connoisseur, proceeds to investigate, at her own financial expense, which perfume exactly in the Dior collection Assia might have worn in 1962: she acquires samples of the vintage Dior fragrances through her connections. By researching the history of Dior perfumes and the attendant advertising campaigns, the author narrows the possibilities to three: Miss Dior, launched in 1947; Diorama, launched in 1949; and Diorissimo, launched in 1956. After analyzing the possibilities, the author's "best guess" is Miss Dior. As she explains, "[Miss Dior] was launched in 1947, the year of Assia's first marriage, and like Assia, Miss Dior is a complex portrait of opposites: both elegant and animalistic, proper and mischievous, mysterious and direct, refined and dirty, fragile and confident; it is, above all, unapologetic." Miss Dior, the author notes, was "intended to invoke a new kind of woman: graceful, fashionable, and daring." In attempting to confirm her hypothesis, the author reached out to Koren and Negev, and they responded that they, too, had tried to identify the fragrance. They had asked David Wevill if he could remember which it might be, but he was unable to do so. The existence of this blog entry showcases the newfound interest in Assia that *Lover of Unreason* sparked as well as the degree to which Assia captivates people in the twenty-first century.

Now I would like to address the phenomena of what I will call "fanfiction," written for Assia as a tribute to her or written about Assia in the spirit of what Assia means to the person or culture producing it. Such writing tends to be uneven in its quality, and so I will highlight only two examples. One is a work in progress; the author, Dina Davis, periodically updates her website to reflect her additions and revisions of a manuscript, titled *Capriccio,* about Assia. Initially, she was writing what she proposes as a novel from Assia's point of view, referencing *Lover of Unreason* each step of the way. The premise of her manuscript is to give Assia a fictional voice, and she intends to show the impact of Plath's suicide on Assia. By all accounts, she is engaged in portraying Assia sympathetically.

On the other end of the spectrum is *Doonreagan: A Private Domain of Ted Hughes* (2013), a published play by Ann Henning Jocelyn; it has been staged in England and Ireland. While it becomes clear that Jocelyn is not sympathetic to Assia, she is nevertheless engaged in producing the phenomenon of Assia fanfiction, having been inspired to write her play after meeting Assia's biographers and reading *Lover of Unreason* and other related texts (21). The remainder of this section will treat *Doonreagan* as a metaphorical bookend to *Your Own, Sylvia: A Verse Portrait of Sylvia Plath* because *Doonreagan* mirrors and has imbibed the same literary-cultural-historical hostility and antifeminist assumptions and stereotypes about Assia that *Your Own, Sylvia* does. The messages conveyed in *Doonreagan* are of the same tune as those in traditional biographies that gesture to Assia, most of which predate *Lover of Unreason*. In spite of the memorial sites for Assia and Shura and the more feminist treatments of them that have sprouted online, *Doonreagan* proves that old narratives are hard to circumvent, even if they are reductive, false, and damaging.

What I have argued throughout this book is that words matter and that they have the power to produce great impact: they shape how we think about ourselves, others, and our world as well as define or illustrate values. Crafted as dramatic literature, *Doonreagan* has reached not only a niche of readers interested in Ted Hughes and his circle but also a theatergoing audience who may not know who Assia Wevill was before attending a performance. Because the play does not delve into the complicated woman she was or the gendered dimensions and constraints of her life, culture, or society, we are left with the impression of Assia as deserving of the poor treatment and reception she has received during her life and after it, even though the play tries to mitigate this aspect some in its recognition that she may have suffered transgenerational trauma in her family's emigration from Nazi Germany. But that idea is not a new one: it can be traced back to the very arguments Hughes made about Assia in *Capriccio*, as we saw in chapter 3. In essence, *Doonreagan* refashions the very arguments and vitriol that Hughes expressed in relation to Assia in his published work and that conventional work on Hughes or Plath has espoused. The subtitle of *Doonreagan* is fitting because while Assia and Hughes are the two main characters in the play, the story line recapitulates what we already know about Assia from past treatments, creative and scholarly; this is a play about Ted Hughes, and it views his world from his purported perspective. Assia is left out of the title of the play that principally concerns her—that features her prominently in every scene, in fact—and this omission is in keeping with the manner in which Assia has historically been important in literary studies: her relationship with Ted Hughes. All of this holds fast in *Doonreagan*, despite Jocelyn's understanding that the life Hughes shared with Assia at the Doonreagan House in Cashel, Connemara, County Galway, in Ireland in 1966 was idyllic for both Hughes and Assia (26).

Assia's character description on the first page of the play alerts readers that Hughes's (and Plath's) characterization of Assia will dominate: in *Doonreagan*, Assia is "aged 38, dark, sensuous, sophisticated, but with a hidden vulnerability" (29). As explored in chapter 3, it is in Hughes's literary output that we encounter the very terms *Doonreagan* exploits. *Doonreagan* molds Assia as despicable and without redeeming qualities; she comes across as immensely unlikable. Assia's fabled elegance and sophistication devolve into crudity and vulgarity in this text from her cursing—not featured in any of her writing across genres or in any literary or biographical accounts of her—to her joke about seducing a priest, which seems very out of character, even for this putative hypersexual character.[11] In scene 1, Assia enters, "out of sorts," wearing a "dressing-gown, clutching a mug of coffee," and she "turns off the music as if the sound hurts her ears" (32). From the very beginning of this play, the author misunderstands Assia and the dynamics of her relationship with Hughes. Assia worked to appease Hughes, and he was clear about his gendered preferences and the division of labor in a household. For instance, the seemingly small detail about Assia starting her day in a dressing gown underscores the obliviousness of *Doonreagan* to the actual realities of

Assia's life: she was responsible for much of the care of three children and the maintenance of the home when she cohabited with Hughes—we know this from *Lover of Unreason* and the archive that contains Assia-related artifacts at Emory University. In keeping with his high standards for Assia's domestic performance, Hughes specifically forbids her from wearing dressing gowns in the morning in an undated letter that contains the "Draft Constitution" of house rules he created; concerning her schedule, he dictates in writing that she cannot sleep past 8:00 a.m., unless he approves. In addition, we also know that Assia would fall asleep to music as a self-soothing technique, it seems, when she was upset, even if the music itself did not strike her. While on a trip with Hughes but left on her own in a hotel for two days, Assia records in her journal that she fell asleep one evening listening to Beethoven's String Quartet No. 13, Opus 130, on the radio, her aversion to it notwithstanding. "I couldn't bear the dark with the quartet playing. It was sinister," she writes to herself (qtd. in Koren and Negev 200–201). And yet she did bear it—with music that made it worse. This journal entry was penned two days before she died, and it appears the music she had formerly loved could not comfort her the way she hoped. This Assia is despairing, but the Assia who appears in a dressing gown as the last one to arise from bed to turn off the music in the Hughes household in *Doonreagan*—the children are outside playing and Hughes is already at work unpacking boxes from their move in scene 1 when she appears—is both impractical and historically inaccurate in light of gendered expectations and realities for Assia in the life she lived, as documented in the archive. But the Assia of *Doonreagan* announces she was "meant for grandeur" after the Hughes of the play updates her about the local household help that Assia did not know existed, which also seems very far-fetched, given that Assia was the one who was most responsible for childcare and domestic work according to the "Draft Constitution."

When Hughes informs Assia that they need to pretend that they are married in order to maintain appearances and good standing in *Doonreagan*, Assia "looks at him," "smiles," and "giggles" in the stage directions before she makes her joke about "seducing" the parish priest: "Oh a priest! Perhaps I should have a go at seducing him?" (33).[12] The Hughes character immediately replies that they need to be careful, which implies that he takes Assia's jest seriously or at least that he views her humor as improper, and rightfully so: Assia retorts (or jests, depending on how her character's behavior is interpreted), "Says who?" (34). Rebelliously opposing norms and propriety, Assia giggles at the idea of their blended family being a "normal English family," as Hughes phrases it before she makes her indelicate joke about the priest. What we might recall from chapter 4 is that, unfortunately, Assia hinged her life on marrying Hughes and being a "normal English family." She would not have been likely to make such jokes or to have taken her personal situation so lightly when her letters to Hughes plead for him to commit to her and Shura, and her journal, will and testament, and suicide note to her father attest to the same desire. Assia wished to make Hughes, herself, and their children a "legitimate" family. For example, although Shura's surname was legally Wevill, Assia inscribed her name as "Shura Hughes" on the back of the photograph of the one-year-old girl celebrating her birthday at Doonreagan in March 1966 (Koren and Negev 155). And Assia listed her own name as Mrs. Hughes in November 1966, while she was living with Hughes at Doonreagan, in her inscribed edition of David Wevill's 1966 poetry collection *A Christ of the Ice-Floes*, even though David Wevill was legally her husband (Bonhams, "Lot 506").[13] As a result, it is strange to read this exchange in *Doonreagan:*

TED:
Remember, this is a chance for us.
To live together.
Have a normal life.

ASSIA:
What's all this about a normal life?

TED:
At least give it a try! (35)

This scene intimates that Assia was somehow opposed to or refrained from striving for a "normal life" with Hughes, when the opposite is well documented in the archive and in *Lover of Unreason*.[14] Worse than the trivialization of the gendered constraints and challenges in Assia's life is the victim blaming that occurs in scene 1, setting the stage, so to speak, for the master antifeminist narratives that have plagued Assia since Hughes set them in motion. While Hughes's *Collected Poems* are not listed in the bibliography of works consulted at the end of *Doonreagan*, his *Selected Poems* are (and some of the *Capriccio* poems were printed therein), as well as *Birthday Letters* and *Letters of Ted Hughes*. It is clear that either what Hughes has related about Assia and/or the ever-present cultural bias toward vulnerable women and female victims has shaped the representation of Assia in this twenty-first-century play.

In scene 1 of *Doonreagan*, Hughes accuses Assia of begetting the trauma of Plath's suicide after she reveals that she feels haunted by Plath and has been having nightmares about Plath's death, possible signs of post-traumatic stress disorder. In *Doonreagan* and the Hughes-Plath-Assia story writ large, Hughes blames the female victim for her victimization. "Really Assia," Hughes tells her, "you've only got yourself to blame." He articulates the reason: "You allowed yourself to get too close." Assia did feel haunted by Plath, as Fay Weldon recounts in *Ted Hughes: Stronger than Death* and as Lucas Myers records in his memoir, but Assia was "too close" to Hughes, not to Plath, and Hughes exonerates himself from blame in the same scene.[15] The Hughes character in *Doonreagan* chastises Assia because she had not "walked away" when Plath died; she should have made herself "scarce," argues Hughes. Of course, the review of Assia's and Ted's correspondence with each other in chapter 4 proves that Hughes took the opposite position; he actively pursued Assia and persuaded her to stay with him. In the play, Hughes is cruel to Assia, but our sympathies strangely reside with him because we are led to think that Assia has brought all her suffering onto herself. Hughes accuses her of being false and acting "as if you'd lost your best friend" when Plath died, although there is no evidence of this behavior anywhere else. He proceeds to add insult to injury by cataloging the ways in which Assia (and no one else) has run afoul of the norms of basic decency (38): she moves into Plath's home, sleeps in her bed, minds her children, and wears her clothes (39). While there is no evidence that Assia wore Plath's clothes, we do know that Hughes moved into Plath's flat because she had prepaid the lease, and Assia went with him, which she could only have done with his approval. As for minding Plath's children, Hughes expected it, and in fact, he detailed in writing the ways in which Assia was to care for Frieda and Nicholas, his children with Plath. Hughes expected Assia to play board games and the like with the children one hour a day and to dedicate all of weekend afternoons to playing with them. She was instructed to maintain their clothes and wash the children, supervising their bedtime rituals. Each week, she was expected to teach two to three hours of German to them. Additionally, Assia was given very specific instructions about what kind of meals and food to serve to Plath's children and Hughes, and Hughes stipulated that Assia was expected to teach Frieda how to cook ("Draft Constitution"). In *Doonreagan*, Assia asks Hughes, "If what I did was so bad, why didn't you help me?" (39). Hughes excuses himself from culpability in response, but we need to wonder the same thing. Only then will we begin to reframe or reset a troubling master narrative concerning Assia specifically and women more generally.

Much of *Doonreagan* continues to maintain what I think of as the official party line constructed by Hughes when he alludes to Assia in his writing, especially his poetry. There will always be multiple verifiable perspectives on any story, but *Doonreagan* does not quite get it right when it has Assia sharply rebuke Hughes for maintaining correspondence with Aurelia Plath, Plath's mother, in scene 2. The factual errors in *Doonreagan* remind us that the basic story being told may be riddled with errors, too, and this is an important ethical reminder when it comes to exhuming and retelling stories or myths (especially about people) that have long held their shape. *Doonreagan* suggests that Hughes was a principal correspondent with Aurelia Plath, but

Assia assumed that role for him, and she was the one who kept Aurelia Plath abreast of the news concerning Frieda and Nicholas Hughes: she became "the channel of information" about Aurelia Plath's grandchildren in what became an "unlikely correspondence" (Koren and Negev 182). According to Richard Larschan, an English professor who served as Aurelia Plath's confidant, he was amazed to see letters from Assia to her. "I remember registering amazement," he admits, "that Assia would write so familiarly to the mother of someone for whose death she, in some measure, could be considered at least partially responsible." He describes Assia's tone in the letters to Aurelia Plath as "very much that of a daughter seeking parental support" and says that Assia's letters revealed "frequent mentions of emotional and physical abuse, some of it, I seem to recollect, sexual" (Larschan qtd. in Koren and Negev 182).[16] Koren and Negev note that Larschan remembers reading similar allegations of domestic violence at Hughes's hands in Plath's letters to her mother, and Larschan remarks upon "the tremendous resemblance between the two women's anguished tone" in their letters to Aurelia Plath (Larschan qtd. in Koren and Negev 183).[17] This scenario reminds us why studying Assia and Plath is relevant in many ways to us now; their lives can function as case studies that show how the personal is political as well as ignite educational discussions about what gendered violence or abuse entails.

Scene 3 of *Doonreagan* delivers the same rehashing of antifeminist sentiments, which, taken together, function to discredit Assia as a victim or as someone we can identify with or feel sympathy toward. Assia proudly declares herself a "femme fatale" in *Doonreagan* (55), and Hughes affirms that Assia possesses a "dark dangerous sensuality" that he is "too weak to resist" (58). In other words, Hughes cannot be accountable for what has transpired with Assia or as a result of being with her. Assia's role as femme fatale and her desirability to men in a patriarchal culture ostensibly transform her into the perpetrator of any crimes that have been committed. *Doonreagan* even assigns her the role of instigator and manipulator of the affair with Hughes in scene 4: she concedes, "I was playing you, like a master fisherman." Laughing, she informs him, "You swallowed it—hook, line and sinker!" The Assia of *Doonregan* lies—Hughes accuses her of lying—and she flaunts her "powers" (68). Her powers include taunting Plath about Hughes the day before Plath commits suicide (70); the Assia of *Doonreagan* implies that she cruelly disclosed she was pregnant to Plath, and Hughes, flabbergasted and horrified, concludes, "That would explain everything!" (73). The play resorts to the antifeminist strategy of pitting Plath and Assia against each other to deflect male involvement, with the end result of the two destroying each other; Plath initially visits Assia to gloat about Hughes returning to her before Assia crushes her with the news of the pregnancy. In general, Assia emerges as the most unlikable character over the course of the play because she seemingly cannot maintain good graces and forms, in contrast to Hughes. Unlike Hughes, who refrains from bawdy talk, Assia continues to make sex jokes at inappropriate times: she likens herself and Hughes to rabbits having sex after he confides in her about his struggle living with Plath (55).[18] In the same scene, she jokes about "lucky Irish girls and their swarthy Spanish sailors," while Hughes recounts the history of Cashel (57). Ultimately, *Doonreagan* scapegoats Assia by painting her as a conniving femme fatale who toys with Hughes and inadvertently kills Plath.

FRIEDA HUGHES'S *ALTERNATIVE VALUES:* "FOR SHURA," "MEMORY LOSS 4: NESTING," AND "MOTHERS"

The epigraph to this chapter comes from the opening lines of "For Shura," from *Alternative Values: Poems and Paintings* (2015) by Frieda Hughes, Plath and Hughes's daughter and a poet in her own right. "For Shura" closes the collection, privileging it as the text that has the last word and highlighting its relevancy—not only is it the closing poem of a masterful collection, but it is timely, as one of her latest poems, and the tone of the poem is highlighted with an accompanying painting. As the only poem that overtly treats Assia and Shura in the collection, it resonates with a pathos that is not easy to dispel.[19] "For Shura" is a poem that propagates the story line created and established by Ted Hughes: in it, Assia assumes the primary role of thief (many times over) as well as the secondary role of cuckoo. The speaker of "For Shura" roundly castigates the memory of Assia in poetic apostrophe to Shura, and in doing so, the speaker continues to (re)draw and mark the contentious and exacting party lines in Plath-Hughes studies for twenty-first-century readers, teachers, and scholars.[20] What is special and unique to the poem is its powerful appeal to pathos, which carries a stark pain embedded in it; this is authored by someone affected by the very tragedies of suicides and filicide described in the poem and by someone who has lived in the aftermath of Assia's decisions, actions, and behavior. It is also authored by a talented poet and painter, who chooses to represent Assia in a poem and an accompanying painting that refuse to bear her name. While the speaker may not represent Frieda Hughes's exact thoughts and feelings in "For Shura," the poem sets in motion, by virtue of its publication in a beautiful art and poetry book and through its unapologetic harnessing of autobiographical and biographical details of real people—namely, Plath, Shura, and Assia—a discourse that refuses to relent in its perpetuation of the narratives of Ted Hughes's *Capriccio* and, to a lesser degree, the binary opposition or polarity of Assia as other and the author or reader as normative subject in Plath's poetry.

The reference to Frieda Hughes's poem in the epigraph to this chapter asks us to consider what Shura and, by extension, Frieda (as a character in the poem) have lost with Assia's choices to take what does not belong to her, specifically Frieda's father and/or mother and Shura's life. The first stanza of "For Shura" is quoted in its entirety here; the speaker wonders, as she addresses Shura, whether she, the speaker/Frieda, has prevented Shura from accessing their father, from claiming even "a father" (1). As half-sisters, Frieda asks Shura rhetorically, in apostrophe, whether she has somehow participated in a kind of traumatic theft of Shura's father, whom we know was notoriously absent as a stable father figure in Shura's life (see chapter 4), in a manner similar to the way that Assia has "denied me mine" (3). In this first accusation, the speaker alludes to Assia, the mother of Shura and the mother figure in the poem who usurps the birth mother's place in the speaker's life. The implication here is that Assia has prevented Frieda from having what is rightfully hers—a mother and, arguably, a father in the ambiguous pronoun antecedent: "Have I denied you a father / As your mother / Denied me mine?" (1–3). These lines could be understood to mean: Assia denied Frieda her mother when Assia became involved with Plath's husband, which, arguably, ruined the marriage and Plath's life and which, in turn, led to suicide. Another interpretation is that Assia denied Frieda a father through Assia's involvement with Ted Hughes, due to his preoccupation with Assia, a preoccupation that would lead him away from home in Devon and take him to London as well as Spain, Germany, Italy, and elsewhere with her (and often Shura). Both readings fit the context and content of the poem. Truly, "For Shura" could have been titled "For Shura and Assia," as Assia is invoked more often than Shura in the poem, but Assia is written out of the title and never named in the poem (though always present and animating the content), just as she has been written out of the official narrative Ted Hughes offered. And like her father, Frieda Hughes argues in her literary work that the responsibility for the fault lines in the Plath-Hughes family unit is attributed to Assia and are of Assia's making, as we will see in the next stanza.

In continuing the narratives set forward by her parents, Frieda Hughes asserts that neither Shura nor Assia resembles the Plath-Hughes family members, and she indicates that Shura will be vulnerable to violent victimization in a way not dissimilar from what the speaker has suffered by Assia's actions. Indeed, Assia, much as she appears in Ted Hughes's *Capriccio,* is portrayed as a thief, an accessory to Plath's murder, and a murderer herself in connection with Shura. Regarding the first two allegations, the speaker explains that the Assia character

> unpicked the threads that wove
> My fabric so she could see
> Right through my holes

To my own dead mother,
Whose place she took uneasily
As if donning a still bloodied human skin

So we children might not smell
Her different scent; the guilty,
Furtive act of replacement. (7–15)

The poem, while indicting and condemning Assia without ever uttering her name, addresses the deceased Shura with the understanding that the speaker and Shura's commonalities lie in blood ties and the shared experience of trauma. Like the speaker, Shura loses her mother, and both losses are attributed indirectly and directly to Assia. The speaker explains that her mother committed suicide, but she points out that the Assia figure assumes the lost mother's place with guilt and furtiveness, suggesting that Assia played a role in Plath's death and/or that Assia wrongfully but knowingly took on the role of mother to the speaker. The trauma detailed by the speaker is couched in figurative language, but the prominent metaphor of a hole resonates with what we know about the condition from trauma studies. The injury is figured as a hole twice over, which indicates that the trauma is a founding trauma—in other words, the basis of her identity (LaCapra 161)—for the speaker: both in the Assia figure's implied metaphorical undoing of the speaker so "she could see / Right through my holes" and in the speaker's acknowledgment of a "mother-shaped hole / That howled in the wind like a cave" (17–18). The accompanying painting *For Shura* by Frieda Hughes features beautifully colored abstract elements that never blend together or bleed into each other. Depicted in the painting are holes that are intersected by abstract lines, but each element retains its unique individuality without taking on the attributes of what is near it or with what intersects it (Hughes, *Alternative Values* 108). The painting functions as the perfect counterpart to the poem.

Much as Shura cannot fit into the Plath-Hughes family, no other "would-be mothers" can fill the hole left by the death of her biological one (23), the speaker explains, and that she and others who experience the same scenario are left behind to endure the would-be mothers'

> thinly disguised aversion to you
>
> As they took your mother's place,
> Unable to ignore the fact
> You wore your mother's face. (24–27)

Assia comes under censure here for her role in Frieda's life, which may account for the hostility directed at Assia in the tone and content of a poem that is ostensibly about Shura but is more about Assia than Shura. Virtually every stanza (nine out of ten, with the exception of stanza 6) mentions the Assia figure. By contrast, five out of ten stanzas directly reference or allude to Shura. The family story narrated by "For Shura" is important in its recognition of the traumatic outcomes following suicide(s) for the bereaved, but it is important, too, in its adherence to the poetic narratives about Assia crafted by Ted Hughes. It continues the stories about Assia embedded in *Capriccio* and carries those from the twentieth century into the twenty-first. But the Plath-Hughes-Assia triangle has always been complicated and contested in scholarship and in the real world, where no easy answers or summations are to be had. For instance, from Ted Hughes's and Assia's accounts in letters and journal entries and in Assia's last will, as we saw in chapter 3, Assia understood herself to be a loving mother figure to Plath and Hughes's children and to her own child with Hughes. Even Ted Hughes admitted as much when he confided in a letter to his brother, Gerald Hughes, that the experiment of escaping England and living with Assia, Frieda, Nicholas, and Shura as a blended family unit in Ireland was successful, from his point of view. According to Ted Hughes, in that April 1966 letter, "This place is a mild paradise for me at present." He continues: "The kids are brimming over. Assia is here with me and a complete success" (256).

Instead of discord, Hughes characterizes his life with Assia and their blended family as idyllic *at the time that he is living it.* It is only after Assia's death, in which Assia assigned him the blame for her suicide, that he needed to figure out what went wrong and to piece together his own life and its narratives among the traumatic fragments in ways that were meaningful to him and others.

But "For Shura" does not speak to a successful blended family dynamic or reference the idyllic time in Ireland. Instead, it focuses on the intrusion of Assia and Shura on a family unit that they have no right to claim as theirs. The speaker declares that Shura is a "Cuckoo" the speaker wants to "undo," much as "your mother [Assia] undid me" (5–6). The denotations of *cuckoo* include applications to a person, especially "in reference to the [cuckoo] bird's . . . habit of laying its eggs in the nests of other birds," and the *Oxford English Dictionary* notes that *cuckoo* has come to mean "fool" or "silly person" in its generic slang sense ("Cuckoo, n. 3"). It also points to a "crazy" person, someone who is "out of one's wits," in American slang ("Cuckoo, adj."). In informing us that Shura is "cuckoo," the speaker wants us to understand that Shura could never have blended into the Hughes family, despite Assia's poaching of a home or family in taking over the nest figuratively, because she is fundamentally or essentially unlike them and because she is perceived as undesirable in both the denotations and connotations of what *cuckoo* means.

In closing, "For Shura" places the culpability squarely on the Assia figure for causing the problems in both the speaker's and Shura's lives. Ultimately, Assia is remembered by the speaker as having committed the unforgettable and unforgiveable act against Shura: "But what she did in stopping breath / Was steal your choice to live a life" (28–29). The speaker holds Assia up as the villain in the story of "For Shura." And for someone as close to the situation as Frieda Hughes, that is certainly understandable. The lives of her family are far more than the texts that literary and women's studies scholars dissect, and academic analyses must seem reductive: heavy-handed and wrongheaded. In the academic tracking of narratives, construction of theoretical frameworks, analyses of contexts, and consideration of significance in existing and new conversations, scholars would approach and understand the texts and contexts differently than someone personally affected by the situation. From my perspective, Frieda Hughes's "For Shura" is a remarkable poem in both literary studies and women's studies: it asks us to consider how we frame and understand the Plath-Hughes-Assia story in the twenty-first century, and it shows us how trauma is an injury that affects the mind, body, and heart. It takes resilience to rebound from trauma, and "For Shura" is a testament to pain and resilience, marking the death of Plath at thirty years old in its thirty lines more than a half-century after the traumatic event.

Frieda Hughes's "Memory Loss 4: Nesting," also from *Alternative Values,* tackles gendered displacement within a home or family unit. In many details, it rings true to Frieda Hughes's biography, lending it special significance as the speaker thinks through what it feels like to be out of place, to feel illegitimate, to question one's rights to the family. Of course, a sense of not belonging and illegitimacy was a source of Assia's distress over her relationship with Ted Hughes and his relationship with their daughter, Shura, but any identification with Assia or Shura is thwarted in this poem. Frieda Hughes would not likely choose to interrogate received and perceived narratives about Assia because she could not and would not identify with Assia—and who could expect her to do so?

The speaker classes herself a "borrowed" child in "Memory Loss 4: Nesting" and assesses her situation with respect to "my father's women" (18), of which Assia was an important one. From their behavior toward her, the speaker concludes that she must be "different" and so "must have been adopted" (19, 20). The sense of displacement within the home is startling throughout the poem, but what is noteworthy about "Memory Loss 4: Nesting," with respect to Plath's poems and Hughes's poems about Assia, is that Frieda Hughes continues the narrative of Assia as an unnatural mother. Though she loved Frieda, Assia emerges in this poem, lumped with Ted Hughes's other women, as a false and untrue mother, someone who fails in mothering and nurturing the speaker.[21] The speaker witnesses her family and their interactions as an outsider in her own home because of the neglect and displacement. "Memory Loss 4: Nesting" is a profoundly sad and moving poem that allows us to see how what I have termed the "good life" for Assia in chapter 4—in short, a unified family and a legitimate home base, both of which contribute mightily to belonging, identity, and security—is what the speaker most desires. The accompanying painting is titled *Memory Loss 4*, and it appears much more textured and rougher than the other paintings that allude to Assia. Compared to the paintings *For Shura* and *Mothers*, it looks chaotic, which fits with the theme of cognitive dissonance in the poem: the speaker knows she is not adopted but wonders whether she might be all the same as a result of her inability to fit in—to be left at odds within a family and a home, both of which should serve as sanctuaries.

"Mothers," another poem in *Alternative Values* and the last in the group of three that allude to Assia, links "Memory Loss 4: Nesting" with "For Shura," making its placement between the two very effective. "Mothers" explores trauma as a founding trauma, the source of an identity, of the great psychological and emotional wound that does not heal with time ("to acknowledge what it was; a bottomless pit / That would always be part of my life / And into which no one would fit" [29–31]). For the speaker, her mother's death leaves her "Lop-sided because of the hole" (2), and the "hole became a kind of cave / In which my cry for my lost parent / Would echo plaintively" (3–5). No one is able to replace the beloved mother, and the implication is that the legacy of the speaker's mother precludes others from ever fitting: the "other women" who fall into the mother-shaped hole perceive the biological mother in the child (8)—"They saw my mother in me, / And heard my mother's voice" (10–11)—when the speaker asks for attention or ice cream from them, sweet requests that underscore the bitterness of the situation for the speaker. The other mothers are finally dismissed with this assessment: they are "Unable to fit, or unwilling to take on the challenge, / Or live long enough" (16–17). Assia is indicted more than once: she does not fit, as we see in "For Shura," and she is perhaps unwilling or unable to take on the challenge in "Memory Loss 4: Nesting." In "Mothers," she is faulted for not living long enough: she and the other would-be mothers (to borrow the language of "For Shura") cannot stop up the "mother-shaped hole" that "let in the wind to chill me," says the speaker (18). Moreover, Assia is an "unrelated woman," and the speaker realizes that "no unrelated woman / Could resolve this" (20–21). Of course, the grand irony is that Assia desperately wanted to be related by marriage and have those familial ties with Ted Hughes and his children. The tentacles in the accompanying illustration of the painting *Mothers* are reminiscent of the tentacles in Plath's poem "Medusa," which is about Plath's mother and Frieda Hughes's grandmother. The painting depicts the scenario of losing a mother and enduring the subsequent mothering from other women as potentially harmful and constrictive; the formidable tentacles fill the slate and appear as barriers to the viewer. Nothing can be seen beyond them, which is a fitting representation of the theme of founding trauma in the poem "Mothers."

THE BBC DOCUMENTARY *TED HUGHES: STRONGER THAN DEATH*

For the first time in documentary history, Assia receives a significant amount of dedicated screen time, approximately ten minutes altogether, in *Ted Hughes: Stronger than Death.* This is a noteworthy development in that Assia, as we have seen in chapter 1, has been essentially erased from literary history, other than as a footnoted villain. The 2015 documentary approaches her as a seductress *and* a victim, thereby complicating the received twentieth-century (and to some extent, twenty-first-century) representations of her. It also positions her as an important person in Hughes's life—so much so that she is introduced in a photograph at the very beginning. The documentary highlights clips from Assia's 1965 Sea Witch commercial, suggesting that she, like Hughes, was accomplished in her respective field. Featured are interviews with her contemporaries, who present conflicting views of Assia, which is fitting as Assia is certainly a controversial and complicated figure in literary history and cultural studies but also was, it appears, in her actual life.

Several examples further the discursive formation of Assia as a villain in the documentary. Edward Lucie-Smith, who worked with Assia at Notley's, comments: "In those days, advertising was regarded as the work of the devil. Yet it's surprising how many poets and writers were employed by the big advertising agencies." This quotation positions Assia in our own day: it considers her as doing the work of the devil (and being very successful at it), but it also indicates that Assia was a talented writer working with other talented and ambitious writers in an era when commercial advertising was denigrated. Lucie-Smith discloses that Assia allegedly thought of herself as a seductress, in that she told him engaging Hughes was "like taking candy from a baby." Apparently, she also divulged details of a sexual encounter with Hughes, prompting Lucie-Smith to dub her a "sexual success." That anecdote and interpretation contribute to Assia's legacy as the hated literary seductress—then and now.[22] Later in the documentary, however, Lucie-Smith infers that Assia became a kind of victim in her adulation of Plath in a startling rhetorical move: he states that Assia tried to emulate Plath, who was a "disastrous model" for Assia. Qualifying his earlier comments on Assia as a brash, sexual creature, Lucie-Smith's take on Assia is that she was always looking for an identity of her own. "Assia," he says, "was essentially a lost soul." For her part, Fay Weldon, a friend and confidante of Assia, recalls what Assia told her about the affair. Offended that Plath had purportedly asked her to peel potatoes like a servant, Assia went down to the garden and "chatted up" Ted, and they kissed behind the beanpoles, which was the start of the affair, according to Weldon, who emphasizes that Assia felt pride at having captured his attention.

In contrast to Lucie-Smith and Weldon, Elaine Feinstein and Ruth Fainlight paint Assia as a victim of Plath's suicide and public censure. Feinstein asserts that Assia felt "quite lonely and hated in the literary world" in 1965, and Fainlight describes the transformation of Assia from "the evil demon incarnate" to a close friend as she felt "more and more sorry" for Assia. She compares Assia to the Eve who is expelled from the Garden of Eden. Returning to Weldon, the documentary spotlights Weldon's story about having tea with Assia, in which Assia claims to see the ghostly Plath. Becoming pale, Assia states that Plath haunts her, and Weldon shares her impression that Assia was filled with fear—not guilt. These interviews and their attendant declarations cast Assia in various guises: she emerges for the twenty-first-century viewer variously in this documentary as a vindictive seductress at the height of her powers (via Lucie-Smith and Weldon); as a devil or demon (via Lucie-Smith and Fainlight); as a vulnerable woman needing validation or affirmation in the eyes of a talented man, such as Hughes (via Weldon and Lucie-Smith); and as a victim (via Feinstein, Fainlight, Weldon, and Lucie-Smith) who knowingly duplicated Plath's tragic suicide out of despair (via Feinstein and Lucie-Smith). What is extraordinary about the mapping of Assia in this documentary is the claim of victim's status for Assia as well as what might be interpreted as a moderate or tempered sympathy for her. Feinstein concludes by remarking upon Hughes's predilection in making "his women" his muse, and we know this is true for Hughes, as chapter 3 argues. Unfortunately for Assia and for women more broadly, we have continued to convey the message through multiple mediums—as we see in this chapter and throughout this book—that some women deserve victimhood, that some lives do not matter as much as others, and that we can do and say whatever we like with few reservations when it comes to the lives and bodies of women.

NEW DIRECTIONS: MOVING FORWARD

How Assia is represented has everything to do with women's studies and literature: engaging such representations has serious repercussions that affect a reading, and nonreading, public inside and outside the classroom because how women are represented—how they are treated, discussed, studied, analyzed, documented, and received—ultimately will influence the ways in which we perceive women. As

Gail Crowther remarks, "Ghosts are not merely alive through remembrance, but alive through their very presence as a transformative potential within our lives; we do not simply remember ghosts and choose to give them voice, but rather they impact directly on our lives, transforming the sort of person we may be, guiding our choices, bringing about positive change and influencing decisions that we may make" (20). In extending this line of argument to the heuristic impulse of this book, I hope that we can stage a feminist intervention for Assia and women like her in the classroom, in our scholarship, in our book groups, on the internet and social media, and more broadly, in the public sphere. Interpreting and presuming to understand Assia and what she has embodied or been made to stand for has more to do with our own values and biases than it does with the actual historical person. As representations of Assia continue to be created, revised, and staged, it becomes apparent to me that we need discussions and additional scholarship about how to move forward in empowering women in abstract and practical ways. We need to address how we talk about women, with an examination into sexism and victimhood and how women are made to disappear or be subjected to abuse and denigration under the guises of scholarship, teaching, entertainment, and the arts more generally, in big and small ways.

In "Literature and Its Publics: Past, Present, and Future," which was his 2016 MLA Presidential Address, Roland Greene makes the case that literary interpretation can be a critical tool in "culture making" and that it "builds collectivities while casting universalism in a critical light" (600). As he observes, the "27,000 members of the MLA will speak to ten or even a hundred times that readership in our classrooms. When we process interpretation to our students, and especially when we enact the office of reading observantly and reflectively, we make a public for our field" (601). I would add that in addition to cultivating a public for our field, we also possess the opportunity to participate in bystander intervention when we ask critical questions about gendered bodies, gendered identities, and victimhood and expect ourselves and others to read closely and thus engage and interpret texts that reflect back to us, through our readings, how we perceive and understand the texts and, by extension, our world, with the intention of complicating or changing the conversations about women and gendered violence. Assia serves as a kind of literary case study in which we can map, track, and challenge how she is represented and why those representations—and challenges—matter now. For my part, Assia has long interested me as a scholar of women's literature, identity politics, and trauma studies. I see her as a figure who has been shaped by antifeminist discourses that set up impossible standards and expectations for women. Additionally, what we encounter when we study Assia are the values of what we like about desirable women and what we condemn in undesirable women; we would do well to problematize and contest those values that circumscribe what it can mean to be a woman personally and professionally. And on a personal level, I take seriously, as surely most of us do, my responsibilities to empower, embolden, encourage, and protect the women and girls, men and boys, in my life because gendered scripts circumscribe everyone. This book will serve its purpose if Assia's life can be viewed and understood as a paradigm that demonstrates the personal is political, that literature and the "real world" reflect and inform each other, and that women's lives and bodies need championing now as much as ever.

NOTES

CHAPTER 1.

RECOVERING ASSIA WEVILL: AN INTRODUCTION

1. Although I concentrate on the period of Assia's life and work following her marriage to her third husband, David Wevill, I will refer to Assia by her distinctive first name, as is common in publications when she is referenced, instead of by one of her more ephemeral last names.

2. See my essay "Interpretations and Implications of Trauma and Narrative in Sylvia Plath's *Ariel.*" *Journal of Literature and Trauma Studies,* vol. 1, no. 2, Fall 2012, pp. 117–46.

3. According to Joan Retallack, "This century's formal investigations into experiences of silence have meant opening up previously inaccessible or unacknowledged or forbidden territory, where the very act of attending entails a figure/ground shift" (111). The situation Retallack articulates is very much at play and is an undercurrent to the recovery efforts of this book.

4. Yehuda Koren and Eilat Negev elaborate: "Amichai's poem 'The Death of Assia G.' was written in Hebrew just hours after he received a phone call from Olwyn [Hughes], telling him of [Assia's] death. It was published a few weeks later in the major Israeli literary magazine *Moznayim* (Volume 29, 1969). Later he included it in his book *Shelo al meant Lizkor* (Shoken Publishing House, 1971). (The Hebrew title of the collection means 'and not to remember'—but the book was not translated as a whole into English.) [Amichai also] included the Assia poem in the 1973 English volume *Songs of Jerusalem and Myself.* The Hebrew title of 1969 stated Assia's full first name ("The Death of Assia G.") while, in English, in the 1973 volume [the title was listed as] 'The Death of A.G.' probably because [Amichai] wanted to protect his very good friend Hughes and make it more obscure for British and American readers, who were more familiar with Hughes" (personal correspondence).

5. Jonathan Bate contextualizes this letter in his Ted Hughes biography: while Plath was angry, hurt, and worried about money, she also had times when she "felt as [Hughes did]" about their separation (202). Bate points out that Plath produced her best work while separated from Hughes, and he explores Plath's complicated relationship with Al Alvarez (202, 313).

6. It is important to note that Assia did feel envious of Plath. She writes of Plath's "muscular brain" and her "envy of [Plath's] splendid brilliance" on 31 November 1966 (Assia qtd. in Koren and Negev 161). While living with Hughes at Court Green, Assia

slept in Plath's bed, used her household goods, and read Plath's notebooks, which invoked, in Assia's words, "a strong sensation of [Plath's] repugnant live presence" (qtd. in Koren and Negev 160). See "Assia Wevill, 29–31 November 1966 [Journal Entries]" for the extant 31 November 1966 journal entry. In a different journal entry, Assia admits to jealousy over Hughes's preoccupations, of which "at the forefront is Sylvia" (qtd. in Koren and Negev 126). As Koren and Negev explain, "[Assia's] sense of inferiority was intensified by Plath's giant shadow and her own place at the bottom of Ted's priorities" (126). In her journal, Assia lamented that Plath "had a million times the talent, 1,000 times the will, 100 times the greed and passion that I have" (qtd. in Koren and Negev 126). After visiting Assia, Anne Alvarez recalled, "She was so beautiful, and kept on talking about Sylvia, and I thought that she had serious identity problems, and is breaking down." As a psychologist, Alvarez expressed concern over Assia's situation and her response to it: "She had no chance, she was doomed from the start. Professionally I would say she had a counter-phobic reaction, and wanted to demonstrate that she was not afraid of Sylvia's demon. For her own good, she would have been much better off not to sleep in Sylvia's bed" (qtd. in Koren and Negev 142). For her part, Assia confided in her journal that she found herself in "this nightmare maze of miserable, censorious, middle-aged furies, and Sylvia, my predecessor, between our heads at night" (qtd. in Bate 221). Murphy remembers: "I had seen Assia in Middlesex Hospital, where she had gone for tests in February 1968 because she feared she had cancer. In fact she was suffering from depression and anxiety, but looked well, reclining on pillows, surrounded by flowers, beautiful as ever" (275).

7. See the letter to Jannice Porter, in which Assia dubs the 23 Fitzroy Road house a "ghost house"; it is reproduced within a series of photographs between pp. 142 and 143 in Koren and Negev's book.

8. Hughes wrote to Assia on 7 February 1965: "Do you know what oppresses me? the thought that you save my letters. You said recently—I forget what, but enough to make me think some day somebody might get hold of those letters & make hay. Assia, I'm foolishly oppressed enough as it is with bloody eavesdroppers & filchers & greedy curiosity, & if you're going to be sitting on all that for some Suzette suddenly to lay her hands on [. . . .] Past experience is bad enough to cope with, but it clears itself—it doesn't really oppose our present lives, whereas those letters & that diary of yours do. They're in our way. They've already caused enough trouble. So please burn all my letters" (236). Assia did not burn his letters to her. As a result, sixty-one letters written by Hughes to Assia were purchased in 2005, seven years after his death, and the acquisition of the letters was a newsworthy event ("Emory Acquires Love Letters of Ted Hughes and Assia Wevill"). Now Assia is part of Hughes's story in a more profound way, especially as other texts by her were also acquired.

9. Ted's sister, Olwyn Hughes, declared in an interview in 2013: "I'm sick of reading that [Ted] left [Plath] for Assia—that's all you get whenever his name is mentioned. Assia."

10. In her March 1967 letter to her sister, Celia Chaikin, Assia confesses to being suicidal. She goes on to state: "I'm clearly ill. The last four years have been a strain, simply too hard to bear" (qtd. in Koren and Negev 163). According to her biographers, Assia "had made a few attempts on her life in the past, but they seemed to be demonstrative, a plea for sympathy." When she was twenty, Assia had her stomach pumped after swallowing aspirins; she had been "shocked and outraged" that her husband at the time, John Steele, had decided to move to Canada from England without consulting her, and she responded in extreme fashion. During her second marriage, to Richard "Dick" Lipsey, Assia swallowed pills in despair in front of her husband on two different occasions because she "felt cheated, thinking she was entitled to a better life" (Koren and Negev 163, 41, 57). Lipsey understood Assia's suicide attempts as "a clear cry for help, and not a deliberate attempt to end her life" (qtd. in Koren and Negev 57). Toward the end, when her life was at its most unstable and insecure, Assia's friends recount that she talked of suicide more than once (Koren and Negev 195–97). Mira Hamermesh, a friend of Assia, recounts: "We had all been through the humiliation of waiting for a man to ring, so we didn't take [talk of suicide] seriously, especially as Assia always said it with a smile, out of the blue, in the middle of dinner. We had all been in therapy, and were told that people who sound the alarm never commit suicide" (qtd. in Koren and Negev 195–96). Assia confided in Chris Wilkins, her former coworker, "that she was worried about her insecurity, and wanted to marry again and settle, but things were not going right with Ted" (Koren and Negev 197). Assia revealed "that she couldn't stand the state of things as they were, and if it didn't change, she would kill herself" (Wilkins qtd. in Koren and Negev 197).

11. Assia remains largely ungrievable in the literary imagination and in popular culture because of her archetypal role as the beautiful but destructive woman who destroyed the Plath-Hughes marriage, herself, and her child.

12. Koren and Negev speculate that Hughes agreed to talk about Assia "maybe because the journalist came from Assia's country, maybe because he thought that an interview in Hebrew would remain obscure and be no risk to his privacy." Koren and Negev comment, "He hardly ever gave interviews, and avoided talking about his personal tragedies, but this time he did" (226).

13. In a striking parallel, Ted Hughes was cheated, arguably, from living a life without critical abuse, especially in relation to Plath's suicide. In her first interview with the BBC in 2015, Frieda Hughes accused feminist critics of abusing her father during his lifetime to such a degree that his life had essentially become co-opted. As Frieda Hughes maintains, "I was appalled that something that happened in 1963 could be carried forward." She explains, "For outsiders—because that's what they are, outsiders—to make judgments that affect somebody in their life, for all of their life, is a sort of horrible form of theft." Further, she adds, "it's an abuse." See news articles citing Frieda Hughes's interview with BBC producers (Furness). Ted Hughes's own anger over intrusive feminist work on Plath and its ramifications for her surviving

family members reveals itself in his poem "The Dogs Are Eating Your Mother" from *Birthday Letters* (*Collected Poems* 1168–69).

CHAPTER 2.

SYLVIA PLATH'S REPRESENTATIONS OF ASSIA WEVILL

1. Though she appears to reinforce notions of what makes a "good woman" and a "bad woman" in terms of traditional femininity, Plath addresses what we would understand as the sexist ideologies of her time in her work and life in various ways, as this chapter will explore. Because Plath was influenced by D. H. Lawrence and Ted Hughes, Plath's poems exhibit an aesthetic indebted to them: a "strong" and "masculine aesthetic" (Clark 20). As she framed it, Plath committed herself to "the great subjects of life: love, death, war" (qtd. in Clark 20). In particular, she appreciated Lawrence's determination to display life in all its facets; Plath quotes Lawrence approvingly: "Even beauty has its thorns and its nettle-stings and its poppy-poison. Nothing is without offense & nothing should be: if it is part of life, & not merely abstraction" (Plath and Lawrence qtd. in Clark 18). Within this aesthetic, Plath produced poems that appear overtly feminist and poems that seemingly entertain a complicated relationship with feminism as Plath both endorsed and critiqued femininity in her life and work.

2. In her short essay styled as a memoir, Linda Gates, an American, provides reminiscences of her time in England in 1964; she arrived in London "almost a year to the day" that Plath died (106). Gates spent time in the company of Ted Hughes and Assia, while Gates was dating Al Alvarez; Assia and Hughes visited them often. As Gates states, "Although Al was very sweet and tried hard, it was really a man's world in those days. Women were referred to as 'birds,' and generally sat quietly and listened to the men talk." Gates recalls that she and Assia were generally left out of the conversations between Alvarez and Hughes (107).

3. For instance, on 20 June 1959, Plath records her disappointment in not being able to conceive a child on a schedule, and she dismisses her career, her worth as a person, her sexual pleasure, her writing, and the value of her childfree body in her esteem of the archetypal earth mother figure. In her assessment of her body-in-situation, Plath seemingly predicates her worth and self-love on being able to conceive a child. Furthermore, in her ideal rendering of her world, she figures Hughes as a patriarch (her word) and herself as a mother. Plath writes in her journal: "I want to be an Earth Mother in the deepest richest sense. I have turned from being an intellectual, a career woman: all that is ash to me." She continues: "Suddenly everything is ominous, ironic, deadly. If I could not have children—and if I do not ovulate how can I?—how can they make me?—I would be dead. Dead to my

woman's body. Intercourse would be dead, a dead-end. My pleasure no pleasure, a mockery. My writing a hollow and failing substitute for real life, real feeling, instead of a pleasant extra, a bonus flowering and fruiting. Ted should be a patriarch. I a mother. My love for him, to express our love, us, through my body, the doors of my body, utterly thwarted" (500). She returns to this discussion a bit later in the same journal entry: "I cried and cried. Last night, today. How can I keep Ted wedded to a barren woman? Barren barren" (501). As we can see, Plath prized the reproductive female body and, in this example, valued it more than her writing: at times, Plath's competing sociocultural-personal identities proved distressing for her.

4. As Clark records, Plath "blame[d] Assia Wevill for Hughes's betrayal, claiming Assia had 'brutalized Ted beyond belief'" in a letter to Olive Prouty, dated 15 December 1962 (164).

5. Women also actively participate in the construction of gender. Judith Butler refers to gender as a "script" with actors ("Performative Acts" 409). As she elucidates, gender is "a constructed identity, a performative accomplishment which the mundane social audience, including the actors themselves, come to believe and to perform in the mode of belief." Changing a gendered script is possible, according to Butler, "in the possibility of a different sort of repeating, in the breaking or subversive repetition of that style" (402). The female body is both a product and an agent in producing femininity (404).

6. Clark maintains that the speakers in Plath's poems "Daddy" and "Lady Lazarus" are actually types of the femme fatale woman (132).

7. Joan Retallack remarks, in "Rethinking: Literary: Feminism," that we will stumble upon the codification of the family romance in twentieth-century narratives. According to Retallack, "The at-large vanishing point for women is simply this: to the extent that we venture onto the post-Oedipal playing field of culture, or the sexual politics of the unreconstructed family constellation, our every role, every move is defined by the 'law of the father' in search of the good wife and mother" (128). In this vein, we will encounter the iterations of Assia as that which is not "good" in Plath's poetry, and these images are used to diminish her and women like her. In spite of the Assia poems, however, we would do well to recognize that Plath lived her life in ways that challenged the sexist assumption that women must forgo family and family life should they hold professional ambitions and wish to cultivate a career. Additionally, the poetic influence of Lawrence on Plath and her themes is explored by Clark in *The Grief of Influence;* the codes and linguistic system Plath employs in her Assia poems are not solely of her making.

8. In her discussion of images related to women, fetuses, and abortion, Susan Bordo invites us to reflect on the "evil mother" archetype. This archetype is "reflective of deep cultural *anxieties* about women's autonomy rather than the *realities* of its exercise," Bordo asserts (95). Bordo reminds us that the female body is a "medium of culture" (165).

9. I would like to note that because we are so immersed in our cultural milieu, it becomes nearly impossible for anyone to completely escape gendered scripts. To that end, we are all products of our cultures, and future generations of feminist scholars will be able to identify, mine, and address the limitations of my approach and that of others to Plath and Assia.

10. Elizabeth Grosz sets forth the problem: feminists have rejected "a fixed concept of the body to contain women" because this concept has been historically and culturally entrenched by men; feminists prefer "to define themselves in non- or extracorporeal terms, seeking an equality on intellectual and conceptual grounds or in terms of an abstract universalism or humanism." Avers Grosz, "The hostility that misogynist thought directs toward women and femininity had been commonly rationalized through the deprecation and derision of women's bodies" (14).

11. Ted Hughes maintained that Plath "was 'Laurentian,' not 'woman's lib'" (qtd. in Clark 34). In other words, Hughes interpreted Plath's views as falling in line with those espoused by D. H. Lawrence, rather than with those held by feminists.

12. Ted Hughes rearranged the collection of poems Plath left behind; she intended to call the manuscript *Ariel and Other Poems*. Hughes's version, titled *Ariel*, was published to wide and great acclaim in 1965. Frieda Hughes oversaw the publication of the facsimile edition of Plath's original manuscript in 2004; it is titled *Ariel: The Restored Edition*.

13. Historically, the event, which informs Plath's poem "Words heard, by accident, over the phone" as well as the biographies of Plath, Hughes, and Assia, has been of interest and significance to scholars. See Feinstein 126–28; Middlebrook 174–75; Bundtzen, "Poetic Arson"; Sigmund and Crowther 20–21; and Bate 188.

14. "In trauma," Cathy Caruth posits, "the outside has gone inside without any mediation" (59).

15. It is interesting to note that, as Bundtzen observes, "all of the biographies and memoirs describe the incident commemorated in 'Burning the Letters' more vividly than the poem itself" ("Poetic Arson" 239).

16. According to Bundtzen, "In the image of the hairy orchid, Assia's crumpled and burning letter (invaginated folds of paper) resembles female genitals, and the hissing is both her name and the sound of the fire" ("Poetic Arson" 247).

17. As Koren and Negev document in *Lover of Unreason*, after Plath died, Assia read Plath's *Double Exposure*, or *Doubletake*, manuscript fragment in addition to Plath's last journals, which all have since been lost. Assia reportedly confided in Nathaniel Tarn that she was disgusted with her depiction as an "icy, barren woman," in contrast to Plath, "who is full of poems, kicks and kids" in *Doubletake*. According to Koren and Negev and Tarn, Assia "hoped that Ted would destroy it all," the novel and the journals (Koren and Negev 117; Nathaniel Tarn Papers). Luke Ferretter points out that poems such as "The Fearful" and "Childless Woman" treat "some of the subject matter

that also went into the novel" (87), and these poems may indicate the focus, treatment, and/or emotional tenor of the lost novel and journals. Citing Suzette Macedo, Feinstein reports, "It was Assia who found and read Sylvia's journal of the last months of her life . . . and [she] was overwhelmed by the spite and malice directed towards herself there" (151). Plath's unhappiness with Assia shows up not only in her final journal but also in her Assia poems.

18. In addition to the Assia poems that are examined in this chapter (e.g., "The Fearful," "Childless Woman," and "The Munich Mannequins"), see also Plath's 1962 poem "The Other," which may be about Olwyn Hughes. "The Rival," also about Olwyn Hughes (Wagner-Martin 97), is a 1961 poem offering a variation on the theme.

19. Ferretter reads these lines as equating to "a moral failure to be a woman" on the part of the Assia character (87), and the moral bankruptcy in terms of gender will become clearer and communicated more stridently as the poem progresses.

20. In a letter to Marcia Brown Plumer, dated 9 April 1957, Plath tells her friend and former college roommate, "I know now that if I want to keep on being a triple-threat woman: wife, writer & teacher (to be swapped later for motherhood, I hope) I can't be a drudge" (*Letters of Sylvia Plath*, vol. 2, p. 110).

21. In her 1963 journal, Alliston writes, "Ted tells me he is going to try with Assia." She continues: "He says he's never in his life found someone so physically attractive. Also she releases his imagination. ie. make a film in ½ hour. She is a rare person. He might be able to save her and she him." She adds, "He is in love with her obviously" (87).

22. *Munich* is an allusion to Assia's German ancestry and background. In his memoir, Gerald Hughes, Ted Hughes's brother, remembers Assia in this way: "Assia, a strangely beautiful woman, had been born in Germany, but her parents had fled to Palestine when she was six—her mother was a Christian, but her father, a respected doctor in Berlin, was Jewish. She had an exotic quality and was artistic, which Ted appreciated" (168).

23. See chapters 3 and 4 for extended discussions of this topic with respect to Assia in both literary and biographical texts.

24. See Plath's 1960 short story "Day of Success" for a treatment of the polarization between the "country wife," with her hair in braids (92), and the glamorous models. Ellen, the protagonist and wife in the story, fears becoming a "deserted wife" when her husband, who is a writer, becomes successful (84). She muses "on the gulf separating her from the self-possessed fur-, feather- and jewel-bedecked [fashion] models" (86). Concerning a woman whom she thinks may be a rival for her husband's affections, Ellen hopes, "*If only she* [the purported rival] *were superficial, empty-headed.*" Ellen's friend Nancy tells Ellen: "Men won't admit it, but they do want a woman to look *right*, really *fatale*. The right hat, the right hair color" (89). Later on, Ellen "couldn't be better pleased" when she realizes her husband, Jacob, "obviously

saw her as the wife and mother type" (91). We can discern several passages in "Day of Success" that resonate with the speaker's attitude in "The Munich Mannequins." The short story and the poem may be read profitably together; they allow us to track the gendered dynamics that reflect cultural gendered expectations of women (as Plath perceived them) at work in both. As a biographical aside, Plath feared being thought of as a "poor country wife" after separating from Hughes; see her 25 October 1962 letter to her mother: "I believe in going through & facing the worst, not hiding from it. That is why I am going to London this week, partly, to face all the people we know & tell them happily & squarely I am divorcing Ted, so they won't picture me as a poor, deceived country wife" (*Letters of Sylvia Plath*, vol. 2, 888).

CHAPTER 3.
TED HUGHES'S TREATMENTS OF ASSIA WEVILL

1. Hughes also refers to Assia as his wife in correspondence with Yehuda Amichai, as Koren and Negev cite (166). Hughes considered Amichai a close friend, and Amichai is the poet whose work Assia translated with Hughes's encouragement. Referring to Assia in this way to one of his confidants is revealing of how Hughes perceived Assia at times.

2. We should be mindful that Hughes must have found it difficult to forgive Assia for taking her own life and that of their child; their story is one of tragedy and trauma, as this chapter delineates.

3. In a letter to Assia's sister shortly after Assia's death, for example, Hughes writes, "I know if I had only moved—if I had only given [Assia] hope in slightly more emphatic words in that last phone conversation, she would have been O.K." (*Letters* 290). To Lucas Myers, Hughes claimed responsibility for the deaths of Plath and Assia, ascribing his "insane decisions" to Plath's situation and his "insane indecisions" to Assia's situation (qtd. in Koren and Negev 215).

4. Assia's suicide note to her father includes this passage:

> The prospect before me is so bleak, that to have lived my full life-span would have entailed more misery than I could possibly endure.
>
> It is the life alone. Insecure, dependent on an au pair to look after my little Shuratchka properly—dependent on the sort of people for whom I work—a very bad, 3rd rate agency who would fire me in case of illness. No husband. No father for Shura.
>
> I've often thought of this—but the pain it would give you, and the criminality perpetuated on my little Shuri—these thoughts often stopped me at the last sane moment, in the past.

> I have lived with the dream of living with Ted—and this has gone kaput. The reasons are immaterial. There could never be another man. Never. (Qtd. in Koren and Negev 204)

See chapter 1, note 9, for a discussion of Assia's suicidal ideations and attempts, some of which preceded her relationship with Hughes.

5. For instance, Hughes plays upon the motif of Assia as a Jew, and yet Assia was not born in Israel and did not identify herself as Jewish, though her father was a Jew. Her biographers make clear Assia's lack of identification in this regard: "Twelve years in Palestine had failed to create a Jewish identity for Assia, and throughout her life she had no strong feelings about her Jewish heritage one way or the other" (Koren and Negev 35).

6. The date of the interview was 8 October 1996, as confirmed by Eilat Negev in personal correspondence.

7. This passage can be found in Hughes, "Notebook 11."

8. While Shura does not figure prominently in *Capriccio*, Hughes does claim her as his daughter to his friend Leonard Baskin in a 16 July 1969 letter and laments her passing: "I have two nice children who make life a great pleasure. [. . .] I had a third, a little marvel, but she died with her mother" (*Letters* 293).

9. Some Hughes critics would consider Hughes's best works to be *The Hawk in the Rain* (1957) and *Lupercal* (1960), along with *Remains of Elmet* (1979). I thank the outside reader who suggested I make this clear to those readers who may wish to seek out more of Hughes's work.

10. As Carol Bere observes, critics tend to overlook the importance of Assia to Hughes and his work. Bere argues: "Any detailed analysis of Ted Hughes's poetic canon should certainly include the Assia poems. *Capriccio*, in particular, is a significant, well realized narrative sequence in its own right. *Capriccio* also provides additional perspective on 'Dreamers' in *Birthday Letters*" (29).

11. Please see Ann Skea's Cabbala readings of *Capriccio* at http://ann.skea.com/CapriccioHome.htm.

12. Bere explains the mythical context of "Capriccios": in summary, Friday is Frigga's day, according to German myth, making Friday the thirteenth and its mythical bad luck even more potent in the poem. While Frigga protects married love (and by extension, childbearing), she suffers the loss of her son Balder with her husband, Odin. Loki, Odin's brother, manages to direct a god to throw mistletoe at Balder, which kills him. Loki, then, is associated with death, and Bere reads death as the "dominant theme" of *Capriccio* (33).

13. An additional interpretation takes into account the figure of the ship as the figurative voyage Hughes embarked on with Assia: *Capriccio* captures those memories, images, and parts of that journey from Hughes's point of view. Also, the "prestidi-

gateur" may reference Assia as the magician or conjurer who wielded power or magic over Hughes during her life and after her death.

14. The series of letters to Assia from Hughes that are archived at Emory University shows Hughes promising time and again that they would be together soon, reunited and, in later letters, living as a family unit. Virtually all of his letters to Assia are peppered with endearments and declarations of his love for her. I will provide bits of summaries from a sample of the ones in which Hughes promises Assia that they will be reunited, that he is committed only to her, and that he will fulfill her dream of a home with him. At times, Hughes delivers explanations about why there has been a delay in doing what he has promised. On 3 October 1963, he declares his love for Assia; he claims he loves her more than ever and that they will reunite soon. On 24 November 1963, he tells her that if she is honest with him about her feelings and takes the world on their terms, they will make it as a couple. On 2 December 1963, he explains that it is only a lack of money that prevents them from being together. On 12 December 1963, he argues that Assia is trying to force a crisis, against him—implying that anything that is not going as it should is her fault, not his. On 15 January 1964, he pleads with her to forgive him for inviting other women (and not extending an invitation to her) to his home in Devon at Christmas: he informs her that no other woman exists as far as he is concerned and that his entire life is staked on her. She is all he has, he posits. He reiterates that he just needs cash and then he will remove the two of them from the damaging influences and jealousy of others. On 11 February 1964, Hughes again gives money as a reason that they have yet to live together and his pressing work as another, but he encourages Assia, despite these obstacles, to wait for him. On 14 September 1964, Hughes promises that they will live together by the upcoming winter if they can find enough room to accommodate Hughes and Assia (and presumably the children). He predicts that there must be some combination, using the metaphor of a lock, that will allow everything to fall into place. On 26 November 1964, he mentions the passing time and speculates that things are better and about to improve even more, seemingly referring to their relationship. Apparently, Assia had used the metaphor of a corridor to define their relationship (its struggles, the time spent waiting), and Hughes embraces this metaphor, encouraging Assia to see their relationship in this very way, implying that they would emerge at the other end together. On 31 August 1965, Hughes closes his letter by emphasizing that they must leave very, very soon and that there can be no mistakes made: she must understand that he can live only with her. On 31 December 1967, Hughes begs Assia to stay with him: he asks her to be patient, to be helpful, and to remain in good spirits. On the condition that she can do those things, he promises that 1968 will be the year they both want. On 7 November 1968, Hughes notifies Assia about what he calls "bad news": the house they had selected went to someone with a higher offer. He promises to look for a new place while offering details about why the house that

got away was not ideal for them. He encourages her to look for homes for them and suggests that maybe a place outside of Devon would be best. He states that it is a pity that her flat is not big enough to accommodate him and Plath's children moving in with her and Shura. Although Hughes usually refrained from signing his name on Assia's letters, this one is signed, indicating that he was very serious about setting up a domestic arrangement together—as late as November 1968. In an undated letter, Hughes declares that he is ready to rearrange life affairs his way, only an unspecified policy attributed to Plath's mother is slowing him down (MSS 1058, Box 1, Folder 52). He assures Assia that nothing else is in the way. In another undated letter, Hughes promises that he loves only Assia and that he cannot live without her and that they will fix an unspecified "it" together (MSS 1058, Box 1, Folder 53). In another undated letter, Hughes urges Assia not to be depressed, just as he is getting clear of what he calls his tangles (MSS 1058, Box 1, Folder 56). In the undated "Draft Constitution," Hughes stipulates house rules for Assia in order to pave the way for them to live together harmoniously; he solicits her feedback, inquiring further as to her intentions in wanting to live with him and asking her to provide her perspective on their relationship as they make plans to move forward in combining their households.

15. Bundtzen notes that there is a line change from *Capriccio* to the *Collected Poems*. "In the version of 'Snow' in *Capriccio*," explains Bundtzen, "he recognizes his inattention to impending doom with the line, 'I watched it [the snow], thinking of something else.' The line is altered in *CP* to 'I watched you. Feeling the snow's touch' (p. 790) as if sensing death's coldness, but remaining intellectually inattentive to its meaning at the time" ("Traumatic Repetition" 143 n. 3).

16. Assia's father was Russian, and her interest in Russian literature and film is evidenced by the books in her personal library. Among books she formerly owned, which are held at the Stuart A. Rose Manuscript, Archives, and Rare Book Library at Emory University, are books by and about Sergei Eisenstein (1898–1948); Boris Pasternak (1890–1960); Alexander Pushkin (1799–1837); and Leo Tolstoy (1828–1910); as well as two books on Russian grammar.

17. All this is discussed in the following chapter, but please see Koren and Negev's chapter 20 in *Lover of Unreason* for a detailed biographical account of Assia's life, especially in this time frame.

18. See chapter 10 in Koren and Negev.

19. I suspect Feinstein is correct in associating the blade of grass in "Fairy Tale," a poem about Plath and addressed to her in *Birthday Letters*, with Assia (235). These lines are the only allusion to Assia in the poem: "You never knew / what a skeleton key I had found / In a single blade of grass. And I entered" (55–57).

20. A different interpretation of "she found us" would reference the fact that David and Assia Wevill responded to Hughes and Plath's advertisement to sublet the flat at 3 Chalcot Square, Primrose Hill, and this scenario was the occasion for Assia's

first meeting with Hughes and Plath. Within the poem, this interpretation would emphasize that Assia pursued the opportunity to sublet 3 Chalcot Square and would minimize the consideration that Hughes and Plath placed the advertisement and brokered the meeting with the Wevills to see the flat.

21. Because this book is indebted to feminist recovery efforts, it is invested in discursive formations of Assia and how they signify. However, the trauma Hughes encountered after Assia's and Shura's deaths—by Assia's hand—would make it difficult, if not impossible, for him to assume a sympathetic view of her or to take on her perspective.

22. Jewish herself, Becker is particularly sensitive to what she sees in "Dreamers" as "sickeningly anti-Semitic" (59). For a full discussion of its anti-Semitism, see chapter 5 in Becker's memoir, which revolves around Plath. Becker also dismisses Hughes's claim that his poetry is curative, and she argues against thinking of him as a victim when he invokes Plath, Assia, and allusions to the Holocaust in "Dreamers." According to Becker, "Hughes's self-exoneration is not merely twaddle, it is blasphemy—if the word can be used in a secular sense, and I think it can" (64–65).

CHAPTER 4.
ASSIA WEVILL AS AUTHOR, ARTIST, AND TRANSLATOR

1. Assia translated the twenty Amichai poems featured in the *Selected Poems* (Cape Goliard), which was published in 1968. These poems, with slight revisions in translation (e.g., the changes in punctuation throughout "Farewell You" and "Farewell, You," respectively), were collected and published the next year in the expanded *Poems* (Harper and Row). *Poems* showcases forty-six of Assia's translations.

2. Assia's timeline is complicated: after becoming romantically involved with Hughes in 1962, she lived with David Wevill, her third husband while, at times, occasionally living with Hughes and taking vacations with Hughes, until she permanently separated from Wevill to live with Hughes in Ireland and Devon, England, from 1966 to 1967. From 1968 until she died, in 1969, Assia headed her own household in London. As for Shura, Hughes is listed as her father on her birth certificate (and he acknowledged his paternity), but David Wevill gave Shura his surname. As Koren and Negev observe, Shura "was both men's daughter, and neither's" (147). For a fuller biographical narrative about Assia, please see Koren and Negev's *Lover of Unreason*.

3. See Wevill, "Will."

4. The stigma of suicide, combined with the appalling act of filicide, may have contributed to the absence of an obituary. For example, likely due to the stigma of suicide, the obituaries that ran for Sylvia Plath six years earlier omitted the cause of death or listed it as viral pneumonia (Fetters and Steinberg).

5. As Brenda Hedden, Hughes's lover at the time, maintains, "Ted was in deep

shock [over Assia's and Shura's deaths], and he was relieved that Assia's death was not in the papers" (qtd. in Koren and Negev 210).

6. The absence of structural, familial, or interpersonal support at home makes her professional success all the more impressive. In fact, Assia was an extraordinarily successful professional. As her July 1968 pay stub from Ogilvy & Mather shows, she made a decent salary as a professional woman at a time when women made approximately 53 cents to every dollar a man earned (Walsh and Wrigley). From what can be determined on the pay stub, Assia earned £208.68 for the "week/month," which equates to a net payout, after taxes, of £153.15. That amount would translate into £2,486.54 in 2016, giving Assia the equivalent, in 2016, of $3,597.54 in American money after taxes. She would have been earning approximately $43,000 (or $81,132 if she had been a man) that year in "take home pay" (in 2016 American dollars) at Ogilvy & Mather, a decent income but one made smaller by supporting a child—which likely accounts for her concerns about money and, in part, her worries about the stability and longevity of her employment prospects. Assia did not receive any form of child support. Conversely, it appears that Hughes did provide Plath with support money (Feinstein 138).

7. The topics Hughes addresses in "Draft Constitution" include directives about childcare, cooking, daily help, accounts, Hughes's friends, a daily schedule, home furnishings, Assia's manners, and her commitment to him. For instance, Assia is instructed to play games with the children an hour a day and to reserve weekend afternoons for the children. She is expected to keep their clothes in repair, to supervise their hygiene, and to instruct them in German for two to three hours per week. As for cooking, Hughes is adamant that he will not cook except in an emergency. Assia is instructed to cook a substantial breakfast every day (without bread). Each week she would need to provide an interesting and fresh supply of pastries for the children, and these were to be made from scratch. Each week Assia would be expected to prepare a minimum of one meal from a new recipe. And she would need to teach Frieda how to cook. Hughes informs her that outside help would be restricted to a half-day, and that she must maintain a daily accounting of expenses. Among her responsibilities, as Hughes sees it in this document, are adhering to his preference that she make a saintly effort in tolerating his friends, the understanding that she never threaten to leave him within the first year, and the expectation that she will never discuss him with anyone. Additionally, she must be out of bed by 8:00 a.m., and she is forbidden to take naps or wear dressing gowns in the morning, except in the case of an emergency or by (Hughes's) agreement. Hughes forbids her from summoning anyone to her bedroom. She is to dedicate herself to tact and detachment. In addition to the "Draft Constitution," Hughes devised "ground rules in order to protect their work" in 1965 (Bate 243): Hughes needed and wanted to write, and Assia was experiencing success in her advertising work. Thus, another perspective on the "Draft Constitution" is that Hughes was articulating guidelines that would allow everyone to function

optimally and create a harmonious household. After Assia moved to Court Green, in 1966, she suffered from how she was perceived and treated by Hughes and his family. Bate concludes, "It was clear that Assia was never going to be one of the [Hughes] family" (223). Perhaps prompted by these developments, Hughes thought he was providing direction to Assia in the form of the "Draft Constitution."

8. Assia aspired to run or participate in a literary salon, and she joined the Group, which was a poetry discussion gathering that formed at Cambridge in 1954 and was attended by many poets (Koren and Negev 65–66).

9. Interestingly, Ted Hughes desired Assia to keep her perceived exotic appeal. In the "Draft Constitution" document in which he lists his preferred house rules, he requests that she aim to be as Israeli and German as possible, ridding herself of her refined English manners.

10. Julia Matcham, a colleague and Assia's art director at work, remembers that Assia commented, "It was nothing to do with me," in reference to Plath's suicide (Koren and Negev 115).

11. Accents can indicate or belie social class standing, something that the Hughes family understood. For his part, Murphy relates in his memoir a memory about introducing Hughes and Plath to his aunt in Ireland: "I wondered would Aunt Bunty pack Ted Hughes off to the kitchen. His voice, with its roots in West Yorkshire, had never acquired the sword-edge used by the gentry to cut down the lower classes and let each other know that they have this power and privilege. To play safe, I introduced him as Sylvia's husband, so he was graciously received" (224).

12. Myers comments: "I thought that within a year or less [Hughes] would be able to resettle with Assia in Scotland and I did not recognize that she might think it was impossible to wait. It seems to me now that she was not in an ordinary state of mind when she committed suicide and that her isolation in London had driven her off a central balance" (135). The animosity Assia faced from Hughes's family throughout her relationship with him, from beginning to end, contributed to the instability of a home base. As Bate reveals, Hughes contemplated living in Heptonstall with Assia after Plath's death in 1963. Bate relates, "[Hughes] told himself that Ma and Pa would get used to the scandal, if it was a scandal, but [his] Aunt Hilda was the main problem: she was horrified by Assia, jealous, angry, panicked, afraid of what people would say, anxious about the effect on Ted's reputation and about whether Assia would drain him of cash and leave him bankrupt. [Aunt Hilda] constantly sniped about Assia, 'with her 3 husbands, her gypsy looks' and her part in Sylvia's death" (223). Such hostility took a toll on Assia's happiness and prevented her from living what she deemed a good life, as her own writing indicates.

13. Please see, e.g., Hughes's 7 February 1965 letter to Assia in *Letters of Ted Hughes* (236–37); and note 8 of chapter 1.

14. In a 9 July 1968 letter to Hughes, Assia beseeches him to commit to her: "Oh Teddy—I see things very clearly at the moment. Clearer than *ever* before *even*[.] For

us to continue living separately feels fundamentally wrong, the reasons for it are abstractions. *We're meant* to be together. And the children need both of us. And we need both of us, and it's worth the effort. Yes, the whole effort. No man's an island, which you're pretending you are, and I'm persuading myself I am. I don't want to be. I want to be with *you*. Don't leave it long, dear love, otherwise there will be no means of return to you. I shall have turned into a salt pillar" (qtd. in Koren and Negev 181).

15. Hughes's contemporaries did speak of his attractiveness and magnetism, from their perspectives.

16. The Ted Hughes archive at Emory houses pieces of "Full House." Assia's illustrations are missing, but drafts of Hughes's poems exist. In one letter, he thanks her for a drawing, praising her lovely work and telling her that they would be wonderful book illustrations. He sends her eight "Full House" poems in the two 1965 letters held by the archive and asks for her opinion about the poems, whether she is stimulated by them. At this time, Hughes was addressing letters to "F. Wall Esq.," wishing to remain under the radar in his correspondence with Assia. See MSS 1050, Folders 35 and 36. (When I last examined them, the manuscripts were in the wrong folders. The letter praising Assia's drawing and containing the queen and king poems were actually in Folder 65. The letter in which Hughes seeks to ascertain Assia's opinion of his drafted poems and which contains the knave poems was in Folder 31.)

17. Her exact words are thus: "So far, everybody but you and I have been dictating our lives—we *need* to be alone, to recover from our Intolerable" (qtd. in Koren and Negev 176).

18. She finds him physically beautiful, enumerating his superb legs and thighs and wondering if God has squandered him on her in a 31 November 1966 journal entry. Studying the hut where he works, she expects to see smoke emanating from it, caused by his presence (journal entries, 29–31 Nov. 1966).

19. Mira Hamermesh recounts the following about a party she attended, at which Assia and Hughes were also present: "The entrance door opened like a gate, and a couple emerged. I've never seen such beauty in my whole life. I asked Ruth [Fainlight], who are these gorgeous people, and she said, Ted Hughes and Assia Wevill" (qtd. in Koren and Negev 167). Koren and Negev explain that "heads turned" and everyone took notice when Assia and Hughes attended literary functions: they reigned as "the royal couple," as was the case at the International Festival of Spoken Poetry in July 1967 (167).

20. For example, Assia, in rage and dismay, writes to Hughes in January 1964: "The only revenge I can take on you is to go to bed with any attractive man who asks me. To hurt your sensations out of my body, if not out of my mind or blood" (22 Jan. 1964; also qtd in Koren and Negev 138). In March 1968, she writes him: "I want to know whether you want to mend us because you still love me, because you feel the animal thing between us" (undated, MSS 1058, Box 1, Folder 71; also qtd. in Koren and Negev 175; Koren and Negev identified the date of this otherwise undated letter

in the archive). In a different undated letter, in which Assia reveals that she has been ill and feels, as she terms it, banished, Assia stridently writes that she has bathed Hughes out of her skin and that, now, she smells safely—her word—of Harrod's best soap. This letter was meant to provoke a reaction from Hughes: she asks him to bring a razorblade so that they can celebrate his birthday in such a fashion that there will never be another like it (MSS 1058, Box 1, Folder 73). And most telling, after a painful bout of cystitis, Assia writes, "If [Hughes and I] can't make love properly again, I'd just as soon not live" (qtd. in Koren and Negev 123).

21. See Assia's letter to Hughes, undated, MSS 1058, Box 1, Folder 71, for the archived letter.

22. Hughes writes to Assia on 9 February 1964:

> When you'd spent Wednesday describing to me how & just how completely you'd planned me out of your future moves, why did you pretend to be angry on Thursday morning at what you interpret as my lack of confidence in you? Something else must have made you angry.
>
> In fact, the more I think about it, the more strange it seems, that on Thursday morning you were ready to tell me to disappear, & on Thursday afternoon & Friday were so affectionate. Maybe those two days were just an illusion.
>
> I wish it didn't all seem so fishy, in retrospect.
>
> There's one explanation for that, and other things, which is that to get your revenge & for self-respect & compensation-just-in-case, you took Liliana's gossip as fact, added it to your general humiliations from last year, & have been investing your Insurance in somebody else. If that's so, it's O.K, but don't go on nursing the dream of our living together—because that dream feeds exclusively on trust, & nothing else will turn it to reality. (Hughes, *Letters* 229)

While Assia was loyal to Hughes, he was involved with other women in addition to Assia.

23. In a revealing letter, a friend and former coworker of Assia's encourages her to be calm while looking for a new job. "You were the only REAL LIVE writer left in that hell-hole [Ogilvy, an advertising firm]," Ann Sample writes. "Be calm. Ted will feel your panic otherwise," she advises (qtd. in Koren and Negev 182). The fact that Sample appeals to Assia's fear over losing Ted when encouraging her friend and propping up her confidence in her writing abilities (and by extension, her chances at landing another job) speaks volumes. The implications here are that Assia needed to be superwoman (i.e., a successful career woman, taking care of herself and her daughter on her own while making it appear easy) and that Hughes was not functioning as Assia's support system in times of great stress.

24. Judy Chicago and Miriam Schapiro echo the connection I see between Assia as a writer-artist and herself as a woman: "There is a contradiction in the experience of a woman who is also an artist. She feels herself to be a 'subject' in a world which treats her as an 'object.' Her works often become a symbolic arena where she establishes her sense of personal, sexual identity" (53). In the Sea Witch commercial, the beautiful sea witches are the ones who are approached initially with hostile intent and stolen from, and yet they are the ones positioned as monsters. To this day, Assia is cast as the beautiful but destructive monster who inserted herself sexually in the Plath-Hughes marriage. Her writing of the Sea Witch spot may well work out the tensions of the pleasures and dangers of femininity from her perspective: culturally, a woman's beauty is prized, but she assumes the bulk of the blame or responsibility for disastrous interpersonal relationships.

25. While they are both Plath scholars working in Plath archives, what Gail Crowther and Peter K. Steinberg maintain about photographs in the Plath archive translates to working with photographs in the Assia–Ted Hughes archive equally well. Crowther argues that "insomuch as photography may be about bringing back the dead, it is also about following and chasing traces. It is about weaving together stories, narratives, and pictures." Steinberg asserts, "Materials in an archive tell their own story, but are flexible enough to allow stories to be constructed about them as well" (Crowther and Steinberg 49).

26. The self-portrait was initially given as a gift to Ted Hughes by Assia. This self-portrait now belongs to the Olwyn Hughes collection at Emory because she obtained the portrait, most likely after Assia died, from Ted Hughes as a memento of a woman who meant a lot to her. Following Assia's death, Olwyn Hughes confesses to Dido and Bill Merwin that she was shattered by the deaths of Assia and Shura (letter, 24 Apr. 1969).

27. In this case, I use *restricted* to indicate that the photographs cannot be photographed or reproduced themselves without permission from the Hughes estate.

28. In her will, Assia stipulates: "To Nicholas Farrar Hughes, since he is too young for possessions, I will all my most tender love. To Freida [*sic*] Rebecca Hughes, I will also my love and all the lace, ribbons and silks she can find, as well as a fine gold chain" (qtd. in Bate 266).

CHAPTER 5.
ASSIA WEVILL IN THE TWENTY-FIRST CENTURY

1. See chapter 1, the introduction.

2. See Elizabeth Compton Sigmund's 22 Apr. 1999 account in *The Guardian*, "I Realised Sylvia Knew about Assia's Pregnancy"; she suspects that Plath may have known about Assia's first pregnancy with Hughes and that the knowledge of it was

devastating. According to Sigmund, "I realised that Sylvia would have known of Assia's pregnancy, and that the thought of Assia giving birth to Ted's child might have offered a further explanation of Sylvia's final ability to face the future." How Sigmund realized Plath "would have known" about Assia's pregnancy is unclear.

3. Because Hemphill's book is set up as an interconnected examination of Plath's biography in verse and because the poems have not been anthologized, I have elected to give page numbers instead of line numbers to make it easier for the reader to locate the sections I reference.

4. In his review of *Lover of Unreason*, Peter Porter remembers Assia thus: "While she was not a poet of genius, as Plath was, she was more than just a beautiful woman who set her cap at a celebrated poet. She had wit, charm and generosity, and while she could be willful and self-dramatising, she was also natural and straightforward—never in my eyes the 'femme fatale.'" He adds, "I found Assia's beauty no strain [on me or my marriage]—she was gestural and extravagant but more usually quiet and serious-minded."

5. See also Hemphill's "Divorce," in *Your Own, Sylvia*, in which Suzette Macedo, identified as a friend of both Plath and Assia, assumes the role of speaker of the poem. Hemphill imagines her confiding to the reader:

> I restrain myself from phoning Assia,
> from holding the mouthpiece
>
> above Sylvia's loud tears
> so Assia can hear
> what unbearable sounds like. (206)

Such lines are somewhat reckless because they demonize Assia, who, as I maintain, is a victim in this tragic mythos too. Assia clearly knew what *unbearable* meant. In a 1967 letter, written two years before she committed suicide, Assia confides in her sister: "The continuing pressure of Ted's mother, the strain that engenders, the isolation, the hostility and, to me, fine contempt of Ted's friends here, are sometimes unendurable." She continues: "I have been literally suicidal. . . . I am clearly ill. The last four years have been a strain simply too hard to bear" (qtd. in Negev, "Haunted by the Ghosts of Love"). In short, Hemphill's poems about Assia, such as "Divorce," are examples of how victim blaming is steeped in an antifeminist, patriarchal culture that repeatedly victimizes and scapegoats women and other underrepresented people and vulnerable populations.

6. See chapter 3.

7. See chapter 4.

8. See chapter 4 for more discussion of how this social setting affected Assia.

9. *Your Own, Sylvia* won a Printz Honor and the Myra Cohn Livingston Award in

2008. As such, the narratives embedded in it are validated to some extent with these awards, and the messages in the book are likely to reach many readers.

10. As of 3 July 2018, approximately 260 notes had been left in memory of Shura, and approximately 60 notes had been left in memory of Assia on the respective *Find a Grave* sites.

11. In *Doonreagan*, Assia has been instructed by a doctor to refrain from sex as a result of her cystitis flare-up, but when Hughes asks about it, she meets his eye and retorts, "Fuck the cystitis" (75). She admonishes Hughes for not having the ability to protect her ("How the hell are you going to protect me from all that?") and for "shitting" himself "over the attacks of American feminists" (81). Assia possesses swagger and vulgarity above and beyond Hughes in the play and speaks in ways that her recorded words do not support.

12. This performance communicates to the audience, from the very start, that Assia is a "bad girl." There may be interesting discussions to be had in the classroom, book groups, or elsewhere about whether a woman can be a "good girl" and be sexual.

13. See the Postmedia News story about the Bonhams auction of David Wevill's and Assia's possessions, which provides insight into what happened to some of Assia's belongings after she died. In an interview in 2013, David Wevill says: "I didn't know after Assia's death what happened to all these things. I didn't know that Assia had all that material, which apparently was then passed on to Ted Hughes." According to the reporter, the artifacts had "once [been] in Assia's possession, then kept by Hughes, and finally added to the vast Roy Davids Collection of Poetical Manuscripts." The reporter describes Assia: "Assia, after separating from her husband in 1962, joined Hughes in an ultimately turbulent and unhappy relationship. Depressed over Hughes's continued philandering, she committed suicide in 1969, also taking the life of the four-year-old daughter she'd had with Hughes" (Boswell). The lot was withdrawn from sale (Bonhams, "Lot 506"), likely because the items belonged in actuality to David Wevill.

14. A similar exchange occurs in scene 4; see Jocelyn 65.

15. As Lucas Myers remembers: "Assia told me that she felt as though Sylvia were haunting her. I don't think she meant that a ghost visited her at night but that the posthumous presence of Sylvia loomed over all her associations and poured over her thoughts" (129).

16. In an excerpt from one of her letters to Aurelia Plath, Assia writes on 4 January 1968: "Ted told me that I was no use to him as an invalid (this was during my post-flu depression and sinus and bronchitis and things), and I thought that was the most brutal thing he'd ever said to me, when I nursed him and his mother for three weeks of his slipped disc. I thought suddenly that that degree of brutality would slowly dement me. That I must perhaps think of living without him completely" (qtd. in Rollyson 240).

17. Plath writes to Ruth Tiffany Barnhouse Beuscher, her therapist, on 22 Sep-

tember 1962: "Ted beat me up physically a couple of days before my miscarriage: the baby I lost was due to be born on his birthday" (*Letters of Sylvia Plath*, vol. 2, 830). Believing what a woman says about gendered violence from the outset is considered a best practice in trauma studies and sexual and domestic violence prevention efforts and work, despite earlier silences or omissions on the part of the victim.

18. And yet a biographical account attests that it would be Hughes who was more likely to make such jokes. According to Assia's biographers, who cite her journal, Assia "was *appalled* by Ted's crudeness when he idly remarked over the breakfast table, in the presence of [his] entire family: 'Have you ever thought, what if you made one quid every time you make love, you'd be very rich by now'" (Koren and Negev 129; emphasis added).

19. In her poem "Assia Gutmann," published in *The Book of Mirrors* and collected in *Stonepicker and The Book of Mirrors* (2009), Frieda Hughes introduces the themes that she will explore more fully in "For Shura," "Memory Loss 4: Nesting," and "Mothers." In "Assia Gutmann," the speaker—who appears to speak for Frieda Hughes in the harnessing of biographical details (the speaker remembers Assia caring for her as a child)—argues that Assia could never understand her ("she never / Translated me" [3–4]) as she could understand and translate the "Jewish poetry" of Yehuda Amichai (1). In the first stanza, the speaker describes Assia's concern with her own appearance, specifically in her longing for youthfulness. "Her beauty frightened me," the speaker admits (14). Even so, the most poignant aspect of "Assia Gutmann" is the speaker's claim that Assia could only see Plath in Frieda Hughes and treated her accordingly:

> I'd no idea
> How my mother's face reflected
> In the polished coals of her eyes
> So that she saw right through me,
> Not to the inner workings of my mind,
> But to the wall behind. (24–29)

20. After perusing the Ted Hughes papers in the archive at Emory, Rollyson clarifies Frieda Hughes's attitude toward her father: "Frieda describes a caring father who helped her keep the memory of her mother alive. That bond with him makes her disdainful of others who have enshrined her mother in their pantheon. She is aghast that her 'more temperate [compared to her mother] and optimistic' father has been vilified." As for Frieda Hughes's take on Assia, Rollyson observes, "[Ted] Hughes never liked seeing Assia's name in print next to his, and Frieda's fealty to him results in turning Assia into 'the other woman' in the preface [of *Ariel: The Restored Edition*]" (268).

21. Sociologists Andrew J. Cherlin and Frank F. Furstenberg Jr. observe that there

is "great variability in how stepparents and stepchildren view each other" (367), and it would appear, from Assia's and Frieda's written words, that Assia (as a stepparent by proxy, in that she was a partner to Ted Hughes and not his legal wife) viewed Frieda with more affection than Frieda viewed Assia. After reading her journal, Assia's biographers assert that Assia "easily added the role of stepmother" to her role as Hughes's partner after Plath's death. They comment that she "enjoyed the domestic scenes" and found Frieda and Nicholas Hughes "touching" (Koren and Negev 123). As for the big picture, Cherlin and Furstenberg report that research shows it takes years for blended families to adjust to a new family structure, perhaps as many as seven years on average for the adjustment process to be completed (370). It may be that Assia did not have sufficient time to develop secure attachments (from Frieda Hughes's perspective) within the Hughes household, given that Assia cohabited with Hughes and his children with Plath sporadically over the six years in which Assia assumed a maternal role, following Plath's death, in the lives of Plath and Hughes's children. Cherlin and Furstenberg also note from existing research that "it can be harder to be a stepmother than a stepfather" (371).

22. And yet in Eugene O'Connell's 2007 interview with Irish poet Richard Murphy, who knew Assia, Plath, and Hughes, Murphy observes, "Sylvia was a troubled woman but likeable, as was Assia of course" (Murphy and O'Connell).

WORKS CITED

Alexander, Paul. *Rough Magic: A Biography of Sylvia Plath*. Viking, 1991.

"Alexandra Tatiana Elise 'Shura' Wevill." *Find a Grave*, https://www.findagrave.com/cgi- bin/fg.cgi?page=gr&GRid=43636930.

Alliston, Susan. *Poems and Journals, 1960–1969*. Introduction by Ted Hughes, Richard Hollis, 2010.

Alvarez, A. *The Savage God: A Study of Suicide*. Random House, 1972.

———. *Where Did It All Go Right?* Richard Cohen Books, 1999.

Amichai, Yehuda. "The Death of A. G." *Songs of Jerusalem and Myself*. Translated by Harold Schimmel, Harper and Row, 1973, pp. 47.

———. *Poems*. Translated by Assia Gutmann [Wevill], Harper and Row, 1969.

———. *Selected Poems*. Translated by Assia Gutmann [Wevill], Cape Goliard, 1968.

Appiah, Kwame Anthony. *The Ethics of Identity*. Princeton UP, 2005.

"Assia Esther Gutmann Wevill." *Find a Grave*, https://www.findagrave.com/cgi- bin/fg.cgi?page=gr&GRid=43639913.

"Assia's Dior: A Mystery." *Perfume Tourist*, http://heathersletters.typepad.com/perfumetourist/2008/02/assias-dior-a-mystery.html.

Barry, Judith, and Sandy Flitterman-Lewis. "Textual Strategies: The Politics of Art-Making." *Screen*, vol. 21, no. 2, 1980, pp. 35–48. Rpt. in *The Feminism and Visual Culture Reader*, edited by Amelia Jones, 2nd ed., Routledge, 2010, pp. 66–72.

Bate, Jonathan. *Ted Hughes: The Unauthorised Life*. HarperCollins, 2015.

Becker, Jillian. *Giving Up: The Last Days of Sylvia Plath*. St. Martin's, 2003.

Bere, Carol. "Complicated with Old Ghosts: The Assia Poems." *Ted Hughes: Alternative Horizons*, edited by Joanny Moulin, Routledge, 2004, pp. 29–37.

Berger, John. *Ways of Seeing*. London: BBC/Penguin, 1972. Rpt. in *The Feminism and Visual Culture Reader*, edited by Amelia Jones, 2nd ed., Routledge, 2010, pp. 49–52.

Bonhams. "Lot 239: (Hughes, Ted [1930–98])—Assia Wevill (1927–69), Assia Wevill's Own Collection of Some 70 Photographs of Herself on Her Own and with Others, and One of Her Father (1940s–1960s)." 10

Apr. 2013. London. https://www.bonhams.com/auctions/20922/lot/239/.

———. "Lot 506: Wevill, David (b. 1935, Canadian Poet) Archive of His Poems, Papers and Photographs Kept by His Former Wife Assia, [1960s]." 8 May 2013. London. https://www.bonhams.com/auctions/20923/lot/506/#/.VsjqwDLNnNo.facebookB.

Bordo, Susan. *Unbearable Weight: Feminism, Western Culture, and the Body.* U of California P, 2003.

Boswell, Randy. "Canadian Poet David Wevill 'Troubled' as Manuscripts Appear at U.K. Auction." *Canada.com*, Postmedia News, 9 Apr. 2013, http://o.canada.com/entertainment/canadian-poet-david-wevill-troubled-as-manuscripts-appear-at-u-k-auction.

Britzolakis, Christina. "*Ariel* and Other Poems." *The Cambridge Companion to Sylvia Plath*, edited by Jo Gill, Cambridge UP, 2006, pp. 107–23.

Bundtzen, Lynda K. "Poetic Arson and Sylvia Plath's 'Burning the Letters.'" *The Unraveling Archive: Essays on Sylvia Plath*, edited by Anita Helle, U of Michigan P, 2007, pp. 236–53.

———. "Traumatic Repetition in *Capriccio*." *Ted Hughes: From Cambridge to Collected*, edited by M. Wormald, N. Roberts, and Terry Gifford, Palgrave, 2013, pp. 130–44.

Butler, Judith. *Bodies that Matter: On the Discursive Limits of "Sex."* Routledge, 2003.

———. *Excitable Speech: A Politics of the Performative.* Routledge, 1997.

———. *Gender Trouble: Feminism and the Subversion of Identity.* Routledge, 2006.

———. *Giving an Account of Oneself.* Fordham UP, 2005.

———. "Performative Acts and Gender Constitution: An Essay in Phenomenology and Feminist Theory." *Writing on the Body: Female Embodiment and Feminist Theory*, edited by Katie Conboy, Nadia Medina, and Sarah Stanbury, Columbia UP, 1997, pp. 401–17.

———. *Precarious Life: The Powers of Mourning and Violence.* Verso, 2006.

Butscher, Edward. *Sylvia Plath: Method and Madness.* Schaffner, 2003.

———, ed. *Sylvia Plath: The Woman and the Work.* Mead, 1977.

Caruth, Cathy. *Unclaimed Experience: Trauma, Narrative, and History.* Johns Hopkins UP, 1996.

Cherlin, Andrew J., and Frank F. Furstenberg Jr. "Stepfamilies in the United States: A Reconsideration." *Annual Review of Sociology*, vol. 20, 1994, pp. 359–81.

Chicago, Judy, and Miriam Schapiro. "Female Imagery." *Womanspace Journal*,

1973, pp. 11–17. Rpt. in *The Feminism and Visual Culture Reader*, edited by Amelia Jones, 2nd ed., Routledge, 2010, pp. 53–56.

Clark, Heather. *The Grief of Influence: Sylvia Plath and Ted Hughes*. Oxford UP, 2011.

"Classic Ads: Sea Witch ['Lost Island']." Online video clip. *YouTube*, 2013 [1965], https://www.youtube.com/watch?v=F1Zs7ag9VaM.

Crowther, Gail. *The Haunted Reader and Sylvia Plath*. Fonthill Media, 2017.

Crowther, Gail, and Peter K. Steinberg. *These Ghostly Archives: The Unearthing of Sylvia Plath*. Fonthill Media, 2017.

"Cuckoo, adj." *Oxford English Dictionary*, 3rd ed., Oxford UP. *OED Online*, http://dictionary.oed.com.

"Cuckoo, n. 3." *Oxford English Dictionary*, 3rd ed., Oxford UP. *OED Online*, http://dictionary.oed.com.

Davis, Dina. *Dina Davis on Writing Matters: Preview of My First Chapter*, https://dinadavis2015.wordpress.com/2015/10/20/preview-of-my-first-chapter/.

Eekelaar, John. "The End of an Era?" *Journal of Family History*, vol. 28, no. 1, Jan. 2003, pp. 108–22.

Enniss, Stephen C., and Karen V. Kukil. *"No Other Appetite": Sylvia Plath, Ted Hughes, and the Blood Jet of Poetry*. Grolier Club, 2005.

Farmer, Richard. "Cinema Advertising and the Sea Witch 'Lost Island' Film (1965)." *Historical Journal of Film, Radio and Television*, 2016, pp. 1–19, http://www.tandfonline.com/doi/full/10.1080/01439685.2015.1129709.

Feinstein, Elaine. *Ted Hughes: The Life of a Poet*. Norton, 2001.

Felman, Shoshana, and Dori Laub. *Testimony: Crises of Witnessing in Literature, Psychoanalysis, and History*. Routledge, 1992.

Felski, Rita. *Uses of Literature*. Blackwell, 2008.

Ferretter, Luke. *Sylvia Plath's Fiction: A Critical Study*. Edinburgh UP, 2012.

Fetters, Ashley, and Peter K. Steinberg. "There Are Almost No Obituaries for Sylvia Plath: A Biographer Explains *The Bell Jar* Author's Unusually Quiet Death 50 Years Ago." *The Atlantic*, 11 Feb. 2013, https://www.theatlantic.com/entertainment/archive/2013/02/there-are-almost-no-obituaries-for-sylvia-plath/273032/.

Furness, Hannah. "Feminists Abused My Mother's Suicide, Says Sylvia Plath's Poet Daughter." *The Telegraph*. Telegraph Media Group, 3 Oct. 2015.

Gates, Linda. "Sylvia Plath and I." *Plath Profiles: An Interdisciplinary Journal for Sylvia Plath Studies*, vol. 5, 2012, pp. 106–8.

Goodspeed-Chadwick, Julie. "Interpretations and Implications of Trauma and Narrative in Sylvia Plath's *Ariel*." *Journal of Literature and Trauma Studies*, vol. 1, no. 2, Fall 2012, pp. 117–46.

Greene, Roland. "Presidential Address 2016: Literature and Its Publics: Past, Present, and Future." *PMLA*, vol. 131, no. 3, May 2016, pp. 594–602.

Grosz, Elizabeth. *Volatile Bodies: Toward a Corporeal Feminism*. Indiana UP, 1994.

Hayman, Ronald. *The Death and Life of Sylvia Plath*. Sutton, 2003.

Hemphill, Stephanie. *Your Own, Sylvia: A Verse Portrait of Sylvia Plath*. Knopf, 2007.

Herman, Judith. *Trauma and Recovery*. Basic Books, 1997.

Hirsch, Marianne. "[MLA] Presidential Address 2014: Connective Histories in Vulnerable Times." *PMLA*, vol. 129, no. 3, May 2014, pp. 330–48.

Hughes, Frieda. *Alternative Values: Poems and Paintings*. Bloodaxe, 2015.

———. *Stonepicker and The Book of Mirrors: Poems*. Harper Perennial, 2009.

Hughes, Gerald. *Ted and I: A Brother's Memoir*. Thomas Dunne / St. Martin's, 2012.

Hughes, Olwyn. "Hughes, Olwyn, London, 24 April 1969." MSS 866, Box 1, Folder 24. Ted Hughes, Letters to Assia Wevill, Stuart A. Rose Manuscript, Archives, and Rare Book Library, Emory University, Atlanta (hereafter cited as "Rose Library").

Hughes, Olwyn, and Sam Jordison. "Interview: Olwyn Hughes, Sylvia Plath's Literary Executor." *The Guardian*. Guardian News and Media, 18 Jan. 2013.

Hughes, Ted. Letters to Assia Wevill, Rose Library.

———. "Astrological Chart, '3rd March 1965, 9.55 p.m.'" MSS 1058, Box 1, Folder 91. Ted Hughes, Letters to Assia Wevill, Rose Library.

———. *Capriccio: Poems*. Gehenna, 1990.

———. *Collected Poems*. Farrar, Straus and Giroux, 2003.

———. "Draft Constitution: For Suggestions and Corrections." Undated. MSS 1058, Box 1, Folder 66. Ted Hughes, Letters to Assia Wevill, Rose Library

———. "Fleeing from Eternity." Undated. MSS 1058, Box 1, Folder 83. Ted Hughes, Letters to Assia Wevill, Rose Library.

———. Letter to Assia Wevill. 3 Oct. 1963. MSS 1058, Box 1, Folder 6. Ted Hughes, Letters to Assia Wevill, Rose Library.

———. Letter to Assia Wevill. 24 Nov. 1963. MSS 1058, Box 1, Folder 8. Ted Hughes, Letters to Assia Wevill, Rose Library.

———. Letter to Assia Wevill. 2 Dec. 1963. MSS 1058, Box 1, Folder 9. Ted Hughes, Letters to Assia Wevill, Rose Library.

———. Letter to Assia Wevill. 12 Dec. 1963. MSS 1058, Box 1, Folder 10. Ted Hughes, Letters to Assia Wevill, Rose Library.

———. Letter to Assia Wevill. 15 Jan. 1964. MSS 1058, Box 1, Folder 13. Ted Hughes, Letters to Assia Wevill, Rose Library.

———. Letter to Assia Wevill. 11 Feb. 1964. MSS 1058, Box 1, Folder 16. Ted Hughes, Letters to Assia Wevill, Rose Library.

———. Letter to Assia Wevill. 14 Sept. 1964. MSS 1058, Box 1, Folder 22. Ted Hughes, Letters to Assia Wevill, Rose Library.

———. Letter to Assia Wevill. 26 Nov. 1964. MSS 1058, Box 1, Folder 25. Ted Hughes, Letters to Assia Wevill, Rose Library.

———. Letter to Assia Wevill. 31 Jan. 1964. MSS 1058, Box 1, Folder 31. Ted Hughes, Letters to Assia Wevill, Rose Library.

———. Letter to Assia Wevill. 31 Aug. 1965. MSS 1058, Box 1, Folder 35. Ted Hughes, Letters to Assia Wevill, Rose Library.

———. Letter to Assia Wevill. 5 Sept. 1965. MSS 1058, Box 1, Folder 36. Ted Hughes, Letters to Assia Wevill, Rose Library.

———. Letter to Assia Wevill. 31 Dec. 1967. MSS 1058, Box 1, Folder 44. Ted Hughes, Letters to Assia Wevill, Rose Library.

———. Letter to Assia Wevill. 7 Nov. 1968. MSS 1058, Box 1, Folder 47. Ted Hughes, Letters to Assia Wevill, Rose Library.

———. Letter to Assia Wevill. Undated. MSS 1058, Box 1, Folder 52. Ted Hughes, Letters to Assia Wevill, Rose Library.

———. Letter to Assia Wevill. Undated. MSS 1058, Box 1, Folder 53. Ted Hughes, Letters to Assia Wevill, Rose Library.

———. Letter to Assia Wevill. Undated. MSS 1058, Box 1, Folder 55. Ted Hughes, Letters to Assia Wevill, Rose Library.

———. Letter to Assia Wevill Undated. MSS 1058, Box 1, Folder 56. Ted Hughes, Letters to Assia Wevill, Rose Library.

———. Letter to Assia Wevill. Undated. MSS 1058, Box 1, Folder 57. Ted Hughes, Letters to Assia Wevill, Rose Library.

———. Letter to Celia Chaikin. 11 Mar. 1970. MSS 1058, Box 1, Folder 3. Ted Hughes, Letters to Assia Wevill, Rose Library.

———. "[Notebook 11], Spiral Bound Shorthand Notebook." Undated (ca. 1968–69). MSS 644, Box 57, Folder 10. Ted Hughes Papers, 1940–99, Rose Library.

———. "Last Letter." Edited by Melvyn Bragg. *New Statesman*, 11 Oct. 2010, pp. 42–44.

———. *Letters of Ted Hughes*, edited by Christopher Reid, Farrar, Straus and Giroux, 2007.

Hunter, Dianne. "Poetics of Melancholy and Psychic Possession in Ted Hughes's *Birthday Letters* and Other Haunted Texts." *Partial Answers: Journal of Literature and the History of Ideas*, vol. 1, no. 1, Jan. 2003, pp. 129–50.

Irigaray, Luce. *This Sex Which Is Not One*, translated by Catherine Porter with Carolyn Burke, Cornell UP, 1985.

Jocelyn, Ann Henning. *Doonreagan: A Private Domain of Ted Hughes*. Oberon, 2013.

Jones, Liz. "Haunted by the Ballad of Ted and Sylvia, Poetry's Most Toxic Love Story: Frieda Hughes Reveals Why Her Parents' Secrets Still Cast a Shadow on Her Own Career." *Daily Mail: Mail Online*, 10 June 2017, http://www.dailymail.co.uk/home/event/article-4587992/Frieda-Hughes-parents-secrets-haunt-her.html.

Kavanagh, P. J. "An Awkward Shyness." *The Guardian*, 12 July 1968, p. 6.

Koren, Yehuda, and Eilat Negev. *Lover of Unreason: Assia Wevill, Sylvia Plath's Rival and Ted Hughes' Doomed Love*. Da Capo, 2007.

Kristeva, Julia. *Powers of Horror: An Essay on Abjection*. Translated by Leon S. Roudiez, Columbia UP, 1982.

LaCapra, Dominick. *Writing History, Writing Trauma*. Johns Hopkins UP, 2001.

Maher, Frances A., and Mary Kay Thompson Tetreault. *The Feminist Classroom: An Inside Look at How Professors and Students Are Transforming Higher Education for a Diverse Society*. Basic Books, 1994.

Malcolm, Janet. *The Silent Woman: Sylvia Plath and Ted Hughes*. Vintage, 1994.

McCloskey, Deirdre. "Paid Work." *Women in Twentieth-Century Britain: Economic, Social and Cultural Change*, edited by Ina Zweiniger-Bargielowska, Longman, 2001, pp. 165–79.

Middlebrook, Diane. *Her Husband: Hughes and Plath—A Marriage*. Viking, 2003.

Murphy, Richard. *The Kick*. Granta, 2002.

Murphy, Richard, and Eugene O'Connell. "An Interview with Richard Murphy: Eugene O'Connell Interviews Richard Murphy on His Eightieth Birthday." *Poetry International Web*, 1 Dec. 2007, http://www.poetryinternationalweb.net/pi/site/cou_article/item/10647/An-interview-with-Richard-Murphy/en.

Myers, Lucas. *Crow Steered, Bergs Appeared: A Memoir of Ted Hughes and Sylvia Plath.* Proctor's Hall, 2001.

Negev, Eilat. "Haunted by the Ghosts of Love." *The Guardian,* 9 Apr. 1999, http://www.theguardian.com/books/1999/apr/10/tedhughes.sylviaplath.

Office for National Statistics. *Social Trends,* No. 40, 6 July 2010.

Plath, Sylvia. *Ariel.* Perennial Classics, 1999.

———. *Ariel: The Restored Edition.* Faber and Faber, 2004.

———. *The Collected Poems.* Edited by Ted Hughes, Harper Perennial Modern Classics, 2008.

———. "A Comparison [Essay, 1962]." *Johnny Panic and the Bible of Dreams: Short Stories, Prose, and Diary Excerpts.* Harper Perennial, 2008, pp. 62–64.

———. "Context [Essay, 1962]." *Johnny Panic and the Bible of Dreams: Short Stories, Prose, and Diary Excerpts.* Harper Perennial, 2008, pp. 65–66.

———. "Day of Success [Story, 1960]." *Johnny Panic and the Bible of Dreams: Short Stories, Prose, and Diary Excerpts.* Harper Perennial, 2008, pp. 80–92.

———. *Letters Home: Correspondence, 1950–1963.* Selected and edited by Aurelia Schober Plath, Harper and Row, 1975.

———. "*Letters Home*—Part Seven." Plath MSS II. Writings. Box 9, Folder 10. The Lilly Library, Indiana University, Bloomington. 4 Nov. 2016.

———. *The Letters of Sylvia Plath,* vol. 2: *1956–1963.* Edited by Peter K. Steinberg and Karen V. Kukil, HarperCollins, 2018.

———. *The Unabridged Journals of Sylvia Plath.* Edited by Karen V. Kukil, Anchor, 2000.

Porter, Peter. Review of *Lover of Unreason,* by Yehuda Koren and Eilat Negev. *The Guardian,* 28 Oct. 2006, https://www.theguardian.com/books/2006/oct/28/featuresreviews.guardianreview8.

Retallack, Joan. *The Poethical Wager.* U of California P, 2003.

Rich, Adrienne. "When We Dead Awaken: Writing as Re-Vision (1971)." *Adrienne Rich's Poetry and Prose.* Edited by Barbara Charlesworth Gelpi and Albert Gelpi. Norton, 1993, pp. 166–77.

Rollyson, Carl. *American Isis: The Life and Art of Sylvia Plath.* St. Martin's, 2013.

Sigmund, Elizabeth. "I Realised Sylvia Knew about Assia's Pregnancy—It Might Have Offered a Further Explanation of Her Suicide." *The Guardian,* 22 Apr. 1999, https://www.theguardian.com/theguardian/1999/apr/23/features11.g21.

Sigmund, Elizabeth, and Gail Crowther. *Sylvia Plath in Devon: A Year's Turning*. Fonthill Media, 2014.

Skea, Ann. "*Capriccio:* The Path of the Sword, An Analysis of Ted Hughes' Use of Cabbala in *Capriccio.*" 17 Oct. 2007, http://ann.skea.com/CapriccioHome.htm.

Sorrentino, Constance. "International Comparisons of Labor Force Participation, 1960–81." *Monthly Labor Review*, Feb. 1983, pp. 23–36.

Stevenson, Anne. *Bitter Fame: A Life of Sylvia Plath*. Houghton Mifflin, 1989.

Sylvia. Film. Directed by Christine Jeffs. Produced by Alison Owen, Focus Features, 2004.

Tarn, Nathaniel. Nathaniel Tarn Papers, M1132, Dept. of Special Collections, Stanford University Libraries, Stanford, CA.

Ted Hughes: Stronger than Death. Documentary. Directed and produced by Richard Curson Smith, BBC, 2015.

Thomas, Trevor. *Sylvia Plath: Last Encounters*. Bedford, England [private publication], 1989.

Walsh, Maggie, and Chris Wrigley. "Womanpower: The Transformation of the Labour Force in the UK and the USA since 1945." *ReFRESH: Recent Findings of Research in Economic and Social History*, vol. 30, Summer 2001, Economic History Society, http://www.ehs.org.uk/the-society/refresh.html.

Weitz, Rose. "A History of Women's Bodies." *The Politics of Women's Bodies: Sexuality, Appearance, and Behavior*, edited by Rose Weitz, 3rd ed., Oxford UP, 2010, pp. 3–12.

Wagner, Erica. *Ariel's Gift: Ted Hughes, Sylvia Plath, and the Story of "Birthday Letters."* Norton, 2002.

Wagner-Martin, Linda. *Sylvia Plath: A Literary Life*. Palgrave Macmillan, 2003.

Wevill, Assia. Journal entries. 29–31 Nov. 1966. MSS 1058, Box 1, Folder 77. Ted Hughes, Letters to Assia Wevill, Rose Library.

———. Journal entries. 6 Sept. 1968, 16 Jan. 1969, and undated. MSS 1058, Box 1, Folder 78. Ted Hughes, Letters to Assia Wevill, Rose Library.

———. Letter to David Wevill. Undated. MSS 1058, Box 1, Folder 74. Ted Hughes, Letters to Assia Wevill, Rose Library.

———. Letter to Lucas Myers. 13 Mar. 1965. MSS 865, Box 1, Folder 11. Ted Hughes, Letters to Lucas Myers, Rose Library.

———. Letter to Lucas Myers. 15 July 1965. MSS 865, Box 1, Folder 11. Ted Hughes, Letters to Lucas Myers, Rose Library.

———. Letter to Lucas Myers. 24 Sept. 1965. MSS 865, Box 1, Folder 11. Ted Hughes, Letters to Lucas Myers, Rose Library.

———. Letter to Richard Gilbertson. 16 Sept. 1968. MSS 644, Box 182, Folder 10. Ted Hughes, Letters to Assia Wevill, Rose Library.

———. Letter to Ted Hughes. 22 Jan. 1964. MSS 1058, Box 1, Folder 68. Ted Hughes, Letters to Assia Wevill, Rose Library.

———. Letter to Ted Hughes. 2 Feb. 1968. MSS 1058, Box 1, Folder 69. Ted Hughes, Letters to Assia Wevill, Rose Library.

———. Letter to Ted Hughes. Undated. MSS 1058, Box 1, Folder 71. Ted Hughes, Letters to Assia Wevill, Rose Library.

———. Letter to Ted Hughes. Undated. MSS 1058, Box 1, Folder 72. Ted Hughes, Letters to Assia Wevill, Rose Library.

———. Letter to Ted Hughes. Undated. MSS 1058, Box 1, Folder 73. Ted Hughes, Letters to Assia Wevill, Rose Library.

———. Pay stub from Ogilvy & Mather. July 1968. MSS 1058, Box 1, Folder 97. Ted Hughes, Letters to Assia Wevill, Rose Library.

———. Photographs. MSS 1266, Box 1, Folder 18. Rose Library.

———. "Self-Portrait." 1967–68. OP1, Olwyn Hughes Papers, Rose Library.

———. Telegram from "Esther" to Ted Hughes. 14 May 1968. MSS 1058, Box 1, Folder 99. Ted Hughes, Letters to Assia Wevill, Rose Library.

———."The Will of Assia Estre [*sic*] Wevill." MSS 1058, Box 1, Folder 100. Ted Hughes, Letters to Assia Wevill, Rose Library.

Wevill, Assia, and Alexandra "Shura" Wevill. Photograph. 1966. MSS 1058, Box 1, Folder 109. Ted Hughes, Letters to Assia Wevill, Rose Library.

Wevill, Assia, Frieda Hughes, Alexandra "Shura" Wevill, and Nicholas Hughes. Photograph. Dec. 1966. MSS 1058, Box 1, Folder 106. Ted Hughes, Letters to Assia Wevill, Rose Library.

Wevill, David. Letter to Assia Wevill. 19 Apr. 1968. MSS 1058, Box 1, Folder 75. Ted Hughes, Letters to Assia Wevill, Rose Library.

———. Letter to Assia Wevill. Apr. 1968. MSS 1058, Box 1, Folder 76. Ted Hughes, Letters to Assia Wevill, Rose Library.

"'Yehuda Amichai,' Poems Translated and Introduced by Assia Gutmann [Wevill] and Read by Ted Hughes." Radio 3. 12 Dec. 1968. MSS 644, Box 122, Folder 22. Ted Hughes, Letters to Assia Wevill, Rose Library.

Young, Iris Marion. *On Female Body Experience: "Throwing like a Girl" and Other Essays*. Oxford UP, 2005.

INDEX